THE LIVES OF CHILDREN AND ADOLESCENTS WITH DISABILITIES

This book will be of interest to undergraduates, postgraduates and researchers in disability studies, childhood studies, medicine and health sciences, and sociology. It also provides insights that will be of use and value to professionals working with disabled children and adolescents in education, health and in disability-specific services.

Opening with four narratives that offer the reader a window into the lived experience of disabled children, adolescents and their families, subsequent chapters explore a range of issues facing disabled children from early childhood through to late adolescence. Topics include family life, early intervention, inclusive and post-secondary education, the right to play, digital participation, the effects of labelling and matters relating to agency and sexuality.

With chapters discussing research from Australia, Canada, Ireland, Italy, Malta, Mexico, New Zealand, Sweden and the UK amongst others, this book:

- contributes to the existing body of knowledge about the lives of disabled children and adolescents, with a focus on socially created disabling factors;
- provides the reader with analysis of issues affecting disabled children and adolescents according to different conceptual frameworks, national contexts and with regard to different types of impairments/disabilities;
- highlights the main issues that confront disabled children and adolescents, their families and their allies in the early twenty-first century;
- highlights the importance of actively listening to the perspectives of disabled children and adolescents.

It provides a rich source of knowledge and information about the lives of disabled children and adolescents, and a variety of perspectives on how their lives are affected by material and non-material factors, social structures and cultural constructions.

Angharad E. Beckett, FRSA, is Professor of Political Sociology and Social Inclusion at the University of Leeds. She is a member of the Centre for Disability Studies (Leeds), where she was for many years Co-Director. She is a researcher and educator in the area of disability and social justice, with a primary focus on rights and inclusion for disabled children. She regularly advises national and international governments and civil society organisations on related matters.

Anne-Marie Callus is Associate Professor in the Department of Disability Studies, Faculty for Social Wellbeing, University of Malta. She lectures, researches and has published on disability rights, empowerment of persons with intellectual disability, inclusive education and disabled children's rights, as well as cultural representations of persons with disability. She is Deputy Editor of *Disability & Society*.

Routledge Advances in Disability Studies

A Historical Sociology of Disability
Human Validity and Invalidity from Antiquity to Early Modernity
Bill Hughes

Defining the Boundaries of Disability
Critical Perspectives
Edited by Licia Carlson and Matthew C. Murray

The New Political Economy of Disability
Transnational Networks and Individualised Funding in the Age of
Neoliberalism
Georgia van Toorn

Design, Disability and Embodiment
Spatial Justice and Perspectives of Power
Janice Rieger

A History of Disability and Art Education
Claire Penketh

The Lives of Children and Adolescents with Disabilities
Edited by Angharad E. Beckett and Anne-Marie Callus

For more information about this series, please visit: https://www.routledge.com/Routledge-Advances-in-Disability-Studies/book-series/RADS

THE LIVES OF CHILDREN AND ADOLESCENTS WITH DISABILITIES

Edited by
Angharad E. Beckett and Anne-Marie Callus

LONDON AND NEW YORK

Designed cover image: Graphics for cover illustration by Ash Loydon
Pic 1: Photo by Alexander Grey on Unsplash, Pic 2: Photo by AnikaMeyer, Pic 3: Photo by Latrobebohs

First published 2024
by Routledge
4 Park Square, Milton Park, Abingdon, Oxon OX14 4RN

and by Routledge
605 Third Avenue, New York, NY 10158

Routledge is an imprint of the Taylor & Francis Group, an informa business

British Library Cataloguing-in-Publication Data
A catalogue record for this book is available from the British Library

ISBN: 978-0-367-61022-7 (hbk)
ISBN: 978-0-367-61019-7 (pbk)
ISBN: 978-1-003-10291-5 (ebk)

DOI: 10.4324/9781003102915

Typeset in Sabon
by codeMantra

CONTENTS

FIGURES

TABLES

CONTRIBUTORS

Rachel Adam-Smith lives in Leeds with her daughter Francesca, a young adult with learning disabilities and complex health needs. Rachel was born with congenital heart disease, and, as a result of her own and her daughter's experiences, she became a disability campaigner on social media. She has also written several articles on congenital heart disease and issues impacting persons with learning disabilities. Rachel completed a law degree at Leeds University, and in 2020, she received the Caroline Gooding Prize for her work as a campaigner and researcher.

Kristin Alfredsson Ågren is a Senior Lecturer at the Department of Health, Medical and Caring Sciences, Linköping University, Sweden. Her PhD project investigated internet use among adolescents with intellectual disabilities. Her ongoing research focus is on digital aspects, participation in everyday life and in research for people with intellectual disabilities.

Claire Azzopardi Lane is a Senior Lecturer in the Department of Gender and Sexualities, Faculty for Social Wellbeing, University of Malta. Research is located around the intersection of sexuality and identities; specifically, the intersection of sexuality and diversity. Her personal research has addressed issues of disability and sexual expression, sexual orientation and gender identity, sexual and reproductive health and sex education, and intersections between identities and positions of vulnerability such as parenting, domestic violence and disability.

Georgette Bajada is currently Head of Department in Inclusive Education within the Secretariat for Catholic Education in Malta. She is also a visiting assistant lecturer in the Inclusion and Access to Learning Department of the Faculty of Education at the University of Malta. She graduated with a master's degree in Disability Studies, focusing her research on disabled students' voices within educational practices. Georgette is presently reading for a PhD within the Faculty for Social Wellbeing at the University of Malta. Her research subject is based on a Foucauldian genealogy of disability in Malta.

Solange Bonello was born in Toronto, Canada, and brought up in Malta. She was diagnosed with congenital nystagmus a few weeks after birth. Solange obtained a first-class degree in Youth & Community studies and a Master of Arts in Sociology from the University of Malta and is currently carrying out her doctoral studies. She has been an activist within the disability and gender equality fields for over a decade.

Clare Carroll is a registered speech and language therapist and Lecturer at the University of Galway in Ireland. She uses a range of qualitative methodologies to study interdisciplinary collaborative working and to support the participation of children, young people with disabilities and their families in research.

Sue Caton is a Research Fellow in the Department of Social Care and Social Work, Manchester Metropolitan University, UK. Her research is with people with intellectual disabilities with a focus on social inequalities, digital inclusion and the impact of the Covid-19 pandemic.

Sue Cranmer is a Senior Lecturer in the Department of Educational Research, Lancaster University. Her main interests are in digital education and social justice with recent research focused on disabled children's digital use practices. Publications include 'Disabled children and digital technologies. Learning in the context of inclusive education,' for Bloomsbury Academic (2020).

Deborah Fenney is an alumna of the Centre for Disability Studies, University of Leeds where she undertook doctoral research into inequalities in disabled people's access to sustainable lifestyles. Her contribution to this chapter was made during her time at the University. She currently works at the King's Fund and is a Fellow in their policy team. She has a particular interest in health inequalities, including those experienced by disabled people in the UK.

Michael Gaffney leads the small early childhood team at the College of Education, University of Otago in Aotearoa New Zealand. He has quite diverse research interests across both schooling and early childhood, especially with respect to children's rights and inclusion. His approach draws on sociocultural theory and the sociology of childhood.

Jesica Paola Gomez Muñoz is an attorney who graduated from Santiago de Cali University. She holds a Master of Law from Icesi University. She is currently a PhD student in Critical Gender Studies at Iberoamericana University and holds a CONACYT scholarship. She is also a member of the Working Group on Imaginations and Representations of people with disabilities of the Ibero-American Network for Research on Imaginations and Representations (RIIR) [Grupo de Trabajo en Imaginarios y Representaciones de la Discapacidad de la Red Iberoamericana de Investigación en Imaginarios y Representaciones (RIIR)].

Miro Griffiths is a Researcher in Disability Studies, within the School of Sociology and Social Policy, at the University of Leeds. His research, primarily, explores disabled people's experiences of activism, social movements and resistance practices. Miro holds several policy advisory positions (government, civil society and private sector) across Europe.

Kerrie Highcock works as the Family Development Manager for a large regional charity in the North East of England. This role involves the management of support for families across the region alongside leading the organisation's autism acceptance award. She completed her Master's in autism at the University of Strathclyde with a research focus on the experiences of young autistic people and how they want to influence positive societal change. She is currently completing her doctorate in education.

Kate McAnelly is a qualified, certificated early childhood teacher who recently completed her PhD at the University of Otago in Dunedin, Aotearoa New Zealand. She works as the lead practitioner within the education consultancy she founded in 2021. Kate's research interests centre on matters of disability, inclusive education, childhood studies, family support and the sociology of diverse childhoods.

Tomas Puentes Leon has a background in sociology and a Master of Arts in Public and Social Policy. He is currently a PhD student at the School of Sociology and Social Policy at the University of Leeds and holds an ANID scholarship (Chile). His research has focused on family relationships and the involvement of young adults with intellectual disability in their transition to adulthood.

Parimala Raghavendra is an Adjunct Associate Professor at Disability & Community Inclusion, College of Nursing & Health Sciences, Flinders University,

Australia. She has over 40 years of global experience working with persons who can benefit from augmentative and alternative communication. She conducted pioneering research in supporting young people with disabilities to use social media.

Maria Edith Reyes Lastiri is a primary education teacher and holds a bachelor's degree in special education and a master's degree from the Research and Development of Education from Iberoamericana University in Mexico. She also has a PhD in Education from the Valladolid University in Spain. She has also trained in psychopedagogical diagnosis at the Iberoamericana University and has a Diploma in Adolescent Psychology and a Diploma in Vocational Guidance from Anahuac University in Mexico. She is an active member of the Technical Council of the Institute for People with Disabilities of Mexico City. She is currently the Coordinator of *Somos Uno Más* [We are one of the same]: Educational and Social Inclusion Program for Youth with Intellectual Disabilities at the Iberoamericana University.

Anna Robinson is a Senior Lecturer in Autism at the University of Strathclyde. She is a psychologist specialising in psychotherapy and her research focuses on emotional psychology, an emotion-focused-experiential approach to psychotherapy and counselling, trauma and post-traumatic growth. Her PhD 'Enhancing emotional processing in Emotion-Focused Therapy for clients with autistic process' received the Outstanding Research Award by The British Association for Counselling and Psychotherapy. Her current research project is #CATS Creating Autistic Trauma Stories.

Alan Santinele Martino (he/him) is an Assistant Professor in the Community Rehabilitation and Disability Studies program in the Department of Community Health Sciences at the University of Calgary. His main research interests are in critical disability studies, gender and sexualities, and qualitative and community-based research. His work has been published in multiple journals, including *Disability Studies Quarterly*, *Canadian Disability Studies Journal* and *Culture, Health and Sexuality*, as well as edited volumes on disability and/or sexualities studies.

Alice Scavarda is a Postdoctoral Research Fellow at the University of Torino. She is a member of Disability Studies Italy and a board member of the European Society for Health and Medical Sociology. Her main research interests include Disability, Mental Health, Vaccines and Qualitative and Creative Methods. Her latest publications are: *Disability Welfare Policy in Europe: Cognitive Disability and the Impact of the Covid-19 Pandemic* (with A. Genova and M. Świątkiewicz-Mośny), for Emerald Publisher, and 'Disability by association for siblings of adolescents and adults with cognitive disabilities' in *Disability & Society*.

Tessa-May Zirnsak is an interdisciplinary researcher at La Trobe University, Australia. Her research centres around understanding how and why disabled people – including people with mental illness – face a disproportional amount of violence. Tessa has worked on health service evaluations, industry and independent research projects. She has a particular interest in research engagement with minoritised communities.

ACKNOWLEDGEMENTS

We would like to thank:

All contributors to this collection for joining us in the (ad)venture of this book. We have enjoyed working with you immensely. This book is a collective product – we did it together.

Our illustrator, Ash Loydon, for his sensitive portraits, which we feel accompany the narrative chapters beautifully.

The team at Routledge – Claire Jarvis and Sully Evans – for helping us to achieve our vision for this collection. We are most grateful.

Tuppence and Perrin, for their furry companionship, actual and virtual!

Our families, for their interest in our project and the many cups of tea delivered, so kindly, when we were deeply engrossed in reading and editing tasks. The task is complete. Now it is our turn to put the kettle on!

1

THE LIVES OF CHILDREN AND ADOLESCENTS WITH DISABILITIES

An Introduction

Anne-Marie Callus and Angharad E. Beckett

The choice of the term 'lives', rather than 'life' in the title of this book, was intentional. Every child and adolescent, disabled or non-disabled, is a unique individual with a particular set of attributes, interests, aspirations and life experiences. Disabled children and adolescents are as diverse as any group of young people. Whilst many will be engaged in similar activities, for example, making their way through education, their experiences of those activities will vary. Impairment does play a role here. The lives of disabled children and adolescents do differ according to the nature of their impairments – at least to some degree. More significantly, however, their lives differ because of the different social, cultural, economic and political contexts in which they live. It is because of this diversity that we chose to talk of *lives*, plural. That 'disabled childhoods' are shaped by different social formations and cultural contexts is starting to be recognised. Further research is needed, however, to truly understand these processes and the impact that they have on children's quality of life and wellbeing. We hope that this book makes a useful contribution in this regard, providing readers with a window into the lives of a diverse group of young people. The chapters in this book also provide insights into the social systems and processes that impact the lives of disabled children and adolescents and the strategies and practices that these young people use to shape their own lives.

We adopt the understanding of disability that is set forth in the United Nations Convention on the Rights of Persons with Disabilities (UN CRPD). This is a social relational understanding. Accordingly, we do not understand disability to equate to impairments (e.g., to a difference of mind or body) but instead to the *interaction* between persons who have impairments and the disabling barriers that they encounter. This means that we are less concerned

DOI: 10.4324/9781003102915-1

with the specific details of the diagnoses of a child or adolescent with disabilities (although not denying the reality of impairment-effects) and are more concerned with the disabling barriers that they encounter in their interaction with other persons and with their wider environment. As we stated above, each child and adolescent with an impairment will encounter the world differently. However, as the testimonies of persons with disabilities over many decades have clearly shown, there are sufficient commonalities to be able to reach an understanding of how living in a disabling world impacts the lives of children and adolescents, as well as adults, with disabilities. Most importantly, they show that the effect of a disabling world on equality and human dignity is profoundly negative.

In choosing to use the term 'with disabilities' in the title, we have adopted the terminology of the UN CRPD. This is a reflection of our commitment to adopting a human rights approach. Preference for, and use of, person-first or identity-first language varies, globally. Both are used within this edited collection and are purposely used interchangeably in this Introduction. Each author has decided which to employ. Although chapter authors use different terms, they all adopt a social relational understanding of disability. They agree that any investigation into the lives of children and adolescents with disabilities must consider the nature and effect of disabling barriers and seek solutions.

Approaching the issue of disability from a human rights perspective also means giving central importance to the perspectives of persons with disabilities, regardless of age. Other perspectives – including those of parents and other primary caregivers, professionals and staff who work with persons with disabilities – are also important. But the starting point needs to be an understanding of disabled people's lived experiences, regardless of age, and type and severity of impairment. For very young children with disabilities, it is often their parents' (or legal guardians') perspectives that are taken as the starting point. Yet, as demonstrated in this book, there are ways of eliciting even young children's perspectives. Finding ways to combine the perspectives of children and adolescents with those of significant others in their lives, carefully and ethically, is essential. Some persons with disabilities, particularly those who have profound intellectual and multiple disabilities, may indeed need others to advocate on their behalf in various regards throughout their lives. Yet again, there will always be aspects of their lives where they are able to have their say and exercise their rights, will and preferences, if given the right support and opportunity.

Whichever way we choose to refer to children and adolescents with disabilities, and however varied their experiences may be, what they share is that their lives are largely shaped by adults. When it comes to disability studies research, their lives are more often than not *narrated* by adults. We acknowledge that it is adults who have authored most of the chapters in this book. It was important, however, that the voices of children and adolescents with disabilities were facilitated and present within this text. Their perspectives are either directly foregrounded or inform the arguments made in most chapters.

The book opens with four narratives. The first, *Kia ora from Ralph* is a co-production, written by Ralph, a four-year-old boy who lives in Aotearoa New Zealand and Kate McAnelly (University of Otego). The second, *Childhood: magic or misery? Childhood: happy or sad?* is written by Rachel Adam-Smith, and it is about her daughter Francesca. It provides us with a parent's perspective on raising and caring for a child with complex dependency needs in the UK and in Portugal. Francesca was happy for her mum to tell this story and helped choose the photograph that was used as source material by our illustrator. She also gave her approval to the illustration and was very excited to receive it.

The third is *The Tale of the Dancing Eyes*, Solange Bonello's retrospective account of growing up with a visual disability. The focus is mostly upon her early to middle childhood, living in Malta. The fourth is another retrospective piece, written by a disabled person who has a physical disability and lives in the UK. In *The Trouble with 'Normal': Finding hope through resistance*, Miro Griffiths offers the reader insights into his teenage years.

For each story, a portrait is presented that seeks to encapsulate the essence of each person's narrative. The process was in itself interesting and is worthy of mention. The illustrator, Ash Loydon, is a member of the Disability Arts community. He identifies as an autistic father, artist and illustrator. He is also the parent of autistic young children. In addition to having photographs from which to work, he read each of the narratives and his interpretations of those narratives informed his illustrations. All illustrations were warmly received by those they represent.

To continue our theme, each narrative is different, *unique*. Yet there are commonalities – the authors' experiences of disabling attitudes and barriers, on the one hand; and on the other hand, of vital, life-enhancing but *precarious* inclusion. The messages conveyed by these narratives resonate across the chapters of the book.

The next two chapters focus on early childhood. *Disabled Children's Active Participation in Early Childhood Education: A story of love, rights and solidarity from Aotearoa New Zealand* by Michael Gaffney and Kate McAnelly discusses the emotional dimensions of learning in early childhood education through a case study about a young autistic child named 'Tama'. The chapter includes four vignettes that bring to life his experience and what matters to *him*. The following chapter, by Clare Carroll – *Positioning the Views of Children with Developmental Disabilities at the Centre of Early Interventions* – extends the discussion on the importance of listening to the views of children with disabilities early in their lives.

The focus then shifts to the experience of children with disabilities within their family. In *A Minority Within the Family: Disabled children and parental perceptions*, Tessa-May Zirnsak discusses the impact on children with disabilities of growing up in a family which comprises non-disabled persons, whose negative preconceptions about disabled people may create inadvertent discrimination within the family itself.

Two chapters then follow, both considering a somewhat neglected aspect of the lives of disabled children and adolescents – leisure, recreation and play. Angharad Beckett and Deborah Fenney explore what is known (and not known) about access to and inclusion for disabled children in nature play – a type of play that is much en vogue. They ask are *Muddy Puddles for All?* and offer a critical (studies in ableism) reading of the way in which nature play is imagined and promoted. Remaining on the theme of recreational activities, Sue Cranmer considers the issues encountered, particularly by children with vision impairments, in accessing the digital environment, in *Disabled Children's Recreational Uses of Digital Technologies in the Context of Children's Digital Rights*.

Next, the spotlight moves onto inclusive education. In *The Individual Education Programme: Who knows best?*, Anne-Marie Callus and Georgette Bajada discuss developments in inclusive education and identify a significant gap – the voice of children and adolescents with disabilities – which, they argue, needs to be addressed for inclusion to truly happen in mainstream schools. The digital theme returns as a focus for the next chapter – *Digital Participation and Competencies for Young People with Intellectual or Developmental Disabilities* – Sue Caton, Kristin Alfredsson Ågren and Parimala Raghavendra consider the important issue of acquisition of the skills needed for digital participation and implications for young people's digital inclusion.

Important issues relating to young people's identities, agency, and resistance are considered in subsequent chapters. In *Autistic Youth as Active Agents for Societal Change*, Anna Robinson and Kerrie Highcock discuss how young autistic persons have agency not only in their own lives but also more widely. In *Normal, Different, or Something in Between? Young people with autism and Down syndrome resisting psycho-emotional disablism*, Alice Scavarda explores how young people with disabilities negotiate their way through stigma and misconceptions, through the use of arts-based methods. In the penultimate chapter, *We Are Sexual Too: Sexuality in the lives of disabled adolescents*, Claire Azzopardi Lane and Alan Santinele Martino consider sexuality, an aspect of life that takes on increasing importance as children move into adolescence and eventually into young adulthood.

The final chapter focuses upon an important point in the lives of all young people – disabled or non-disabled – but which can be a particularly fraught time in the lives of disabled people (and their families): the transition to further and higher education and/or employment. Focusing upon the experiences of young persons with intellectual disability, Jesica Paola Gomez Muñoz, Maria Edith Reyes Lastiri and Tomas Puentes Leon's chapter entitled *Challenges of the Somos Uno Más [We are one of the same] Programme in the Access to Higher Education and Preparation for Adulthood of Young Persons with Intellectual Disability in Mexico* closes this collection.

Taken together, the 15 chapters attest to the rich lives of children and adolescents with disabilities, the intricacies of the disabling barriers – both attitudinal and environmental – that they encounter and the many ways in which barriers can be dismantled and support provided to ensure that their rights are respected and they are included in all aspects of life. At the same time, the complexity of the lives and barriers encountered by disabled young people means that no book can expect to provide a comprehensive picture or coverage. It is hoped, however, that this book highlights a number of the main issues, brings home to the reader the importance of appreciating the lives of each child and adolescent with disabilities *from their own perspective* and acts as a prompt for further research and social innovation to ensure the human rights of, and inclusion for, these young people.

2

KIA ORA FROM RALPH[1]

As narrated by Kate McAnelly

FIGURE 2.1 Ralph is sitting on a mat reading a book. Rex, his toy dinosaur, is just behind him, also reading a book

DOI: 10.4324/9781003102915-2

Hi everyone, my name's Ralph, and I'm four years old. I live with my Mum Tamora, Dad Felix and sister Vanellope in Aotearoa New Zealand. Something you might not know about me is that I'm autistic. Being autistic is something Mum and Dad have always talked to me about and encouraged me to be proud of.

I attend my local kindergarten Monday to Friday, and the kindergarten community helps me to feel proud of being autistic too by telling, and showing me that they value my diverse meaning-making, views and opinions. The kindergarten community asks lots of questions of my Mum and me because, as my teachers say, we're the experts on me and my life, and so the best place to start is always to ask us what we think and want. By doing this, they've helped me to learn, grow, thrive and achieve the best I can!

Asking lots of questions helped my kindergarten community to quickly realise which knowledge was valuable to support my participation, learning and inclusion. A big part of this is I enjoy being social and love to have fun, but that I sometimes find it hard to understand the 'rules' of social relationships. Mostly I'm left to ask for support as and when I think I need it, and I'm free to say yes please or no thanks to any support that people might offer. I really like routine and knowing what's going to happen next. My Mum told my teachers this when I first started at kindergarten. They give me as much warning as possible if anything different is going to happen during the day, so that I won't get too stressed.

For me, sound, touch and heat are senses that I experience really strongly. Kindergarten is easier for me if I can have a comfort item – usually my favourite toy dinosaur, Rex – with me. Rex helps me feel calm and safe, and holding him or having him nearby means I can join in whatever learning is interesting to me. People know that Rex is important to me, and why I take him everywhere. Everyone in the kindergarten community is patient and kind to me and gives me lots of time to make sense of my learning. I feel safe, secure and like I belong at kindergarten because they do this.

I know what learning is important to me and how to go about it, and I have a voice I like using and often it is about the things I'm interested in and affect me within the kindergarten community and environment. A great example of this was when I helped co-plan the kindergarten Christmas party. I was so excited about this and was very proud of the job I did.

The kindergarten community listens to all the different ways I communicate (there are lots!). This makes me feel like they love me, and I belong there.

My family has helped me to be proud of being autistic and the people at my kindergarten do the same. Being me is the best!

Love from Ralph.

Note

1 Ethics approval (18/021) for this piece of work is provided by the University of Otago, Dunedin, New Zealand.

3

CHILDHOOD

Magic Or Misery? Happy Or Sad?

Rachel Adam-Smith

FIGURE 3.1 Francesca and her mother Rachel are walking along a country path with the coat-of-arms of Portugal in the background

DOI: 10.4324/9781003102915-3

Introduction

As a mum to a child with disabilities, I had no idea childhood would be so challenging and society so inaccessible. Any mum just wants her child to have a happy childhood, to be included, to have friends, to be invited to parties, to have toys to play with and to learn from those experiences. I never imagined that society would make childhood for a child with disabilities so difficult, that the difficulties we'd face would reduce Francesca's ability to have a childhood as others do. The failure of society to enable children to play as other children do, to be able to access the environment and interact with others, to freely go out for the day with no worries about where they will park, if there will be accessible toilets or a playground with accessible equipment, has reduced Francesca's ability to have a childhood as others without disabilities experience. Childhood is meant to be a happy time. Francesca did experience happy times, but there have been many sad times; this should not have been the case. This chapter illustrates the happy and sad times of a child with learning disabilities growing up.

Schooling

'You might as well face it now; your daughter will be in a special needs school for the rest of her education'. When the developmental paediatrician said this, Francesca was two years old. No one could have known her potential at that stage of her life, particularly because she had a chromosome disorder unique to her. It was upsetting the way this professional delivered her news, the decision she had seemingly made for our daughter without our input. She was just two years old; Francesca had not been diagnosed at this stage, she would not have been diagnosed until she was six years old; therefore, how did she know what Francesca's future held or what she could achieve? This professional had already put Francesca's name down for a particular special needs school, and I was urged to go and see it. I did not want to do so. I wanted to enjoy her childhood and visit nurseries and primary schools as other parents were doing, but I was suddenly forced into looking at a special school that a paediatrician had decided Francesca would attend. I went to see it; for me, it was an upsetting experience. The school felt like an institution. The door handles were high up, out of reach to a child. It smelt like a mixture of lunch and bowel movements. The play areas were not play areas, but concrete areas with tall fencing. There was nothing colourful, no play equipment, nothing sensory, just a slab of concrete. It was reminiscent of a prison yard and incredibly depressing. I did not see how this would be stimulating to Francesca. The environment seemed to have no joy for a young child learning to play. I wanted her to be included in society, to engage with other children both disabled and non-disabled and to be pushed to reach her potential. I wanted her to experience colour, water, sandpits and sounds. To be able to use play equipment, as other nurseries or schools had, and to be able to learn from other children who were non-disabled, for those children to learn from her, and for her to be accepted into society, I did not see how solely going to a special needs school would enable her to learn and to have experiences as other children.

In the end, I won one of the first arguments we would face over the next 20 years, and Francesca attended a local nursery. Prior to Francesca starting nursery, she had Portage. This made me feel somewhat pressured into doing purposeful play to help her progress. It felt as though the play was being turned into therapy and I realised that the Portage worker was reporting her progress back to the paediatrician. It created pressure; I felt as though I was being judged and it took the joy out of 'just playing and developing'. Some of the games we played, such as using a scarf to play peek-a-boo, were games I would have played with her anyway but other play that she would ask us to do, such as playing with farm animals, putting them into a stable or the rider onto the horse, never worked and became frustrating for Francesca as she could not do it. Sadly, until around the age of 13, she was still pushed to try to achieve these types of tasks; it was only around this age that she was diagnosed with cerebral vision impairment. It now made sense as to why she was never interested in play that was more intricate. She had been pushed for years to try and do something that she could not do due to her vision impairment. She must have been so frustrated and upset that she had repeatedly been asked to do something that was just impossible for her to achieve. I think this should have been recognised far earlier and then time would not have been wasted in pressurising her to achieve unrealistic goals. I do not think Portage achieved anything for us, other than making play feel pressurised.

During her time at nursery, I enthusiastically tried to join local groups for Francesca, such as gymnastics, dance and music classes. Parents of non-disabled children would have little difficulty joining these groups, but for me, it was a challenge trying to get them to accept Francesca. Repeatedly, I had to explain her disability, but they would often say it was not suitable or they did not have the staff available. Francesca loved gymnastic–type activities, but we were not able, or not allowed – I am not sure which – to join the local group, and instead did private trampoline lessons after the main gymnastics class had finished. We would arrive early; Francesca would sit on the side, totally mesmerised by the class that was taking place and clearly wanting to join in. She was very sociable and loved the interaction of others, but she was denied the opportunity to join them. She enjoyed her trampoline lessons; she did well, but it was always sad that she had to do this by herself. I appreciate her disability limited her mobility, but she was so keen to join in, it broke my heart that she could not be given the opportunity to just be included, and I am not sure what it taught her about society at such a young age. Shortly after Francesca finished nursery, when she was five years old, we moved to

Portugal for a period of time. It is here that I have the happiest memories of Francesca's childhood.

Portugal

From the minute we moved to Portugal, we felt included. It was the end of August, the weather stayed warmer and the days lighter, which helped, but more importantly the Portuguese people just seemed more accepting. I had been coming to Portugal since I was a child, so I was familiar with the country. Francesca attended an international school. It was small, with about seven pupils in the class, and the school was based in a little complex of around five villas. Francesca was accepted from day one, and I was accepted by the other parents. Within days we were included in invites, the first being to the beach after school for the children to play and have a picnic. Not only was this inclusion but it was also physiotherapy for Francesca (walking on the sand). She was invited to all the children's birthday parties and to swimming after school, and I was invited to book clubs at the parents' home in the evening and for coffee after morning drop-off. Both of us were being included. Potentially, I think this was because the class size was so small, and there was no ability to ignore just one child, but people's attitudes were also more relaxed. Francesca was part of that class and pushed to learn as any other child would be. She seemed very happy. She seemed part of the gang. After school, once a week we would go swimming with one little boy called Adam. Afterwards, we would get dinner. All the staff knew and accepted Francesca. She would sit with Adam, and as she watched him dipping his chips into the ketchup, she would do the same, sucking the end of the chips. She was learning from being around children, as children do, but something not often afforded to special needs children. Francesca would have swimming lessons and go to the riding centre to take part in hippo-therapy. It is a form of physiotherapy on horseback. This was fantastic for her, and it was run by therapists from the local cerebral palsy centre (you did not have to have cerebral palsy to receive therapy from them). As well as being a good physiotherapy, it also gave her a sense of freedom. We would then go to this therapy centre for physio and occupational therapy once a week. It cost only two euros for an hour's session. Quite incredible when you compare the cost and accessibility of services vital to disabled children in the UK.

Francesca really progressed during her time living in Portugal. Sadly, we had to move back to the UK. We continued for many years to go back for the summer holidays (we had the benefit of my mum's home there). Rather than sitting at home during the holidays with nothing to do, we could take part in gymkhanas at the riding centre, something that's never been possible in the UK. Francesca loved these, as did I. The sense of pride on Francesca's face when she was placed was wonderful to see. Whilst there in the summer, we could just relax, swim and do hippo-therapy again (with no long waiting lists as there often are for riding for the disabled in the UK). New shopping centres that had popped up since we had lived there had created fantastic playgrounds that were accessible, giving Francesca more ability to play and improve her physical strength and coordination. Francesca had her favourite restaurants, and all the staff knew her, accepted her and would be happy to blend her meals, so she could choose her own meals. You did not fear asking the question, 'can you blend her food?' (Blending meals for those with disabilities seems so difficult to achieve here in the UK, stopping people from being able to go out with family for a meal and make a choice from the menu, as others do). I miss those days living in Portugal, I miss the inclusion and I am sure Francesca does also. I think her time in Portugal was the happiest time of her childhood and the most inclusive.

Parties and Friends

'Watch this dad, I will end up being the nanny to all the other children whilst the parents all sit and chat'. I was going to a party that Francesca had been invited to (when she was around seven years old). My dad was staying with me, so he came also. I explained to my dad how I would need to support Francesca at the party for her to be able to play and be included, but I realised from experience that I would end up looking after everyone else's children, whilst their parents sat, had a drink, and chatted. Sure enough, that is exactly what happened. I would be on the bouncy castle supporting Francesca and the other children whilst their mums (and dads) sat around drinking champagne and oblivious to the fact not only was I supporting Francesca to play but also their children. I remember spending nearly the entire two hours on that bouncy castle; Francesca would not get off as she enjoyed it so much, and nobody offered to take over, if only for ten minutes to give me a break. I left the party not having talked to anyone and exhausted. A similar issue arose when I would take Francesca swimming in Portugal with other children. Those children could swim, so their mums seemed confident their children were safe in the pool, but I often wondered if they relied on the fact I was with Francesca. They'd often walk through just to check on their children, and say, 'looks like you are doing a great job', 'you should be a nanny'.

There were occasions throughout Francesca's early years when she was invited to parties. Those invites disappeared the older and 'more disabled' she became. Her inability to verbalise was often the reason a child who had been friends with Francesca lost interest. I endlessly invited children to ours when she was in a mainstream school, but the invites would rarely be returned; no doubt those children found it harder to interact with Francesca the older they got and developed other interests. They would start to cancel, mostly last minute, parents saying their child had been asked to go somewhere else, and they had gone. People never seemed to think anything of not returning the invites to parties or tea or cancelling at the last minute because their child got a better offer. Francesca's feelings never seemed to matter.

People would stop inviting us around to their house after one visit because they'd realise I could not sit and have a coffee whilst the children played, and Francesca could not play by herself with their child. I could not just leave Francesca either, as other parents might leave their children at other parents' houses (as they got older). It was no different when Francesca started special school. Even though the class sizes were small, similar to the situation we had in Portugal, the experiences were not the same. In a way, going to a special school became more isolating because many children were transported to school, so you would miss the interaction parents would normally get with other parents at the school gates, and there were no invites as there had been in Portugal to meet up after school or at the weekend. I think the reason for this is that many families with disabled children are not living in accessible homes. They might have no accessible outside space; one child in a special school might need an accessible bathroom, or ramped access, whilst another child's disability might not require that provision, making the ability to invite others around very difficult, and of course, we could not go to the park to play as so many are inaccessible.

For the last eight years of Francesca's schooling, she attended a special school. During that time, she was only ever invited to one party. The invite was to a bowling party. I knew Francesca would not be able to bear the noise, or enjoy it, but I went anyway, as I did not want to look ungrateful or stop Francesca being included, and I hoped for once that she might enjoy it. However, it was a disaster; we spent a vast proportion of that party lying on the floor, as Francesca was so distressed by the noise; we left early. I think the lack of inclusion over the years, meaning that going out and doing normal things as other families do, has created fear that might not have existed if she could have been included more in normal everyday life. The less Francesca was included in society, the more she grew to fear things that she used to love. Whilst special schools have their place, my fear is she went from a mainstream setting, where she was known by many people (in the village), interacting with non-disabled peers, enjoying trips out with school, being included, particularly when we lived in Portugal, to mainly staying behind the gates of the special school and not actually experiencing life and experiences as other children do.

Toys and Play

Francesca's main love now is the computer, she loves watching YouTube and playing games on CBeebies. The computer is something she can do; she can use the mouse independently, which I am sure gives her confidence, but she also enjoys interacting and playing on it with the young carers. I think Francesca views the younger carers that she has as friends and is very excited when they arrive. Francesca is very sociable; she loves engaging with other people. She would love to have friends. The carers I employ do become part of the family, but they move on to university, other jobs, and whilst they stay in touch from time to time, they are no longer coming around to play as they did. That must be hard for Francesca to understand and cope with. She has suffered a lot of loss throughout her life. She won't be aware that the person coming to play games with her on the computer is paid to do so and eventually moves on to other work.

Francesca has enjoyed playing with dolls throughout her childhood, still now in adulthood she wants to go to see the babies in the supermarket or toy shop. She's also enjoyed matching games and has been very good throughout her life at playing these games; some of these games I've needed to simplify for her and play in another way to enable her to understand and join in. There is a lack of toys on the market that are simpler to understand. With activity books, there is too much information on one page, making the pages too busy for Francesca to follow or see. In the early years, she enjoyed her pretend shop, but she was never interested in her doll house or the figures and home furniture I bought for it. I realise now her visual impairment impacted her ability to play with some toys. The games Francesca enjoyed the most were when I incorporated physiotherapy or occupational therapy into her play, such as building an assault course in the garden in Portugal, or role play with the babies, changing their clothes, putting them in the bath, feeding them and putting them to bed. Her teddies have been her favourite toys throughout her life. I and Francesca's Grandma have regularly brought the bears to life to help Francesca follow instructions. We've probably looked somewhat strange at times when out in public, talking as if we were the bear, asking Francesca to do something. But it has helped Francesca understand when 'Lily Bear' brushes her teeth, takes her medication, gets out of the car at hospital or eats her dinner first. Lily Bear even had an operation, to help desensitise Francesca to hospital procedures. Reflecting on play throughout her childhood, play for Francesca has always involved some form of therapy or desensitisation.

Playgrounds

One of the biggest issues restricting my Francesca's ability to play and have a childhood has been the lack of accessible playgrounds. When Francesca was very young, her mobility was not as severe, so she managed with support to access most of the playground equipment. The swing was Francesca's favourite; I think she loved the feeling of freedom it gave her. As she got older, and bigger, she needed a swing with support but could no longer fit into the 'toddler swings'; there were no other options other than the normal swings that parks have for older children. These swings were not suitable as she would often let go to communicate something to me using her hands, or her physical disabilities meant that she struggled to balance herself and was at risk of falling off. Accessible swings exist now in some playgrounds; however, in many parks, there is only one, a 'token' swing for those with disabilities which, from my experience, is always being used by other non-disabled children. The lack of suitable swings reduced her enjoyment of parks, and she started to switch off from going. Sadly, despite where we live having three playgrounds, none is accessible to us.

Francesca is very sociable and enjoys watching other children play. Whilst she enjoyed this, I wondered what she was thinking; it made me sad, as she could not get on the equipment and experience childhood as those children were. She wanted to be independent, to be able to go on equipment without 'mum', and she should have been able to access the park as other children do. She was denied this basic provision.

The lack of accessible playgrounds made my daughter and me feel excluded from society. We would attempt to go up the slide, only for other children to get frustrated and push past us; this would disrupt Francesca's concentration, and she would not want to go, become upset or would miss her turn. Children and their families would often stare at us, particularly, when I had to climb up and down the slide with her; it was not a nice feeling. Families would often be sitting around a picnic table engaging with each other, or families after school would arrange to meet up at the park, but those invites or that inclusion was rarely extended to us. When I picked my daughter up from school, whilst I would hear mums saying to others, 'are you coming down the park?'; we were rarely included in those invites. If we were, I would not be able to sit with other parents, chat and have a drink, as other parents did, as I needed to support Francesca on the equipment. Because of this, we never experienced childhood as others do. Throughout Francesca's childhood, we have often been excluded from things that other families take for granted. As my daughter got older, she became more frustrated by her inability to access the equipment as she used to do; she would not want to stay as long or would give up after a couple of attempts. As a parent, this is a very sad thing to witness because it could have been so easily fixed to ensure all children are able to play and have a childhood. If the playground had been accessible, I think this would have changed people's attitudes towards her. The playground should have been a place where Francesca could have enjoyed, played and made friends. It could have given her the opportunity of incorporating physiotherapy into her play; sadly, this was never possible.

4

THE TALE OF THE DANCING EYES

Solange Bonello

FIGURE 4.1 Solange as a young child, with pigtails and glasses, is smiling. An aeroplane is in the background

DOI: 10.4324/9781003102915-4

Puppet Show

One of my first childhood memories is sitting on a green wooden chair in the school hall watching a puppet show. I was sitting at the front next to my first-grade teacher who always systematically placed the quieter children in the first row to keep up appearances, as we were always told that quieter students represented the school. I remember laughing out loudly, clapping and cheering as if it were the greatest show ever made.

This was, however, not down to being entertained by the puppeteer; it was rather a result of myself imitating my classmates' actions. If they laughed, I made sure to laugh louder; if they clapped, I waved my hands and clapped twice as hard. I was only five years of age at the time but I had already mastered the ability to hide my insecurities by pretending to be like my peers.

In reality, I could barely see past the main stage and could only see silhouettes of what were supposed to be puppets but that didn't matter to me. I had an eagerness to fit in, to enjoy the activity as my peers appeared to be doing so easily. Hence, at a very young age, I learnt that if I wanted to enjoy life's puppet show.... I had to improvise.

Airline Pilot

Every year on my birthday before we make our way through some homemade cake, my parents always narrate the same anecdote. They recite all the memories from the moment I was born up to my impairment diagnosis. A narrative that, despite having listened to it for over three decades, I still look forward to it every year for it is a reminder of how even in the midst of pain and heartache, the wonder of life is always present.

I was born in the late 1980s in Toronto, Canada, to Maltese parents. My mother recounts how, after only a few weeks of having given birth to me, she could observe that I struggled to focus visually. After seeking medical advice she was told not to fuss as first-time mothers tend to do and my lack of visual engagement was put down to normal stages of development.

As more weeks passed by, my parents noticed that my eye pupils would move uncontrollably whilst I cried for hours on end because of what seemed like irritation and restlessness. Having persisted with medical professionals that something wasn't right, I was referred for further testing at one of the largest children's hospitals in Toronto. The results confirmed that my parents' intuition was indeed correct. I was diagnosed with congenital nystagmus, a visual impairment that results in involuntary eye movement with some degree of vision loss. Since at the time I was only a newborn, the extent of my vision loss could not be determined. At a later stage, it was eventually established that I had severe vision loss. The only certainty was that no cure was available.

What my parents recall, every year on my birthday, is how they sat at the consultant's office after the news had just been broken to them, feeling like life had just come to a halt. At the time they were in their mid-20s, living in a country far away from their family and support system. My mother recounts how the first thing she asked the consultant was how the impairment would impact my life and what I would be able to do. The consultant brusquely replied that I would never be an airline pilot. Feeling distraught and in need of more answers, my father narrates his frequent visits to one of Toronto's main libraries, where he would look up the diagnosis in search of more information. This was at a time when the luxury of online research was still non-existent.

A year after my diagnosis my parents decided that relocating back to Malta would be the best way forward in terms of emotional support. My mother always recounts how being surrounded by family and friends eased the anxiety of the unknown and how coming back to Malta gave them more emotional security, knowing that, even if the world would come crumbling down once again, they would be physically surrounded by unwavering love and support.

Not a Disability

Despite understanding that my visual impairment would impact my life in one way or another, my family was not made aware by medical professionals that the severity of my impairment could actually be classified as a disability. Therefore, growing up I very well understood my visual limitations but always referred to the situation as having limited eyesight and needing thick spectacles to get on in life. In this regard, until I was 18 years of age, I never identified myself as being disabled nor did we as a family seek assistance from any particular support services.

The reality of not having been given a disability label until later on in life has had both its advantages and disadvantages with the former being the most palpable. As a child and in my pre-teens, I went about my daily life thinking and genuinely believing that I was no different to anyone else. I still experienced episodes of insecurities when carrying out tasks that challenged my eyesight, but the anxieties were not a result of feeling self-conscious around my peers but rather internal frustration of not being free to carry out particular tasks, just as I had desperately wanted to enjoy the puppet show in that Grade One class.

In retrospect, the benefits of not having been given a disability label at a young age gave me the opportunity to attempt life without prejudice, pity or overprotectiveness. Guidance and assistance were given to me both at home and at school solely when needed. I was never seen as a child whose entire life prospects were based on a particular disability. I was a child like my sibling, cousins and peers, who all needed guidance for one thing or another just like any child would at different stages throughout their childhood. Consequently, the concept of disability, as it was understood then, did not overshadow my childhood. I had the opportunity to experience what it felt like to be seen as everyone else did, whilst being supported solely when required.

Nevertheless, not being registered as a disabled person during my childhood did have its drawbacks. First, my parents would have benefited from financial assistance that would have lessened the cost of medical treatment and equipment. Second, at times when disability is not particularly visible, it is difficult to prove the extent of what is needed and what is yours by right. In this regard, having a confirmation on paper would have been of great help during different scenarios.

First Row

I attended a small Catholic school from the age of five until I was 16 years of age. The school staff were made aware of my visual impairment without it being labelled a disability, and I was always given unwavering support when required. My schooling journey started in the early 1990s when learning support assistants were not common practice, and thus, my teachers were exclusively responsible for my needs. The school was a relatively small one with a tight-knit community, and I had the same classmates through the majority of my 11 years in primary and secondary education. This environment made it easier for my needs to be met, and thus, my visual impairment was a reality that my peers were familiar with from the age of five until we parted ways at the age of 16.

I can never recall feeling excluded or bullied as my inclusion was part and parcel of daily school life. The first row was always reserved for me by my peers, and I was allowed to sit at the front during activities and outings. This of course does not necessarily mean that I fully enjoyed every activity as many a times sitting at the very front did not automatically mean I could see well enough. Nonetheless, I felt loved and supported and that really did surmount everything else as it eased in some ways the frustration of not being able to participate fully during activities and outings.

Teachers provided handouts in large print, and anything written on the blackboard (and eventually the whiteboard) would be dictated to or written down for me. When teachers were tight on time, one of my peers would be asked to copy the notes for me, and it was always a competition of who would be honoured with the task. When we had sports and other activities, I was a terrible team member as my vision would limit my ability to participate fully. Still, I never recall being left out as one of my peers would be appointed to assist me, and the task would be accepted without any hesitation.

Furthermore, as a child, I was very quiet yet friends with all of my classmates and was selected a number of times as class prefect by my peers. This feeling of respect and appreciation did boost my confidence and did ease to some extent my internal anxieties throughout my school years.

Nevertheless, despite having a very positive school experience, I still recall my daily struggles of trying to keep up with the rest of my peers academically and during extracurricular activities. I genuinely enjoyed studying and was at the majority of times at the top of my class in terms of grades. However, this achievement came with its own fair share of struggles and exhaustion. Visually, I was not able to concentrate for long hours at a stretch, and reading and writing were exhausting, and at times, the smallest of things seemed like a mammoth task. Therefore, studying always meant much longer hours than my peers needed to put in and planning ahead.

During my primary school years, my parents would assist me in my studies in a myriad of ways, and I attribute my love for academia as a result of their love, dedication and perseverance. Nevertheless, as the years went by and I grew older, I had to start fending more for myself, and it became more difficult to keep up. Still, I was never given a free pass by my parents. I remember complaining that I would be visually exhausted when studying or carrying out endless amounts of homework and my mother would encourage me to rest but would make it clear that I would have to continue where I left off right away. At the time I may have not appreciated their approach as much as I do now, as it is now clear to me that if I had been looked upon with pity and allowed to give in whenever I felt that I couldn't achieve something, I most probably would have done so.

In addition, particularly in secondary school, having different teachers for each and every subject meant different styles of inclusion which may have been lacking at times yet the tight-knit community made sure not to leave anyone behind, and thus, my struggles were always addressed in one way or another.

Looking back at my years in primary and secondary school with my present understanding of inclusion, I can highlight a number of instances when inclusivity might have been lacking. Such as some teachers thinking that placing a visually impaired student in the front row is meeting all of their needs or not thinking about accessibility issues when watching educational video clips on small television screens. Nevertheless, I remember being loved, cared for, respected and surrounded by my peers. This made me proud to belong to a community where I felt safe and most of all was seen as an individual. In this regard, I will always look back at my schooling experience with very fond memories for it was a community where I could just be myself without having a disability mark stamped all over everything I did.

Driving Lessons

Up until I was 18 years of age, I was still not registered as a person with disability and had accomplished most of life's milestones just as my peers had done. For this reason, I genuinely believed that – just like all other instances in my life – I would be able to drive a car with some adaptation. Thus, my ultimate goal was to start driving lessons so as to become more independent.

I can still picture clearly the expression on my ophthalmologist's face when I asked him to sign the required paperwork to apply for driving lessons. It was as if I had just asked him to give me the green light to operate a rocket into space. He had been my ophthalmologist since we had arrived from Canada and was the kindest, most gentle doctor with a welcoming smile and always full of encouragement. This was the very first time in nearly two decades that he seemed lost for words and saddened by what he was about to say. Even though 15 years have passed since that particular consultation, I remember his exact words as if they were uttered yesterday:

> I have been your doctor since you were just a baby and it hurts me to have to tell you this as I care and respect you as if you were one of my very own grandchildren. I cannot sign this paperwork, for your eyesight is too severe to allow you to drive. No vehicle adaptation or glasses prescription can ever give you that opportunity. You have a disability and if I sign the paperwork I would be signing your death sentence.

It was the very first time in my 18 years of living that the possibility of disability crossed my mind. In the span of a few seconds, a countless number of feelings ensued ranging from shock to disbelief. Suddenly the consultation room that I had been visiting for nearly two decades was no longer familiar. It felt like I was being re-diagnosed with a visual impairment that I knew nothing about.

The pain my parents had felt when being informed of my visual impairment back in the late 1980s felt somehow tangible to me. As the ophthalmologist continued to speak, I remember feeling like I was being handed down a life sentence of dependence, for at the age of 18, I genuinely thought that my ultimate goal in life was to obtain a driving license. It felt like the stability I had experienced throughout my childhood was being ruptured by the term disability.

During this period in my life, I was re-visited by the internal anxieties I experienced as a child, yet this time around it was coupled up with anger, depression, bargaining and denial. The intense feeling of denial continued to increase my anxiety, and I visited five other ophthalmologists in a period of six months in an attempt to challenge my own ophthalmologist's conclusions. As I desperately searched for someone who would untie me from this heart-breaking reality, to my own dismay, I was given the same answer by all of the other ophthalmologists.

It is evident to me now that, at the age of 18, I was experiencing the mourning stages of being diagnosed with a disability. My experience is also a pure illustration of how the journey of acceptance comes at different phases in life and that the multifaceted stages of mourning are fluid and intertwined.

Even though I had lived all my life with a visual impairment, it is clear that the way I experienced life during my childhood, pre-teens and most of my teenage years was somewhat different from my life after being confirmed as a person with disability. I was free from labels, free from feeling different, free from stigma, and free from self-consciousness around others.

As a child, I never recall feeling self-aware of my eye pupils moving rapidly when people looked into my eyes. For my family and schoolmates, it was part of who I was, which meant that for the majority of the time, I also forgot how fast my pupils moved. Yet, during this particular period in my life, having been newly labelled as having a disability, I started becoming more aware of how others looked at me and became much more self-conscious. I remember looking down as much as I could to avoid eye contact whenever possible and started to question everything around me.

It felt like my disability had been dormant and had now taken life through a stamp on a document. I kept resisting the idea of having a disability, yet it seemed to chase me wherever I went. I yearned for my childhood when the complexity of disability was not present, when I was allowed to live with my visual impairment without too much fuss. I grieved the life I had lived until now; it was as if I had woken up to a different life in an unknown environment.

Onwards and Upwards

Through the unwavering support I received from my family and closest of friends, I slowly started to come to terms with the notion of having a disability. It took years for me to comprehend that acceptance doesn't necessarily mean feeling grateful for my disability but rather learning to live with the reality of a life-changing experience. By the time, I realised that my emotions were valid as I was a human being trying to make sense of life, and thus, the first step towards acceptance was allowing myself to feel all the emotions that at times took over.

Nevertheless, over time it became more evident that having been diagnosed with a disability also had its advantages. Now that I had official documentation that proved that I had severe visual limitations, I was able to apply for services such as access arrangements during my tertiary education and join support groups for visually impaired individuals, amongst others. It also made me feel seen in terms of my difficulties and that my visual struggles needed to be addressed in each and every scenario.

In addition, I started to appreciate how fortunate I had been to have had a beautiful experience during my primary and secondary school years. This was instrumental towards my love for inclusion particularly in educational settings. I was eager to share my own experience and to learn more on how educational settings can improve their current inclusive practices. I obtained diplomas in *Early Years Education* as well as *Inclusive Education* and furthered my studies with a first degree honours in *Youth & Community Studies* and a *Master of Arts in Sociology*. I have currently also embarked on my doctorate specialising in gender and disability studies.

Having had the opportunity to live a life where disability was not always the main focus allowed me to appreciate that having a disability was part and parcel of my life but not in its entirety. This perspective fuelled my work in the activism sector both within the disability and gender fields as I took a particular interest in the rights of women and girls with a disability. Through my activism work, I continued to enhance my understanding of the underpinnings that truly make up an inclusive society, particularly when addressing those in power and privilege.

As I look back, particularly at my childhood experience, I realise how often we take the stability of inclusion, love, support and care for granted. I have been blessed to have crossed paths with a number of individuals who have been there to soothe the anguish in a myriad of ways when I felt like my life was collapsing into pieces. These individuals include my family, close friends, colleagues, university lecturers and classmates who have supported me and encouraged me to carry on even when I felt that I couldn't cope during different stages in my life.

Reflecting on my own disability journey has always been somewhat bittersweet as it has hurt me and healed me all at once. Yet, throughout time I learnt to work with my disability rather than against it, for I now understand that both myself and the notion of disability are perpetually developing together.

Consequently, on the days when it is difficult to find hope, I lean on those who have walked similar paths and who have thrived in spite of their trauma. My disability journey has given me a number of highs and lows but, above all, it has shown me the true meaning of fortitude and the importance of support and acceptance so as to be able to live freely and according to one's own free will.

5

THE TROUBLE WITH 'NORMAL'

Finding Hope through Resistance

Miro Griffiths

FIGURE 5.1 A young Miro in his motorised wheelchair is in the foreground, with a portrait of the adult Miro in the background

How do I start a chapter reflecting on my years as a disabled teenager? Let us start with the context. I lived on the Wirral peninsula, in a semi-detached house surrounded by the smell of fertiliser on the nearby farmlands. The property had been adapted to accommodate my needs around the age of

DOI: 10.4324/9781003102915-5

ten; prior to this, my parents would carry me around the house and *plonk* me down in different environments – bed for sleeping, dining room chair for eating, living room floor for gaming and the bath for washing. My power wheelchair could not manoeuvre around the house due to narrow hallways, narrow doors and tight turning corners. I lived with my father as my parents had divorced when I was ten, although my mother still lived in the same village and my brother had left the family home to gain enlightenment from university.

Thinking back, as a teenager, I yearned for a normal life, an ordinary life, with people not acknowledging my impairments. I was desperate to be forgotten about. Every stare of curiosity felt like a growing twinge of pain. I would be embarrassed if people referenced the wheelchair. I wore clothes that could hide my atrophied body, and I apologised for everything. I mean *everything*. It was my fault if a building was inaccessible, and I felt compelled to apologise to the proprietor for the inconvenience I was causing by trying to enter. I was the nuisance that caused peers to move their chairs when I entered the classroom. At the time, it never occurred to me that the design of the classroom, organised around the assumption that everybody in that space would walk on two legs, could be the reason for asking people constantly to 'make way for Miro'.

I would apologise through my inner voice or non-verbal communication signs. I remember struggling to feed myself in the school canteen. The weight of the cheese-pickle-bread combination, along with the weight of the shirt and jumper sleeve fabric, made eating an ordeal. The pursuit of wanting to be normal, or even just ordinary, meant rejecting, outright, the offer for my school assistant to feed me. I did not want that. I believed it was childlike to be fed when everybody around me could feed themselves. I did not want to be different. Different meant deviant. It meant becoming an outsider. Nobody would consider me normal if they saw me being 'different'. I struggled. I dropped the sandwich, and the pickle juice stained my white school shirt. The cheese tumbled and became trapped between my legs and the wheelchair seat. My eyes darted around the open hall and my inner voice apologised to every student, teacher and kitchen staff worker.

> I'm sorry if you saw that. I am sorry if *I* embarrassed *you*. I am sorry for bothering you and I'm sorry for being here. What I did was *not normal*, but I will correct it.

These thoughts played on a loop whilst my assistant blotted the stain and searched for the grated cheese.

I feel quite angry as I speak the paragraph above.

I do not type, I cannot type. I have dictated all my writing through voice recognition software since the age of 21. I am now 33 years old, and I think and feel very differently from my teenage years. People's stares, which are still a constant, no longer embarrass me. I love the premise of disruption now, so if I have disrupted somebody's gaze or pattern of thoughts then that is an accolade I embrace. I am content with how my body is, despite the occasional day of contemplating 'getting beach body ready'. My partner, Emma, affectionately calls my atrophied arms her 'noodles', and my dog appears best pleased using my prominent belly – caused by the weakening of my stomach muscles – as his pillow.

My power wheelchair is a valuable asset, which I love to sit in and manoeuvre every day. My personal assistants, which I have 24 hours a day and seven days a week, are essential for realising self-determination, choice and control. They move me, they bathe me, they dress me, they feed me, they administer my medications and therapies, they take direction from me and they assist me to *be who I want to be*. For me, carrying out such tasks independently, to demonstrate self-sufficiency, is no longer something I desire. I have no interest in walking (I consider it overrated), I have little regard for demonstrating normal (conformity is exhausting) and I no longer accept responsibility for the exclusions I experience throughout society (I will not apologise for the unnecessary restrictions imposed upon me).

I have come to realise that the normalcy I desperately wanted in my teenage years is so deeply toxic. It was, and always will be, toxic to every atom of my being. The normalcy I yearned for, and the persistent feeling that I needed to conform to the expectations of others, was poisonous. The crackles of my internal Geiger counter intensified as I searched, desperately, to be accepted and fit in with those I considered to be 'normal'. The closer I found myself to achieving normalcy, the more I felt ashamed of my impairments and access requirements. I did not realise, at the time, that the more I searched for normalcy, the further I moved away from the path to liberation. Thankfully, this period was a detour. It was imperative that this changed for my wellbeing and sense of self. I am in no doubt that, left unchallenged, I would have destroyed myself.

It did change. The turning point was when I became aware of disability activism and politics.

It should be noted, before I describe my personal trajectory through activism and resistance, that my parents were politically active throughout my early and teenage years. My mother had grown up in Yugoslavia, under the rule of President Tito, and my father had been active in the UK Ecology Party. There was a general emphasis on accessibility, inclusion and participation in our family. Participation in the community was important, opportunities to play and form friendships were encouraged and celebrated and there were regular attempts to remove restrictions through changes to the environment around me.

My upbringing was at odds with the narratives and perspectives articulated by medical professionals, who became involved extensively in my life after my diagnosis at 18 months old (a condition that causes progressive muscle weakness from the neck down). Professionals, with their authority and assumed credibility, were popping up everywhere. They were in my school. They were in my home. They would interrupt me when I was playing with my friends. They would chair the many meetings about me and make the decisions. Forget being in the driving seat! I was not even a passenger. *I was luggage in the car boot.* I was picked up, prodded, scrutinised, and made to repeat tests and my (impairment-focused) stories – often to people who never introduced themselves and who I would never see again. What hurt the most, for me and my family, were the pity and the repulsion. People – from doctors to co-workers, to neighbours, to family members – were very quick to express their views. The paediatric consultant, on verbalising my diagnosis, followed this up immediately by telling my parents 'Technology these days…It is amazing what people can do with their eyes'. One of my father's co-workers, on hearing the diagnosis news, said 'well, you will be rolling in money, considering all those benefits those disabled people get'. Neighbours, and some family members, would talk about the sorrow and the shame that I wasn't healthy, that I wasn't like *their* children. To them, I was something they did not desire.

After my diagnosis, professionals started discussing the benefits of segregated services (school, respite services and segregated play centres for disabled children). They claimed that in such spaces, I would be better supported; I would have quick access to service provision; and I would be safe. Protecting disabled children was paramount. It was the priority. To be safe, according to them, meant being incarcerated in segregated environments.

My parents pushed back against these narratives. They started to become familiar with disability politics, particularly the social model of disability and independent living philosophy. They happened upon this by chance, through their own research and study. The realisation was stark. To live, and to thrive, Miro needed self-determination. Here, they arrived at a crossroads. We could strive for self-determination by prioritising rehabilitation, building hopes for a cure and aspiring for self-sufficiency. Alternatively, self-determination could be pursued through prioritising support, responding to access requirements and building environments that accommodated all forms of participation. My parents followed the second road.

Shortly after my parents reached this understanding, my mother marched around the corner from the family home to the local primary school (which my father had attended) and knocked on the headmaster's door. In her rather stern-sounding Slovenian accent (which has not softened to this day), she said:

My youngest son is disabled. He is a wheelchair user. He *will* come to this school. You have several years to prepare. There need to be ramps, there need to be support assistants, there need to be parking bays. *All* children will learn together, he will *not* be segregated.

She walked out of the headmaster's office before waiting for a response. Several years later, I started at that local primary school.

My parents emphasised the importance of participating in the community and of having the necessary support (assistive technology, mobility equipment and support provision) so that I could do the things that I wanted to do with my life. Having a power wheelchair from the age of three provided me with the agency to influence who I would play with, where I would go and what I would do. Building friendships with disabled and non-disabled peers meant we, organically, found our own ways to support each other and determine inclusive practices when we played and studied together.

I would drive my power chair up and down the avenue where I lived, playing games with other children who lived there. We would get into quite a lot of mischief. One of our favourite games was to shake apple trees in the avenue and see how many apples would fall onto the roofs of nearby cars. I was always the champion because I could swing the back of my power chair quite fast into the tree trunk, causing the apples to rain down and bounce off the expensive vehicles. My friends chanted my name until the car owners would come out of their homes, shout and chase us away!

In primary school, my classmates supported me during activities and study periods. If my hand became tired from writing and my support worker was unavailable, students would take it upon themselves to write for me as I dictated to them. They would raise my hand up if I wanted to get the teacher's attention and would clear pathways on the way out of the classroom without any teacher prompting them.

Despite all this, my early childhood and teenage years were subjected to persistent questions over my legitimacy to exist and participate in the local community. I became aware, as I aged, that my behaviours, actions and choices were being scrutinised by professionals and practitioners. My parents had to *exhaustingly* justify the reasons for requesting access to services or resources. My needs had to be outlined, but they also had to be defended when the onslaught of questions and challenges materialised. The starting point for most conversations was never *how* to prioritise participation. Instead, it was *why* is participation necessary?

I would sit in meetings with professionals as they debated the cost implications for my access requirements. Every interaction would include statements such as: *How much will this cost? Who is paying for this? How will this meet his [insert health, educational, well-being et cetera] outcome?* I felt reduced to a prescriptive set of outcomes, which were constantly 'under review'. This meant it was near impossible to propose alternative pathways to the one I had been advised – or told – to follow. I received the same answer if I wanted support provided differently or if I wanted to pursue different opportunities from the one present: *no, it is not possible.* Professionals would tell me how much time, resources, and money had been pumped into the current set of activities. Changing it would be costly, and complicated, so it is *best to continue with the way things are.*

During my teenage years, I had to find, and articulate, the value and worth associated with my participation. As stated, I apologised to everyone around me for the inconvenience caused by my presence. I also became fixated on watching people, scrutinising their behaviours, to witness the signs of their intolerance. I presumed everybody was intolerant to my being. Sighs, eyes rolling, squirming, avoidance or even smirks would form part of my watch list. These feelings intensified as I tumbled through secondary school and college. The joy of play, bonding and nurturing friendships, which appeared so essential to early childhood, started to dissolve for me. It was replaced with toxic displays of self-sufficiency and aggressive competition amongst peers. These displays were everywhere: from friends, strangers and from within my body. Fitting in became a survival tactic and, coupled with the incessant need to apologise, I believed the only way to survive was to assimilate with others and 'perform normal'.

Have you spotted the irony in my story thus far? My parents placed me on the path towards celebrating interdependency, prioritising accessibility and emphasising change within social organisation. It was *me* who rejected their approach despite all their efforts. I felt *compelled* to follow the alternative path, which I now consider to be deeply harmful to the lives of disabled people – and their families. In fact, I consider the quest for normalcy to be an act of violence against all communities across the globe. Chasing normal means living in desperation. It means desiring anything other than who you are now. It stifles creativity. It ignores the celebration of variance and diversity throughout existence. It rejects the experiments to build accessible, inclusive, safe and participatory societies.

I do not blame myself, nor will I ever blame anybody who yearns for assimilation and who fixates on their performance to pass as normal. I have lost count of the number of disabled people, often young and/or who are new to the experience of impairment, who tell me their dream is to *not* be disabled. 'Of course', I respond, 'but how do we stop being disabled?' I can guess their answer before they communicate it. They tell me the fix is to feel ordinary, to be perceived as ordinary by others, to fit in, have the same opportunities and be treated like everybody around them. I feel desperately sad by this answer.

My feelings of sadness manifest because of the insight I have gained through disability activism and politics. It was around the age of 15 when I first became aware of disability politics. Prior to this, I had become entangled in a few traditional charity campaigns, where I would speak passionately about *triumphing over adversity* and the cruelty of being *trapped* in a wheelchair. One day, a prominent disabled activist approached me after I had finished giving a public talk on behalf of a charity. We sat together for an hour and debated our understanding of disability, what constitutes inclusion and the pitfalls of ordinariness. The more I listened and reflected, the more I realised my views were becoming conflicted. I needed time to consider the activist's perspective further. They sent me material to read on the social model of disability, independent living philosophy and the politics of disablement. I will never underestimate how a single, albeit fleeting, conversation affected my understanding of my body, the positions I occupy throughout society and my identity as a political subject. (*Please, I beg you, remember that all conversations have the potential to transform individual, and collective, lives.*)

It was a struggle to find local disabled activist networks. I did not know who to search for, and I lacked the confidence to approach them, so instead I immersed myself in the writings of disabled activists nationally and internationally. The social model of disability and the independent living philosophy became – and still are – the core of my activism and politics. They provided me with an awareness, a passion and a vocabulary for investigating the injustices experienced throughout society. I could no longer accept responsibility for the restrictions imposed upon me because these restrictions were unnecessary. They were unnecessary because they were socially produced. Possibilities always exist to reimagine, and reorganise, the social world. The world, in its current forms, was reproducing the barriers, the restrictions, the intolerances and the injustices encountered by disabled people. I no longer had ownership of disability – I was not a person 'with disabilities'. I was a person who had and has an impairment, but disablement was being, repeatedly, done *to me*, imposed *upon me* by a disabling society. Disablement and disability were produced through social organisation and 'owned' by society.

I realised that chasing normal was causing me to be exhausted, lonely and sad. I began to question what the fixation on normal would achieve. There is so much frustration, anger and desperation in our societies. I thought about how the world, in its current organisation, was not working for most people. We (disabled people) want to be accepted, and tolerated, for who we are, yet most of us are trapped into attempting to achieve this acceptance, this *acceptability*, through assimilation.

But there is variation throughout all forms of existence. There is variation in our bodies, in our processing, in the reasons for our participation and in the approaches we take to participate. There is variation everywhere, and acceptance – indeed, celebration – of variance should remain at the core of our social organisation. Societies, surely, can progress beyond merely tolerating one's existence.

This is what I want to achieve through my activism. I want to explore alternative avenues and multiple possibilities for (re)arranging our societies. I want us to use our activism to build communities on principles of accessibility, participation and acceptance of variation. The point of our activism is not to imagine a world where we, disabled people, can *just* fit in. We need to use our activism and politics to produce ideas for reimagining inclusive societies that benefit *all*. We can use our experiences and understandings of inclusion, exclusion and accessibility to establish spaces where *all are welcome*.

I cherish the moment when I realised, as a teenager, that resistance and transformation are always possible.

In closing, I return to the memories of those arduous and painfully bureaucratic meetings with professionals who would determine the opportunities that would be afforded to me. I said the starting point for most conversations was never *how* to prioritise my participation. Instead, it was *why my participation was necessary*? If I were to return to my younger self, then I would propose they answer a different question: *why is Miro's participation being denied?*

6

DISABLED CHILDREN'S ACTIVE PARTICIPATION IN EARLY CHILDHOOD EDUCATION

A Story of Love, Rights and Solidarity from Aotearoa New Zealand

Michael Gaffney and Kate McAnelly

Introduction

In Aotearoa New Zealand, the national early childhood curriculum is called *Te Whāriki* (Ministry of Education, 2017, p. 10), which is the indigenous term for woven mat where:

> [k] aiako [teachers] in ECE settings weave together the principles and strands, in collaboration with children, parents, whānau [families] and communities, to create a local curriculum for their setting. Understood in this way, the curriculum or whāriki is a 'mat for all to stand on'.

This last phrase is important in relation to disability studies because it reflects the notion that all children belong and have a place in Aotearoa New Zealand's early childhood settings. Elsewhere in *Te Whāriki*, there is acknowledgement that:

> [a]ll children have rights to protection and promotion of their health and wellbeing, to equitable access to learning opportunities, to recognition of their language, culture and identity and, increasingly, to agency in their own lives.
>
> *(Ministry of Education, 2017, p. 12)*

We see these ideas as expressing the aspiration that many advocates of children's rights in Aotearoa New Zealand hold (Smith, 2013; Smith, 2015; Te One, 2011), which is that the innate competence, strength and power of all children be recognised and affirmed (Bevan-Brown et al., 2015; Rameka

DOI: 10.4324/9781003102915-6

and Soutar, 2019). However, turning this aspiration into reality for all is where work still needs to happen, as too many disabled children's experiences continue to be counter to *Te Whāriki's* inclusive intent (Purdue et al., 2020). Critics have noted that *Te Whāriki* is not without its ableist tendencies by not referencing disabled children and their families directly and leaning towards normative expectations when diversity should be the norm (Macartney, 2019).

In this chapter, we outline the work that we have done to support the shift that we propose is required to achieve these curriculum aspirations. We do this by making visible the affective potentials of love (Thomas, 2012) within disabled children's experiences of active participation, inclusion and citizenship in early childhood settings. Our work set out to define what active participation (McAnelly and Gaffney, 2017) looks like for disabled children based on observing it in an early childhood community of practice. We use community of practice terminology here as the early childhood setting in question met Wenger's (1998) definition. There was a group of people who shared a concern and interest as part of a joint enterprise, in this case, to create an inclusive early childhood setting. Collectively they learned how to be more inclusive as they interacted regularly and negotiated their shared practices as part of their ongoing mutual engagement based on by all, for all democratic notions of participation and learning. Over time, shared repertoires of meaning emerged that became a resource to support negotiating practices in response to new scenarios and defined them in terms of what participation could be.

We have come to understand active participation as consisting of three elements, each contributing to the shared repertoires of meaning for a community, they are the:

> Pedagogic [where] all members of early childhood communities of practice enjoy responsive, reciprocal relationships with each other that value different ways of being, doing and knowing....
>
> Ecological [where] all members of early childhood communities of practice are able to realise an image of themselves and each other as capable, competent, powerful learners and contributors to the world around them....[and]
>
> Equitable/inclusive [where] all members of early childhood communities of practice are supported to have an equitable voice in decision making processes about the things that effect them there.
>
> *(McAnelly and Gaffney, 2017, p. 20)*

Next, we wanted to more closely examine the underlying features of active participation, and how this was supported by the intentionality of the members of the early childhood community of practice. The main focus of this work was in identifying how disabled children's active participation and learning could be evaluated in relation to the affordances of the early childhood learning environment. We ended up with a framework which asserts that when:

> A meaningful and inviting learning environment has been made available; within which the practices are based on a culture of rights and inclusive belonging and contribution; and people adopt a pedagogy of participation promoting engagement and growth; then a learner's identity reflects confident, competent and resilient citizenship.
>
> *(McAnelly and Gaffney, 2019, p. 1090)*

Enacting Love, Rights and Solidarity as Features of Active Participation

What we have reflected on more recently is that there is a prominent affective feature to enacting love, rights and solidarity (Thomas, 2012), which we have not incorporated in an explicit sense within our framework of active participation. We can see links between rights and the equitable/inclusive element, and solidarity and the ecological. But what of love and the pedagogical? In Aotearoa New Zealand, we know that relational pedagogies are fundamental to understanding the 'how' of inclusive early childhood education (Hedges and Cooper, 2018; McAnelly and Gaffney, 2020; Tesar and Arndt, 2019; Warren, 2014) and affirming the whole child (Macartney, 2019). *Te Whāriki* suggests that the affective element is front and centre of the curriculum with principles of relationships/ngā hononga, holistic development/kotahitanga, family and community/whānau tangata, along with aims of belonging/mana whenua, communication/mana reo and contribution/mana tangata.

However, there still tends to be an emphasis on cognitive rather than affective dimensions of active participation and learning. We consider that the affective is defined by the 'intimate, personal, warm, trustful, compassionate, emotional and reciprocal' (Quiñones, Li and Ridgway, 2021, p. 142) relationships with people, places, things and practices that have a substantial positive impact (or negative impact in the case of the absence of these things) on active participation and learning. We also acknowledge that there are other affective elements to learning such as passion, flow and curiosity (Carr and Lee, 2012). To that end, Carr and Lee (2012, p. 138) made a call for assessment in early childhood to record the affective in the form of 'excitement, enthusiasm, exuberance and élan' of children.

It was Thomas (2012) who provided childhood studies the means to widen the notion of participation by drawing on Honneth's (1995) theory of recognition. This conceptualisation draws on love, rights and solidarity (Thomas, 2012) to frame recognition intersubjectively. It fits well with the sociocultural nature of *Te Whāriki* and a child-rights–focused framework of participation that sees the relational nature of active participation and learning as a holistic experience (Smith, 2002). In this conceptualisation, love is used to describe the many relationships that show respect based on the emotional attachment of those involved. Spending time together in collective effort where:

> these relationships are the site of complex emotional interactions, of which the most significant are affection, attachment, trust, and the struggle to achieve a balance between symbiosis and self-assertion.... Many things can go wrong in such primary relationships; but the outcome, when they are successful, is a mutual recognition of independence 'supported by an affective confidence in the continuity of shared concern'
>
> *(Thomas, 2012, p. 456)*

We see love as a key feature of the relationships that teachers have with children in early childhood settings, just as children do with each other. This approach to practice teases out the notion, embedded in *Te Whāriki*, that 'children learn through responsive, reciprocal relationships with people, places and things' (Ministry of Education, 2017, p. 17). It makes for an interesting debate as to whether teachers should love the children they teach, as they can shy away from such a level of connection for fear it could be construed as 'unprofessional' (Page, 2018; Rouse and Hadley, 2018). In this chapter, we will use the definition of love offered by Thomas (2012) which is made up of primary relationships between people whereby recognition is achieved intersubjectively. These relationships between people are based on affection, attachment and trust. However, we acknowledge children's strong affective attachment to people, places, things and practices that might allow us to use the term love beyond a restriction to between people.

The second element of recognition is rights, which we have become much more familiar with over the last 30 years since the promulgation of the United Nations Convention on the Rights of the Child (1989) and the development of the United Nations Convention on the Rights of the Persons with Disabilities (2006). In line with children's rights and disability rights is the idea that self-respect emerges when rights are recognised in the context of social respect. That is, respect should be freely given rather than having to be demanded. This aligns with the image of the capable, competent child that underpins *Te Whāriki*.

Lastly, solidarity is the means by which people are recognised for their diverse contributions to society or 'various forms of self realisation' (Thomas, 2012, p. 457) and is reflected in the social esteem they are accorded by others as part of that recognition. *Te Whāriki* asserts that social esteem that results is a fundamental expectation of 'a curriculum [that is] for all children' (Ministry of Education, 2017, p. 12), where diversity is construed as a strength and drawn into everyday modes of living and learning in ways that support the realisation of citizenship. However, we know that feelings of solidarity and being at one with their communities of practice can be problematic for disabled children navigating early childhood education in Aotearoa New Zealand because their experiences are more often those of marginalisation, discrimination and exclusion (Macartney, 2019; Purdue et al., 2020).

A central dynamic of inclusive practice that values the alterity of the Other (Moss, 2007) is the reciprocity generated within communities of practice, whereby we:

> look at children not only as recipients of care and affection but also as givers of care and affection, and as rights-bearers and rights-respecters, and as potential, if not actual, members of a community of solidarity based on shared values and reciprocal esteem.
>
> *(Thomas and Stoecklin, 2018, p. 78)*

In Aotearoa New Zealand, the indigenous term of ako is used to reflect how this reciprocity occurs in the social contexts of all learning and teaching. These contexts are expected to be embedded in te ao Māori (Māori worldview) ways of being, doing and knowing (Ministry of Education, 2011). Ako moves us away from stereotyping the adult teachers in a one-way relationship with children as learners and the receivers of teaching. Instead, in any moment, children and adults are engaging in both teaching and learning (Carr et al., 2010). The notion of ako also presumes children's competence, provides the opportunity to equitably distribute power amongst all members of communities of practice and avoids othering some kinds of children as less deserving (Bevan-Brown et al., 2015; Reedy, 2019).

Percy-Smith (2018, p. 162) summarises the three dimensions of love, rights and solidarity as:

> children cannot participate fully if they do not feel warmth and affection, if they are not respected as rights holders and unless there is mutual esteem, solidarity and a sense of shared purpose.

While in the past we have worked to highlight how the reciprocity of active participation has a basis in rights (McAnelly and Gaffney, 2017) and solidarity within early childhood communities of practices (McAnelly and Gaffney, 2019), the purpose of this chapter is to speak to the relational element through Honneth's acknowledgement of love being just as important as rights and solidarity (Thomas, 2012).

Researching within an Early Childhood Community of Practice

So as to be able to explore the realisation and practice of disabled children's rights and citizenship in the context of inclusive early childhood education, an ethnographic case study was undertaken in an early childhood community of practice. The case study sought to understand the ways in which all members of the community of practice, children and adults alike acted in support of a disabled child's active participation and inclusion in the local curriculum there.

A local early childhood organisation was approached for consent to carry out the research in one of their services, once ethics approval for the project had been granted. There were two inclusion criteria for a service to be a part of the project. One was that a minimum of one disabled child must attend the service, and the other was that the service needed to walk the walk as well as talk the talk of inclusive practice with disabled children. The senior leadership team of the organisation made some suggestions of likely fits with regard to participant services. One such service was then approached and the teaching team there consented to participating in the project. Then a family was asked if they would like to participate. The child was asked for ongoing assent, rather than assuming their initial assent would apply to their participation in the research across time (Powell and Smith, 2009).

The children and teachers of the early childhood service chose the name Ātaahua (the word for 'beautiful' in the Māori language indigenous to Aotearoa New Zealand) as a pseudonym. The service was located in a suburb of a regional New Zealand city. Reggio Emilia philosophy (Thornton and Brunton, 2015) was well embedded in practice within the service, especially the ideas of: the capable and competent child; respecting and honouring children as possessing multiple modes of communication, meaning-making and expression beyond the verbal (Edwards, Gandini and Forman, 2011); and democratic participation (Moss, 2007), where everyone had a hand in decision-making about the things that interested and affected them. Tama, a five-year-old autistic boy who attended Ātaahua Kindergarten, became the focus child of the project. We choose to use identity first language of 'disabled child' and 'autistic child' in this chapter to refer to Tama, in honouring Tama's feeling that autism was a fundamental component of his identity and the ways in which he viewed and experienced the world (Botha, Hanlon and Williams, 2021; Loud Hands Project, 2012).

Strong relationships are fundamental to early childhood practice (Macartney, 2019; McAnelly and Gaffney, 2017), and so the first few days in the setting were spent getting to know Tama, his family, the teaching team, other children and the wider kindergarten community. Once the month-long data collection period got officially underway, ethnographic observations and interviews provided an understanding of how the members of the kindergarten community of practice supported Tama's active participation and inclusion as well as – ultimately – Tama's ability to realise and practice citizenship. Field notes were written up as a record of observations made and some photographs accompanied these. Two semi-structured interviews, one with the

Ātaahua teaching team and another with Tama's parents, were conducted towards the end of the data collection period. It was agreed that a 'sit down' interview was not appropriate for Tama, as this possessed the potential to stress and disorient him. However, there were plenty of opportunities to engage with his thoughts, feelings and opinions through observations. For the purposes of this chapter, we reviewed the observation data in order to identify moments when affect was central to the reciprocity of teaching and learning.

Evidencing the Affective

The data was reviewed for those moments when Tama was overtly emotionally engaged in some activity. We have then selected the following four vignettes to highlight different features of affect as they relate to Honneth's theory of recognition based on love, rights and solidarity (Thomas, 2012). We have deliberately provided full vignettes, so readers have a good sense of the context, relational interaction and affective outcomes from the perspective of the ethnographer. Building on Thomas's work we looked for moments of intersubjective recognition where within the relational reciprocity the collective listening, creation of options and solving problems and the intense positive affect were important for explaining the success of each vignette presented below.

VIGNETTE 1   Affective Meaning-Making at Bush Kindy

In the enclosure (at the bush kindy – an Aotearoa New Zealand interpretation of the forest schools popular in Europe and elsewhere – site where the Ātaahua children chose to spend the majority of their morning this particular day), there was lots of mud as well as water. Tama seemed to be immediately drawn to one area of mud, which was on a slope and had a gap in it that ran the full downwards length of the slope. He looked at it for quite a while. It was evident that he was carefully deliberating inside as to what the purpose of this gap could be. All of a sudden, a knowing smile lit up his face and he loudly announced 'Tama know, a slide!'. He sat himself in the gap and wiggled himself around, giving a thumbs up to indicate it was a good fit. Then Tama tried pushing off...but there was no movement. He tried pushing off again a number of times, but he stayed sitting where he was. He got up off the 'slide' with an annoyed/confused expression on his face. William had been watching Tama's attempts to get down the slide and came over. 'Tama, I think I can help you find an answer, would you like me to help you?' he said. Tama nodded in agreement. William continued 'I think getting some water and making it slippery could be a good idea. Should we try it out?' Tama nodded in agreement again and said 'yes, Tama like'. 'Let's go and get some water with these containers' (pointing to some floating down at the edge of the pond), William then said. He took Tama's hand and they went down and filled up the containers, then brought them back up to the slide, tipping the water down it. 'Now you give it another try' William encouraged Tama, 'then I will have a go after you'. Tama sat back down at the top of the slide and pushed off. This time the water helped him sail three-quarters of the way down the slide almost effortlessly. He got off and watched William have his turn. William only reached the three-quarter mark too. Once William got off, Tama said to him 'more water'. William agreed that was a great idea, so off they went to get more water to pour down the slide. This time when Tama and William tried it, they slid all the way down to the bottom. They laughed a lot, gave each other massive high-fives and continued to practise this new skill/knowledge for some time, sharing it with the other children as they came to join in too.

In this vignette, the mud and slope had suggested to Tama that they could be used as a slide. We tend to think of the learning environment speaking to children in this way and it is interpreted as children using their imagination to inspire play. Wenger (1998) says imagination sits alongside engagement in supporting the creation of belonging within communities of practice. In this vignette, imagination is an important part of supporting joy (as an outcome of love). Tama was able to imagine possibilities (for play), which is something that is often unjustly said to be beyond the capacities of autistic children (Wolfberg, 2015). Key to this vignette was the reciprocity and intersubjectivity shown between Tama and William that characterised their mutual engagement and emphasised their solidarity in support of each other's right to participate. The vignette does not reflect a new way of working or new practice but rather is part of the shared repertoire of practice that acts as a resource to realise the potential within the outdoor space. These features are inherent in the community of practice and form what adults call learning, but was explicitly referred to by the children as fun.

The intersubjectivity embodied in the form of high fives is a reflection of their mutual engagement and is also in support of adding the disposition of working together to their shared repertoire of practices which they, and others, can draw on in the future. This is one feature of how friendships form over time (Gaffney, 2020). Working together to find an outcome that made sense to them was based on the empathy that was generated through positive reciprocity and intersubjectivity. This empathy has its own trajectory that was reflected in the boy's ongoing relationship with each other over time and across their experiences at Ātaahua Kindergarten. The activity drew in other children, curious to see 'what all this noise [was] about' (field notes, 8 August 2016) and to hopefully realise similar feelings of fun by having a go on the slide as well. This moment of engagement gave other children the opportunity to draw on their shared repertoire of practices. To miss out on such opportunities constitutes a form of exclusion. While this vignette required a disposition of persistence to achieve success, the next one was much more open-ended, and the outcome was unknown in terms of what success was going to look like.

VIGNETTE 2   Affective Meaning-Making Courtesy of a Chance Rain Shower

Tama was outside playing in the long grass with his peers Derek, Punch and Jazzy. They then decided to lie back on the grass with their hands behind their heads at Tama's prompting, relaxing and looking up at the sky, which is something Tama really enjoys. They lay there for a while just quietly contemplating what they were seeing, when Tama felt something land on his face. He batted at it. 'Wet, it's the rain!' he told Derek, Punch and Jazzy, and pointed at the sky with urgency. They reached their hands up towards the sky to see if they could feel it too. 'It is wet!' Jazzy declared. The conversation turned to 'what is rain?', a question Punch asked. Tama ventured the first opinion 'rain...water coming from the sky'. The others agreed. Derek thought rain was 'a Mum crying because her kids weren't doing what she asked'. Tama found this hilarious and dissolved into giggles. No-one said anything else during this time and joined Tama in his giggling. The rain continued. Then Tama asked 'we go in, stay out?' meaning should the group go inside or stay outside. They mutually agreed to stay outside and enjoy the feeling of 'the soft rain falling gently on our faces' (Derek).

The imagination of the children also appears central in this second vignette, as a key driver of reciprocity and intersubjectivity. There was no set direction to the experience, just open-ended shared sensory meaning-making and dialogue in which Tama was one of many active participants. The ways in which the grass, sky and rain acted upon Tama and the other children made visible their 'sensitivity to the agential power of the nonhuman...in the outdoor environment' (Merewether, 2019, pp. 114–115). This view of the learning environment being able to act on and upon children changes our view of what is curriculum by highlighting the potentials within the environment and how these 'spoke' to Tama's affective meaning-making and that of the other children. By collectively listening and responding to each other in this quiet moment of intersubjective reflection (acknowledging both the place of rights and solidarity), the children's imaginations created something that was unlikely to be produced by one child on their own. Mutual engagement and intersubjectivity are formed within the novel embodied physical, cognitive and emotional experience for each child, and the imaginative is also feeding into the shared repertoire of practice. The collective reciprocity and shared decision-making generate the positive learning outcomes of laughing and giggling (love) that for many children is a legitimate end in and of itself (Naraian, 2010). Such outcomes are unlikely to arise if the children are not practising a pedagogy of listening to each other or being authentically responsive to each other's thoughts, ideas and feelings (Carr et al., 2010). In the next vignette, adults are present in the mutual engagement.

VIGNETTE 3   Affective Meaning-Making While AWOL (Away Walking Our Land)

On Thursdays, a small group of children goes on a walk with a teacher to a nearby patch of land popularly known as the 'magical forest' as part of the kindergarten's AWOL (Away Walking Our Land) community exploration initiative. Today Tama was asked if he'd like to go to the magical forest, and he enthusiastically consented. The opportunity to be in relation with the mud and puddles seemed to be more exciting than the magical forest to Tama, who started stimming up a storm with spinning and flapping as he squealed 'muddddddd and puddlesssssssss!'. Other children and teachers watched this stimming and smiled, as did I. William told me 'this is how Tama shows us he's excited, it kind of looks different but it makes sense to him'. Tama saw me watching him and said to me 'before the mud and puddles, the Pop Goes the Weasel pole'. I was a bit confused as to what he meant, but as we set off on our walk to the magical forest, it soon became clear. We had to cross a car park that had some power poles at its perimeter before we got to the magical forest. As we got to the corner of the car park, I noticed the teacher and the other children slow down as Tama made a mad dash for one particular power pole. He wrapped one arm around it and started slowly moving around it as he hummed a tune. The teacher and the other children then started singing the song Pop Goes The Weasel.

Half a pound of tuppenny rice
Half a pound of treacle
That's the way the money goes
Pop! goes the weasel

Tama's face lit up as he skipped around the pole, his arm still wrapped around it, for exactly three repetitions of the song (being encouraged and cheered by his audience all the while) before he stopped and said 'we can go now'. We were then able to move through to the former school site where the magical forest was situated. Later, I talked to Pania (the teacher) about it and she shared with me that this was accepted to be part of Tama's environmental meaning-making while out on walks to the magical forest, so time and patience from all was accorded to him working through his ritual with the power pole and the song. Conversations with the other children on the walk revealed comments such as 'if Tama's happy, then we're all happy', 'I like it when I see such a big smile on Tama's face singing his song and doing his spinning round the pole', and 'he needs to do that (singing and spinning round the pole) before we can keep going, so we just wait patiently and watch and sometimes even join in…because it's actually a lot of fun'.

Unlike the other vignettes, this one highlights how regular routines create opportunities to show that the world can be consistent in the way it responds to Tama and Tama to it. Over time, other children and teachers support Tama to have the time and space (and right) to introduce an important piece of subjective meaning-making into the regular routine of going for a walk to the magical forest. Through a patient and unhurried approach being taken with Tama's embodied expression, Tama's active participation within the event was sensitively supported (Brodzeller et al., 2018). A demonstration of solidarity within this mutual engagement did not require all children to join in with Tama or to understand his meaning-making, although some had noted that they had in the past and recognised its potential for fun. His right to engage on his own terms meant that his agency was supported, his choices affirmed and his actions accepted as part of Tama being Tama (rights), and the children and teacher understood the goal of collective joy (love) in how they enacted their assumed responsibilities as agents of inclusion (solidarity) (McAnelly and Gaffney, 2019). This was an explicit democratically oriented approach to practise that recognised Tama's active 'participation [as] an important criterion and right of citizenship' (Moss, 2007, p. 3). While the focus in this vignette was on Tama, it was identified that this idea applied equally to all the children. What is more, the outcome of this activity being seen as fun makes it worthy in its own right, such that others contribute by drawing on their shared repertoire of practice by slowing down in anticipation as they approach the pole and then sing along with Tama. In the following vignette, the teacher and Tama have to work together to intersubjectively establish a solution to a problem that Tama has identified. It does not reflect fun as seen in the other vignettes, but it does show love beyond the definition by Thomas (2012).

VIGNETTE 4 Affective Meaning-Making and Being an Environmental Guardian

The weather hasn't been very kind in town lately. There's been lots of rain. At Ātaahua Kindergarten, though, there is a mantra of 'there's no bad weather, only bad clothing'. So children are still able to go and play outside in rainy stormy weather (it's recognised that there's lots of learning to be had there!) so long as they're properly prepared and dressed in warm clothes, wet weather gear and gumboots. A downside of this has been that a big patch of grass in the playground has been turned into mud from being so waterlogged and having children constantly trampling all over it. This was obviously bothering Tama today. When he went outside this morning he immediately saw how muddy the area had become. He was careful to walk around the edge of the area several times, looking at the mud with a concerned look on his face. Some other children went to run through the mud and Tama put his hand out and said, 'No, stay 'way'. They shrugged their shoulders, said, 'OK Tama', and went off. Tina (one of Tama's teachers) noticed this and came over to Tama. 'What's happening buddy? Is there something about this mud that's bothering you?' she said, crouching down to his level, but not looking for eye contact. Tama emphatically nodded and pointed at the mud several times over, eventually venturing, 'Big mess, not OK'. 'Well Tama', Tina said, 'have you got any ideas about how we could fix the mess?' Tama thought about this for a while. Tina waited for him to articulate a response, then Tama said, 'Fence, stay 'way'. 'Do you think we should put a fence around the edge of the mud to keep the children away?' she asked, further adding, 'What a fantastic idea Tama!' Tina and Tama went off to find some suitable materials for the fence, eventually deciding on some stakes and a rope. Tama assisted Tina in pushing the stakes into the ground, and also with twisting the rope around the stakes. Tama chose red rope because he knew red means 'No go here'. He then stood sentinel for quite some time at the perimeter of the fence, helping his peers to understand what he'd done and telling off those who snuck under the fence to play in the mud, saying, 'Pease no, big messy mud' when they asked why they couldn't. They appeared to respect Tama's argument in saying 'OK Tama, we understand' and went and found something else to do.

This vignette highlights how Tama's disposition to take care (love) of the grassed area in the kindergarten was given recognition in a moment of sustained shared thinking between Tina, the teacher and himself. The outcome of this mutual engagement was that he was supported to realise and practice citizenship through putting his decision-making (right) into action. His concern (love) for the state of the grass was visible in his interactions with the other children, which Tina had observed and deduced by taking a moment to listen. She could see that Tama wanted the means to protect it in some way. Tama was able to make a series of decisions, with Tina's support, based on what he wanted and thought would work as a fix. He was then very keen to explain the rationale behind erecting the fence to the other children, who in turn respectfully listened to and abided by Tama's wishes (in solidarity). They did this even though they did not necessarily understand all his ideas, but they did recognise that Tama was someone who was capable, expert and could be trusted to make appropriate decisions (McAnelly and Gaffney, 2017). This shared repertoire of practice reflected the democratic principles of the Reggio approach within early childhood settings (Moss, 2007) and provides the resource upon which future moments of mutual engagement can be negotiated.

The Affective Elements of Learning and Its Inclusive Role

The first three examples show the importance of children participating in play and being playful. This is just as important for Tama, a disabled child, as for any other. His imagination is fostered in multiple contexts, which includes contributing to a collective sense of imagination, identified as play. It has been suggested that autistic children can sometimes struggle with empathy and being part of a group (Douglas et al., 2021; Jordan, Roberts and Hume, 2019). However, for Tama, this was well within his repertoire of participation in this community. An interview with his parents indicated that other early childhood communities he had been a part of had not been able to affirm his sense of self as a capable, competent learner, but Ātaahua was able to support his diverse modes of understanding and meaning-making as part of the mutual engagement that formed participation within this setting. Each of the vignettes offered evidence of Tama enacting his right to be who he wanted to be, with the acceptance of his peers characterising their mutual engagement as one of solidarity. When applied across the community, this demonstrated that all children were seen as 'competent and confident learners and communicators, healthy in mind, body and spirit, secure in their sense of belonging and in the knowledge that they make a valued contribution to society' (Ministry of Education, 2017, p. 6). This is the realisation of the inclusive aspiration of Aotearoa New Zealand's early childhood curriculum *Te Whāriki*.

All of the vignettes provided highlight how the high level of intersubjectivity characterising mutual engagement, supported by the embedded practice across the community of a pedagogy of respectful listening, formed an important resource – a shared repertoire of practice – within the early childhood setting. It was this very same intersubjectivity that revealed the differing forms of love evident in each vignette. There was the joy of having fun in being successful together, being given the space and time to practise one's own meaning-making, having concern for the environment and sharing imaginative moments with each other. Each moment was a significant outcome in its own right that can get lost in the world of play framed by learning rather than fun, especially if having fun is a reflection of the level of love that community members have for each other (Percy-Smith, 2018).

In our theorising learning, we see the affective as an opportunity to learn from children as to what forms of diversity are important to them. We are sure they would remind adults that play and fun are an important part of love and friendship and therefore adults should acknowledge them as key features of current thinking and practice to which society should pay substantially more attention. As exemplified by Tama, the affective is an important part of explaining active participation and learning in the four vignettes. These threads are inherent in his play and provide a means of understanding how important love is to theorising the pedagogic, alongside rights in making sense of the equitable, and solidarity in relation to the ecological, that form our active participation framework (McAnelly and Gaffney, 2017). We can also see that love can be expanded beyond the idea provided by Thomas (2012). It must be between people and also look at how people, places, things and practices can operate intersubjectively to recognise each other in support of inclusion.

Te Whāriki has been able to acknowledge many of these elements of inclusion when it became the first bicultural national early childhood curriculum in Aotearoa New Zealand (Reedy, 2019). The relational elements (whānaukataka), the connection of people to place (mana whenua) and the spiritual (wairua) dimensions (rather than religious) have created more space for disabled children, such as Tama, to realise and practise their right to belong in early childhood settings. From Tama's perspective, rather than define participation in terms of love, rights and solidarity, he is more likely to equate participation with play, which is about fun, free choice and friends. This reinforces the idea that rights to enrolment and attendance on their own do not guarantee an inclusive experience for children (Purdue et al., 2020). It also supports Carr and Lee's (2012) suggestion that the affective element of participation is an important part of constructing learner identity, for both children and adults, such that it could be a central measure of a successful community of practice.

Conclusion

Te Whāriki makes many references to play as being important for children's learning, and while it describes different sorts of play, it never defines the nature of that play. In particular, the curriculum mentions the importance of imaginative or spontaneous play, and how teachers should be 'knowledge-able about play-based curriculum and pedagogy' (Ministry of Education, 2017, p. 59). However, there are only two uses of the term fun, and this is in relation to playing with language. We want to draw teachers' attention to the importance of children playing for fun and all the emotions that come with it, and the contribution it makes to the formation of shared repertoires of practice. Doing so has allowed us to highlight the important role that love, alongside rights and solidarity (Thomas, 2012), plays in supporting disabled children's active participation in play-based early childhood settings.

References

Bevan-Brown, J., Berryman, M., Hickey, H., Macfarlane, S., Smiler, K. and Walker, T. 2015. *Working with Māori children with special education needs He mahi whaka-hirahira*. Wellington: New Zealand Council for Educational Research.

Botha, M., Hanlon, J. and Williams, G. 2021. Does language matter? Identity-first versus person-first language use in autism research: A response to Vivanti. *Journal of Autism and Developmental Disorders*, 50(2), pp. 691–693.

Brodzeller, K., Ottley, J., Jung, J. and Coogle, C. 2018. Interventions and adaptations for children with autism spectrum disorder in inclusive early childhood settings. *Early Childhood Education Journal*, 46(3), pp. 277–286.

Carr, M. and Lee, W. 2012. *Learning stories: Constructing learning identities in early education*. London: Sage.

Carr, M., Smith, A.B., Duncan, J., Jones, C., Lee, W. and Marshall, K. 2010. *Learning in the making: Disposition and design in early education*. Rotterdam: Sense.

Convention on the Rights of the Child. 1989. [online]. [Accessed 17 August 2021]. Available from: https://www.ohchr.org/en/professionalinterest/pages/crc.aspx.

Convention on the Rights of Persons with Disabilities and Optional Protocol. 2006. [online]. [Accessed 22 July 2021]. Available from: https://www.un.org/disabilities/documents/convention/convoptprot-e.pdf.

Douglas, P., Rice, C., Runswick-Cole, K., Easton, A., Gibson, M.F., Gruson-Wood, J., Klar, E. and Shields, R. 2021. Re-storying autism: A body becoming disabil-ity studies in education approach. *International Journal of Inclusive Education*, 25(5), pp. 605–622.

Edwards, C., Gandini, L. and Forman, G. (Eds.). 2011. *The hundred languages of chil-dren: The Reggio Emilia experience in transformation*. Santa Barbara: ABC-CLIO.

Gaffney, M. 2020. Peer reciprocity and friendship in the classroom: A disabled stu-dent's experience. *Ethnography and Education*, 15(4), pp. 462–478.

Hedges, H. and Cooper, M. 2018. Relational play-based pedagogy: Theorising a core practice in early childhood education. *Teachers and Teaching*, 24(4), pp. 369–383.

Honneth, A. 1995. *The struggle for recognition: The moral grammar of social con-flicts*. Cambridge: Polity Press.

Jordan, R., Roberts, J. and Hume, K. (Eds.). 2019. *The SAGE handbook of autism and education*. London: Sage.

Loud Hands Project. 2012. *Loud hands: Autistic people, speaking*. Washington, DC: Autistic Press.

Macartney, B. 2019. Moving *Te Whāriki* from rhetoric to reality for disabled children and their whānau in early childhood education. In Gunn, A. and Nuttall, J. eds. *Weaving Te Whāriki: Aotearoa New Zealand's early childhood curriculum document in theory and practice* (3rd ed.). Wellington: New Zealand Council for Educational Research, pp. 119–134.

McAnelly, K. and Gaffney, M. 2017. He waka eke noa: A case study of active participation for a disabled child in an inclusive early childhood community of practice. *Early Childhood Folio*, 21(1), pp. 16–21.

McAnelly, K. and Gaffney, M. 2019. Rights, inclusion and citizenship: A good news story about learning in the early years. *International Journal of Inclusive Education*, 23(10): pp. 1081–1094.

McAnelly, K. and Gaffney, M. 2020. Producing an understanding of autistic tamariki in early childhood settings: The case for a new materialist approach. In Gunn, A., Surtees, N., Gordon-Burns, D. and Purdue, K. eds. *Te Aotūroa Tātaki Inclusive early childhood education: Perspectives on inclusion, social justice and equity in Aotearoa New Zealand* (2nd ed.). Wellington: New Zealand Council for Educational Research, pp. 109–125.

Merewether, J. 2019. New materialisms and children's outdoor environments: Murmurative diffractions. *Children's Geographies*, 17(1), pp. 105–117.

Ministry of Education. 2011. *Tātaiako: Cultural competencies for teachers of Māori learners*. Wellington: Ministry of Education.

Ministry of Education. 2017. *Te Whāriki: He whāriki mātauranga mō ngā mokopuna o Aotearoa. Early childhood curriculum*. Wellington: Ministry of Education.

Moss, P. 2007. Bringing politics into the nursery: Early childhood education as a democratic practice. *European Early Childhood Education Research Journal*, 15(1), pp. 5–20.

Naraian, S. 2010. 'Why not have fun?': Peers make sense of an inclusive high school program. *Intellectual and Developmental Disabilities*, 48(1), pp. 14–30.

Page, J. 2018. Characterising the principles of professional love in early childhood care and education. *International Journal of Early Years Education*, 26(2), pp. 125–141.

Percy-Smith, B. 2018. Participation as learning for change in everyday spaces: Enhancing meaning and effectiveness using action research. In Baraldi, C. and Cockburn, T. eds. *Theorising childhood: Citizenship, rights and participation*. London: Palgrave McMillan, pp. 159–186.

Powell, M.A. and Smith, A.B. 2009. Children's participation rights in research. *Childhood*, 16(1), pp. 124–142.

Purdue, K., Gordon-Burns, D., Rarere-Briggs, K., Stark, R. and Turnock, K. 2020. Key factors in supporting the development of positive identities in young children with disabilities. In Gunn, A., Surtees, N., Gordon-Burns, D., and Purdue, K. eds. *Te Aotūroa Tātaki Inclusive early childhood education: Perspectives on inclusion, social justice and equity in Aotearoa New Zealand* (2nd ed.). Wellington: NZCER Press, pp. 109–125.

Quiñones, G., Li, L. and Ridgway, A. 2021. Affective pedagogies for infant-toddlers' education and care. In Quiñones, G., Li, L. and Ridgway, A. eds. *Affective early childhood pedagogy for infant-toddlers*. Cham, Switzerland: Springer, pp. 131–144.

Rameka, L. and Soutar, B. 2019. Te hōhonutanga o Te Whāriki: Developing a deeper understanding of Te Whāriki. In Gunn, A. and Nuttall, J. eds. *Weaving Te Whāriki: Aotearoa New Zealand's early childhood curriculum document in theory and practice* (3rd ed.). Wellington: NZCER Press, pp. 45–56.

Reedy, T. 2019. Tōku Rangatiratanga nā te Mana Mātauranga: "Knowledge and power set me free...". In Gunn, A. and Nuttall, J. eds. *Weaving Te Whāriki: Aotearoa New Zealand's early childhood curriculum document in theory and practice* (3rd ed.). Wellington: NZCER Press, pp. 25–44.

Rouse, E. and Hadley, F. 2018. Where did love and care get lost? Educators and parents' perceptions of early childhood practice. *International Journal of Early Years Education*, **26**(2), pp. 159–172.

Smith, A.B. 2002. Interpreting and supporting participation rights: Contributions from sociocultural theory. *The International Journal of Children's Rights*, **10**, pp. 73–88.

Smith, A.B. 2013. *Understanding children and childhood: A New Zealand perspective* (5th ed.). Wellington: Bridget Williams Books.

Smith, A.B. 2015. Early childhood education in New Zealand: Progress and challenges in achieving children's rights. In Smith, A.B. ed. *Enhancing children's rights*. London: Palgrave Macmillan, pp. 80–94.

Te One, S. 2011. Implementing children's rights in early education. *Australasian Journal of Early Childhood*, **36**(4), pp. 54–61.

Tesar, M. and Arndt, S. 2019. Re-reading and re-activating Te Whāriki through a posthuman childhood studies lens. In Gunn, A. and Nuttall, J. eds. *Weaving Te Whāriki: Aotearoa New Zealand's early childhood curriculum document in theory and practice* (3rd ed.). Wellington: New Zealand Council for Educational Research, pp. 181–194.

Thomas, N. 2012. Love, rights and solidarity: Studying children's participation using Honneth's theory of recognition. *Childhood*, **19**(4), pp. 453–466.

Thomas, N. and Stoecklin, D. 2018. Recognition and capability: A new way to understand how children can achieve their rights? In Baraldi, C. and Cockburn, T. eds. *Theorising childhood: Citizenship, rights and participation*. London: Palgrave McMillan, pp. 73–94.

Thornton, L. and Brunton, P. 2015. *Understanding the Reggio approach: Early years education in practice*. London: Routledge.

Warren, A. 2014. 'Relationships for me are the key for everything': Early childhood teachers' subjectivities as relational professionals. *Contemporary Issues in Early Childhood*, **15**(3), pp. 262–271.

Wenger, E. 1998. *Communities of practice: Learning, meaning, and identity*. New York: Cambridge University.

Wolfberg, P. 2015. *Play and imagination in children with autism*. New York: Teachers College Press.

7

POSITIONING THE VIEWS OF CHILDREN WITH DEVELOPMENTAL DISABILITIES AT THE CENTRE OF EARLY INTERVENTIONS

Clare Carroll

Introduction

Childhood and disability are now increasingly reconceptualised in terms of voice, agency, competency and rights. The voices of children who have autism, intellectual disability, communication and language difficulties and cerebral palsy (CP) – among others – are often left out (Carroll and Twomey, 2021; Kelly, 2007; Leahy and Carroll, 2021; Lyons et al., 2022). There is a pressing need to include children who are neurodiverse, particularly young children, as participants in research and practice in order to understand their contexts. Including children with disabilities in research may take more time and preparation, and their input is valuable (Carroll et al., 2020). We need to explore ways to make their participation in research about their early interventions (EIs) a reality. Their inclusion in research can subsequently inform how the voice of children with disabilities can be realised in professional practice, which is extremely important for practitioners working on EI and school-aged disability teams.

As a speech and language therapist, working both in clinical practice and in academia, my goal is to support children to communicate and participate in their daily lives. In my teaching and research at the University of Galway, Ireland, my aim is to bring disabled children's voice in EI to the fore and to move away from deficit-based and medicalised interventions. EI 'encompasses a range of different supports to promote optimal child development, such as interventions targeted to improve child and/or family outcomes' (Sapiets et al., 2021, p. 696). Supports can include preventative interventions and service provision following a diagnosis of a developmental disorder. The International Classification of Functioning – Child & Youth Version

DOI: 10.4324/9781003102915-7

[ICF-CY] (World Health Organization [WHO], 2007) has been used as a framework in EI. As a framework, it can support the different professionals and families to have and share a common language. Within it, participation is considered a key outcome (Bjorck-Akesson et al., 2010; Imms et al., 2017). The WHO (2007) defines participation as involvement in life situations. Using this framework, parents and professionals can discuss a child's activities and their participation, in these activities, within different contexts. In order to achieve this outcome of participation in life situations, the multiple constructs of participation need to be considered in the EI process as well as the child's perception of these constructs (Bjorck-Akesson et al., 2010).

Given that EI aims to improve people's level of Activities and Participation, as outlined in the ICF-CY (WHO, 2007), more ecologically valid studies are required to assess the functional impact of EI (Dunst et al., 2008). Many factors contribute to client and parental engagement such as receptiveness, willingness and self-efficacy (King et al., 2013). For children with disabilities, a family-centred model is associated with increased positive functioning by parents, family, and child (Dunst et al., 2007). Parents often have their own hopes for their child and their own priorities which need to be recognised by professionals when building relationships and planning how to facilitate the child and family (O'Neil and Palisano, 2000). However, while parent needs and views are important, we also need to create space for the child to share their hopes and priorities. Children have the right to express their views, participate in decision-making and share responsibility and power. However, these rights are not always realised (Merrick et al., 2019).

This chapter considers why it is important that health and social care professionals foreground the voice of young children in family-centred practice. Family-centred EIs are the services and supports that may be needed by a child with developmental needs and their family to take part in various activities in their daily lives. Taking part in these daily activities can be difficult because of their motor, sensory or communication needs for example. Professionals need to ensure that the services and supports are supporting the child and their family to participate in meaningful routines and activities. The child's participation in family and preschool daily life is the key to children's development, learning and wellbeing (Dunst and Espe-Sherwindt, 2016).

EI philosophy is in line with upholding children's participation rights and therefore, it is important to discuss how the voice of young children is included in the EI context. There is a need for health and social care professionals to commit to a rights-based approach giving the child the right to express their views, exploring voices from hard-to-reach groups, recognising the child as an experiencing agent (Kelly, 2007) and listening to their voice as a source of understanding. This chapter draws from seven studies involving 14 preschool children with developmental disabilities. These studies included a variety of data collection tools, for example, auto photography, observations and interviews, to explore the experiences of the children engaging and participating in interventions with health and social care professionals. This chapter contributes to our understandings of family-centred practice by focusing on the child's view. By focusing on the child's view, the child becomes an experiencing agent. Through the child's agency, we have knowledge about his/her world and about how he/she participates in intervention from his/her perspective. Adding this perspective values the child as a partner in the intervention journey and acknowledges what daily participation looks like from his/her point of view. Furthermore, this chapter extends the discourse that acknowledgement of a child's perspective creates new priorities for everyone involved and allows interventions to be both functional and inclusive.

Understanding Children's Lives

A child is knowledgeable about their own life and the issues that affect them (Clark, 2005). A child's life includes their immediate environments – the microsystem – and the connections between these different environments – the mesosystem. Looking at a child's life through the lens of Bronfenbrenner's (2005) bioecological model can help professionals to consider the child's microsystem, where they spend most of their time (e.g., family, nursery or preschool or school or crèche, extended family, neighbours, peers, health and social care services), and the child's mesosystem, where two or more of the child's influences in their microsystem interact (e.g., family and school, family and health services, school and health services, school, family and health services). Furthermore, considering the bioecological model of a child's life can enable professionals to look beyond the child's impairment and consider their family and community contexts. Additionally, this approach supports family-centred practice as interventions can be informed by the child's daily life and led by what is meaningful for the child. Children's views are valid even though they may see the world differently (Harcourt, 2011). Regularly, adults make decisions on a child's capabilities and on a child's level of participation (Bloom et al., 2020). Health and social care professionals, and educators among others, must engage with children to ensure our understanding of their lives is not fragmented (McCormack, Baker and Crowe, 2018).

A child who is neurodivergent may have secondary speech, language and communication needs (SLCN). SLCN is defined by Bercow (2008, p. 13) as an umbrella term to describe 'difficulties with fluency, forming sounds and words, formulating sentences, understanding what others say, and using language socially'. Lyons et al. (2022, p. 548) state that we still know very little about 'the impact of SLCN on everyday activities or participation or the personal and environmental factors that may impact on functioning from the children's own perspectives'. Bloom et al. (2020) found in a critical review that there is a paucity of research stating the effective methods to enable a child with SLCN to participate in research about their school learning experiences. Participation is important for a child's health and well-being, as evidenced by its prominence in the ICF-CY (WHO, 2007). The meaning of participation has been debated, with disagreement over the level of involvement required before being considered participation (McNeilly et al., 2015). Participation can include everything from attending passively to actively impacting decisions (McNeilly et al., 2015). Participation of children in research and practice is essential, supporting the view of children as competent social actors, with their own agency and voice, acknowledging children as experts of their childhood (Carter, 2009). Singer et al. (2020) argue that the concept of 'communicative participation' is new in the field of childhood SLCN. The term 'communicative participation' has been defined as 'communication in life situations where knowledge, information, ideas or feelings are exchanged' (Eadie et al., 2006)

Understanding the life of a child, who is neurodiverse, will support practitioners in planning interventions that are both child-centred and family-centred. Shifting the focus to examining the participation of younger children with SLCN in EI interventions, appropriate strategies can be identified to enhance participation, in particular, communicative participation. Children's views are valid even though they may see the world differently (Harcourt, 2011). Researchers must engage with children to ensure our understanding of their lives is not fragmented (McCormack et al., 2018). Regularly, adults make decisions on a child's capabilities and on a child's level of participation (Bloom et al., 2020). Bloom et al. (2020) found in a critical review that there is a paucity of research stating the effective methods to enable a child with SLCN to participate in research about their school learning experiences.

Coyne et al. (2016) argue that, in healthcare, when we adopt a family-centred approach a child's parents/guardian are the key players, whereas when we adopt a child-centred approach the child's rights are more recognised. Furthermore, they do assert that children are part of a family and the 'family is the emotional unit and families are systems of interconnected and interdependent individual' (Coyne et al., 2016, p. 497). Moreover, within EI, collaborative teamwork is very important and we must recognise the child, their family and their practitioners as key players on the team. Lundy (2018) recommends that adults acknowledge the preferences and views that children express and, in line with Article 12 of the United Nations Convention on the Rights of the Child (1989), give these views due weight.

Although we may acknowledge that a child is adept in communication and can make sense, Dockett and Perry (2005, p. 508) declare that 'rarely are young children recognised as holders of expert knowledge, or even experts on their own experience'. Children communicate in multiple ways (Merrick et al., 2019). Children, who are neurodiverse, have many ways of communicating and researchers and practitioners need to do more to provide all children with opportunities and means to express their voice by being innovative (Merrick et al., 2019; Twomey and Carroll, 2018). McCormack et al. (2018) share that a child who has difficulty communicating may not be listened to or heard because of their lack of voice Therefore, 'in the absence of voice a different form of expression is required' (Twomey and Carroll, 2018, p. 3). For those who find verbal communication challenging, participation in interactions in their daily lives in life can prove difficult (McLeod, 2018). Traditionally, studies on children's lives have often focused on adult interpretations instead of treating children as active participants and collaborating with them (Clark and Moss, 2017).

Participation of Young Children in Research

Tisdall (2018), Merrick et al. (2019) and Roulstone et al. (2011) argue that for us to understand children's activity and participation in society from their own perspectives, researchers need to explore and use age-appropriate, child-friendly and innovative methodologies. As discussed above, very little research explores the perspectives of young children with disabilities. In a scoping review by Carroll and Twomey (2021), to understand more about how researchers are including the voices of children with neurodevelopmental differences [in particular, intellectual disability, autism spectrum disorder, attention deficit hyperactively disorder and CP] in research, they found five studies that included children under 6 years old and 14 studies that included children between 6 and 13 years old. Therefore, it is important that they are given the opportunity for their voices to be heard and their own personal experiences to be included in research. We need to learn from the children themselves so that their voices can be included in collaborative practice (Carroll, 2018). Researchers need to do research 'with' rather than 'on' children as a priority, supporting children with cognitive, communication, social, physical or medical difficulties to have a voice, in whatever way that may be represented (Kelly, 2007).

Clark (2004) designed the listening framework Mosaic approach within the early years setting. Researchers continue to use the Mosaic approach to support their research with children as it combines quantitative and qualitative data, includes visual methodologies, uses a range of methods to build a picture of the project and avoids reliance on written and spoken word. The Mosaic approach (Clark and Moss, 2011) uses both visual and verbal methods to explore children's perspectives (Azunre and Sowrirajan, 2021; Lyons and McAllister, 2019). Psaila (2017) used the Mosaic approach with a seven-year-old boy with a physical disability to create a holistic approach to his life. The methods used were drawings role-plays, photographs and interviews. Additionally, Carroll and Twomey (2021) found a range of qualitative multimodal methods that can be used with children and young people with

SLCN, for example, interviews or focus groups supplemented with visual methods, open-ended question surveys and ethnographic approaches such as participant observation.

There are diverse types of visual data that can be collected (e.g., videos, photographs, drawings, artwork, and observations). In photo-elicitation, visual images (e.g., photographs, paintings and cartoons) are used to generate more in-depth discussion from participants about a topic (Verdon et al., 2021). Using participatory visual methods such as a wearable camera (Microsoft® SenseCam), Talking Mats (Murphy, 1997), digital photography, supported collage making and Draw and Talk (McCormack et al., 2022) can support researchers and professionals to gain a more in-depth understanding of a child's view and their lives. It is important that the voices of young children with SLCN and those with developmental disabilities are heard, particularly in research. Byrne and Carroll (2021), in a scoping review, found six studies that used participatory visual methods to include children and young people with Down syndrome in research. One of the studies by Carroll and Sixsmith (2016) involved eight children, aged two to four years, with developmental differences who took photos using a SenseCam, a tool for auto photography. Another study by Lundqvist et al. (2019) used draw-and-talk methods to include 26 children, aged five to seven years, with special educational needs to learn about the children's lives in their educational setting. A further example by Press et al. (2011) used multiple methods within a Mosaic approach, such as a baby cam for digital footage to record and represent the everyday lives of young children with SLCN. In addition, Roulstone et al. (2011) used a KiddyCam, observations and interviews to include the voice of preschool children with SLCN. Another interesting use of photographs was by Paige-Smith and Rix (2006) where they used narrative observations and photographs of daily events as a tool for engaging children. Their non-participatory observations created data through the writing of vignettes or first-person narratives.

McCormack et al. (2010) and O'Neill and Moore (2016) report that arts-based research encourages expression and goes beyond the limitations of spoken communication to produce understanding and information that would otherwise not be expressed. Furthermore, McCormack et al. (2022) used drawing to elicit the views of 124 young children with speech-sound dif-ficulties about their talking. Several studies found drawing allows children to communicate their thoughts (Dockett and Perry, 2005; Einarsdottir, 2005). Moreover, McCormack et al. (2010) included 13 preschool children and 21 of their significant others. They used drawings, interviews and questionnaires as methods, which supplied rich data.

Exploratory Case Studies

As mentioned earlier, this chapter shares and discusses data from 7 studies involving 14 preschool children with developmental disabilities, specifically

Down syndrome. These children have a double disadvantage from being included in research because they are young and have SLCN and other needs.

Six exploratory case studies conducted by some of my speech and language therapy students at the University of Galway, considered the participation of young children with developmental disabilities in a communication group intervention (Hannon et al., 2018). The EI communication group had been running for 18 years. It involved fortnightly group sessions with six children and their parents targeting communication skills. The sessions were facilitated by a speech and language therapist and a community nurse. Previously, O'Loughlin et al. (2010/2011) explored the views of six parents about their involvement in this group intervention; however, child views were not included. While parents' views are important, I was keen to understand the views of the children who attended the group. Further details on the parents' views can be found in a paper by O'Loughlin et al. (2010, 2011).

The qualitative case studies used multiple observations and visual methods involving six preschool children with Down syndrome and interviews with their parents. The studies wanted to gain an understanding of the experiences of children with Down syndrome when engaging and participating in an EI communication group intervention. Imms et al. (2017) proposed a Family of Participation-Related Constructs, a framework to help us understand participation at the level of the individual in their context. The observations, in the six exploratory studies, were structured by an observation checklist adapted from Imms et al. (2017)'s framework. Imms et al.'s (2017) framework describes intrinsic and extrinsic factors that can influence, and are influenced by, participation and describes the connections between these factors. Intrinsic factors include the child's activity competence, their sense of self and preferences. Activity competence 'can be measured as capacity, capability or preformed skill' (Imms et al., 2017, p. 20). Extrinsic factors include the context, which relates to people, objects, place, activity and time, and the environment, which consists of social and physical structures (Imms et al., 2017). These extrinsic factors are linked to the microsystems of Bronfenbrenner's (2005) bioecological model that I mentioned earlier. For example, the environment, the toys used and the time of day might affect the child's participation. The observations were structured and involved the students observing the children in their group intervention and in their homes. These two environments are part of each child's microsystem.

The adapted checklist from Imms et al. (2017) Family of Participation Constructs, included: Being There (attending, frequency, duration), Involved (belonging, engaged, focused, interacting), and Prerequisites (activity competence, preference in child). The exploratory studies wanted to delve into these intrinsic and extrinsic factors mentioned above within the context of the EI communication group. Hannon et al. (2018) found that children's personal preferences, abilities and learning styles affected when and how they took part in activities. They were more engaged with toys and activities that they chose and with activities involving movement. For one of the children, Chloe (two years and six months) who has Down syndrome, her own preference often determined whether she participated in activities or not. Using toys she liked led to a more immediate focus on the activity and increased interactions with other children in the group. She was less distracted when she chose the activity and when it involved movement. She used multiple modes of communication including vocalisations, Lámh signs and actions effectively, supporting Branson and Demchak's (2009) research review findings that using a variety of augmentative and alternative communication methods can facilitate children with SLCN to communicate with others effectively. For example, Chloe's involvement in sessions improved when visual props like a puppet were used, whereas other children in the group responded better to auditory stimuli like music.

For another child, Paul (aged three years), his mood varied, and this affected his involvement in the intervention with his mum sharing that 'some days he can be fully engaged with everything and other days he just has no interest'. The more familiar Paul was with the materials, the greater was his participation. He engaged more in the activities, by exploring the toys and taking turns. Some observations indicated that there were more opportunities for the children to participate when there were fewer children in the group. There were differences too in terms of participation in the different settings. For example, Paul's mother shared that 'he's different in the group compared to at home'. She noted that he was more vocal at home and quieter in the group. He could focus on activities more at home, whereas in the group, he found focusing on activities harder.

All methods of communication and approximations of speech were accepted and applauded. For example, Emily (aged three years) performed a labial trill (blowing a raspberry) in the place of shouting 'boo!' during the 'peekaboo' activity which effectively completed the exchange. The child received praise for this, and her mother was assured by the group leaders that this was good progress. This inclusive environment not only provided comfort to the parents of these children, as they celebrated their small but significant achievements, but also gave the children confidence to participate. Additionally, this increased participation enables the children to obtain more benefit from the sessions. The group leaders modelled how to support each child's communication, which helped the latter engage and participate in the group. This modelling helped the parents to support their child's communication in the home setting. In turn, this support enabled the children to participate in the activities learned in the group in the home setting. Seeing the child at home and in their intervention setting allowed for the exploration of participation in multiple contexts.

The seventh study, mentioned earlier, involved eight young children with neurodevelopmental disabilities (Carroll and Sixsmith, 2016). The children successfully engaged in the research and communicated their experiences through pictures, auto-photography, SenseCam photographs and through interactions with the researcher. In Carroll (2018), I highlight how one of these children shared interests that did not come to the fore in discussions with his parents, such as the importance of pets in the child's world. Using a data collection tool that facilitated auto photography gave a real sense of the child's world. Using visual methods added value to my research and opened another view of the child's daily life, thus confirming the value of using such methods as discussed above. The benefits of using visual methods point to the importance for professionals working with children to look at other ways to understand a child's world.

Participation of Children in Practice

Encouraging children to participate in research has the dual effect of empowering young children and providing data from research that may influence future practice (Birbeck and Drummond, 2005). We need to understand the lives, preferences and perspectives of children with SLCN to inform practice. The research studies by Carroll (2018), Carroll and Sixsmith (2016) Hannon et al. (2018) found that identifying children's preferences as well as their individual competencies may help to support their engagement in intervention. Supports which could benefit a child's participation may be identified through observing the child across contexts and engaging in discussion with a caregiver. Knowledge of the child's world, their microsystem and mesosystem and their participation in their intervention can add their perspective as a partner on the EI intervention journey. Their voice becomes part of the intervention process. Clark (2005) showed that by listening to children, they can be involved and empowered to participate in decision-making in their setting.

When planning EI services for children who are neurodiverse, practitioners need to tailor the intervention for each child, and this is not an easy task. Seeking the views of the child can facilitate the process as it can help ensure that practitioners understand the child's perspectives. Furthermore, the involvement of the child enables practitioners to appreciate how a child who is neurodiverse uses unconventional means of communication, and that they are knowledgeable about their life and can share their experiences. The children in the studies I was involved in used different ways to express themselves to make choices and demonstrate enjoyment. In terms of the context, the studies identified that the individuals who interacted with the child as well as the techniques and strategies they used within activities also affected participation. Potential implications for practice include adopting a total communication approach (Fargas-Malet et al., 2010) when interacting with young children with SLCN as well as identifying children's preferences and individual competencies to support engagement in intervention. We need to embrace a child's preferred mode of communication and use multiple modes of communication. Participation, in the case studies, involved using movement and a range of communication types. In practice, using a total communication approach could include the use of picture boards to communicate, picture-based communication apps, writing, drawing, keyword signing, photographs, vocal signals, sounds, words and sentences.

These case studies also demonstrate that autonomy is a vital component of participation with self-governance leading to enhanced participation. This is consistent with the work by Hoogsteen and Woodgate (2010) who found that having a choice is necessary for successful participation. D'Arrigo et al. (2017) suggest that attending to a child's need for autonomy by allowing them to choose therapy activities, for example, is one way of enhancing engagement. D'Arrigo et al. (2017) also suggest that this approach will support meeting the child's need for relatedness, which involves the therapeutic relationship, and competence. In practice, offering choices for activities enhances participation. When defining participation among children with disabilities, Hoogsteen and Woodgate (2010, p. 325) state that the child must take part in 'something or with someone'. They must have a sense of inclusion and some control or choice in what they are participating in. Moreover, they must be working toward a goal that has personal or social meaning to them. For all children, participation promotes the development of friendships, communication and other life skills (Law et al., 2007).

Complementary to the child's autonomy and preferences is their experience of enjoyment or fun. The case studies highlight that the element of fun is also integral to the children's participation in the group. In areas where the children demonstrated strengths, they appeared to participate more, whereas factors such as reduced attention tended to restrict a child's participation. The element of fun can be described in ICF terms (WHO, 2001) as relating to both personal factors and participation (Rosenbaum and Gorter, 2012). A sense of enjoyment also relates to the affective component of engagement (King et al., 2020). The case studies indicate that fun was identified as an integral aspect of participation and the children engaged better in activities they enjoyed.

Adult support allowed the children's skills to expand and develop with the use of strategies such as repetition, structure and routine in the environment. Preferences, as identified by Imms et al. (2017), are among the intrinsic factors which influence and are influenced by participation in children with disabilities. When a choice was given, the children demonstrated the ability to choose and subsequently demonstrated enhanced involvement with these chosen activities or toys. The case studies above outlined how a child's preferences, including their enjoyment, as well as activity competence and relevant supports can impact participation in a group intervention setting. These findings link to Imms et al.'s (2017) constructs of persistence, affect and engagement.

The studies highlight the complexities of participation and how each child is an individual. The impact of familiarity within interactions is interlinked and required to achieve participation. Observations of the child in the group and in the home and the use of multiple data collection tools allowed for the exploration of participation in multiple contexts and the inclusion of the child and their primary carer allowed for multiple perspectives to be included. Tisdall (2018) suggests that researchers need to seek alternative ways of eliciting voice other than language, e.g., art, building materials and music. Participation must be studied with the aim of determining children's everyday functioning and according to Pinto et al. (2019) knowing more about participation will provide greater information than a specific diagnosis. Considering this view, we need to look beyond diagnosis, and we must all consider the child's participation in everyday functioning and position their views at the centre of EI. We must consider the child's environments and understand the child's microsystem and mesosystem. Supporting the child to share their views about their lives is very important.

McCormack et al. (2022) argue that the use of drawing can create child-centred practice within speech and language therapy and be used as a method for children to express their views. This method could be used by all practitioners working with children creating an opportunity for them to share their views on their lives. Lyons et al. (2022, p. 5) acknowledge that:

> children have an active role to play in letting the practitioner know what communication is like for them and in negotiating the desirable outcomes and practitioners should remain open to all courses of action.

Therefore, practitioners can learn from methods used in research to acknowledge a child's perspective and explore how their communication rights can be realised. Children with disabilities may choose not to partake in activities in which they are less competent than their peers (Imms et al., 2017). If limited opportunities for choice are available to those with disabilities, children may become less adaptable in new environments (Imms et al., 2017). Acknowledging the child and family perspective will create new priorities for everyone involved and allow their intervention to be both functional and inclusive. Therefore, practitioners working with children need to create opportunities for all children to share their views about their lives and about interventions.

McLeod (2018, p. 4) argues that:

> the importance of communication rights goes beyond just enabling freedom of opinion, expression and language. Once these rights are realised, people are more readily able to realise other human rights.

Conclusion

This chapter shows that we need to understand how a child participates in their everyday lives. We need to understand more about their participation in different contexts. When we understand how they participate using multiple methods, in particular visual methods and observations, we can understand their needs better. Communicative participation is key to realising other human rights. For children, who are neurodiverse, their communicative participation can be impacted. Participation must be studied with the aim of determining children's everyday functioning Acknowledging the child and family perspective will create new priorities for everyone involved and allow intervention to be both functional and inclusive. Therefore, practitioners working with children need to create opportunities for all children to share their views about their lives and about interventions.

References

Azunre, G.A. and Sowrirajan, T.M. 2021. The mosaic approach as a tool to facilitate participatory planning with children: Insights from Milan, Italy. *Education 3–13,* 49(5), pp. 529–544.

Bercow, J. 2008. *The Bercow report: A review of services for children and young people (0–19) with speech, language and communication needs.* Nottingham: DCSF Publication.

Birbeck, D. and Drummond, M. 2005. Interviewing, and listening to the voices of, very young children on body image and perceptions of self. *Early Child Development and Care,* 175(6), pp. 579–596.

Bjorck-Akesson, E., Wilder, J., Granlund, M., Pless, M., Simeonsson, R.J., Adolfsson, M., Almqvist, L., Augustine, L., Klang, N. and Lillvist, A. 2010. The *International Classification of Functioning, Disability and Health* and the version for children and youth as a tool in child habilitation/early childhood intervention - feasibility and usefulness as a common language and frame of reference for practice. *Disability & Society,* 32(S1), pp. S125–S138.

Bloom, A., Critten, S., Johnson, H. and Wood, C. 2020. A critical review of methods for eliciting voice from children with speech, language and communication needs. *Journal of Research in Special Educational Needs,* 20(4), pp. 308–320.

Branson, D. and Demchak, M. 2009. The use of augmentative and alternative communication methods with infants and toddlers with disabilities: A research review. *Augment Altern Commun,* 25(4), pp. 274–286.

Bronfenbrenner, U. 2005. *Making human beings human: Bioecological perspectives on human development.* Thousand Oaks, CA: Sage.

Byrne, E. and Carroll, C. 2021. Involving children and young people with down syndrome in research through the use of participatory visual methods: A scoping review. In: *Irish Association of Speech and Language Therapists Biennial Conference, 09.09.21, Virtual.* IASLT.

Carroll, C. 2018. Let me tell you about my rabbit! Listening to the needs and preferences of the child in early intervention. In: Twomey, M. and Carroll, C. eds. *Seen and heard: Participation, engagement and voice for children with disabilities.* Oxford: Peter Lang, pp. 191–242.

Carroll, C., Linehan, S., Scott, S. and Quinn, G. 2020. Children with Down syndrome and their communication partners participating in research about communication. *Social Work and Social Sciences Review,* 22(1), pp. 103–118.

Carroll, C. and Sixsmith, J. 2016. Exploring the facilitation of young children with disabilities in research about their early intervention service. *Child Language Teaching and Therapy,* 32(3), pp. 313–325.

Carroll, C. and Twomey, M. 2021. Voices of children with neurodevelopmental disorders in qualitative research: A scoping review. *Journal of Developmental and Physical Disabilities,* 33, pp. 709–724.

Carter, B. 2009. Tick the box? The ethical positioning of children as vulnerable, researchers as barbarians and reviewers as overly cautious. *International Journal of Nursing Studies,* 46(6), pp. 858–864.

Clark, A. 2004. The mosaic approach and research with young children. In: Lewis, V., et al. eds. *The reality of research with children and young people.* London: Sage, pp. 142–161.

Clark, A. 2005. Listening to and involving young children: A review of research and practice. *Early Child Development and Care,* 175(6), pp. 489–505.

Clark, A. and Moss, P. 2011. *Listening to young children: The Mosaic approach.* 2nd ed. London: National Children's Bureau.

Clark, A. and Moss, P. 2017. *Listening to young children, expanded third edition: A guide to understanding and using the Mosaic approach.* London: Jessica Kingsley Publishers.

Convention on the Rights of the Child. 1989. [online] [Accessed 20 October 2022] Available from: www.ohchr.org/en/professionalinterest/pages/crc.aspx

Coyne, I., Hallström, I. and Söderbäck, M. 2016. Reframing the focus from a family-centred to a child-centred care approach for children's healthcare. *Journal of Child Health Care,* 20(4), pp. 494–502.

D'Arrigo, R., Ziviani, J., Poulsen, A.A., Copley, J. and King, G. 2017. Child and parent engagement in therapy: What is the key? *Australian Occupational Therapy Journal,* 64(4), pp. 340–343.

Dockett, S. and Perry, B. 2005. 'You need to know how to play safe': Children's experiences of starting school. *Contemporary Issues in Early Childhood,* 6(1), pp. 4–18.

Dunst, C.J., Trivette, C.M. and Hamby, D.W. 2007. Meta-analysis of family-centered help giving practices research. *Mental Retardation and Developmental Disabilities Research Reviews,* 13, pp. 370–378.

Dunst, C.J., Trivette, C.M. and Hamby, D.W. 2008. *Research synthesis and meta-analysis of studies of family centered practices.* Asheville, NC: Winterberry Press.

Dunst, C.J. and Espe-Sherwindt, M. 2016. Family-centred practices in early childhood intervention. In: Reichbow, B., Boyd, B., Barton, E. and Odom, S.L. eds. *Handbook of early childhood special education.* Cham, Switzerland: Springer International, pp. 37–55.

Eadie, T.L., Yorkston, K.M., Klasner, E.R., Dudgeon, B.J., Deitz, J.C., Baylor, C.R., Miller, R.M. and Amtmann, D. 2006. Measuring communicative participation: A review of self-report instruments in speech-language pathology. *American Journal of Speech-Language Pathology,* 15(4), pp. 307–320.

Einarsdottir, J. 2005. Playschool in pictures: Children's photographs as a research method. *Early Child Development and Care*, 175(6), pp. 523–541.

Fargas-Malet, M., McSherry, D., Larkin, E. and Robinson, C. 2010. Research with children: Methodological issues and innovative techniques. *Journal of Early Childhood Research*, 8(2), pp. 175–191.

Hannon, E., Keane, N., O'Connell, A., Caulfield, M. and Carroll, C. 2018. An exploration of young children with down syndrome's engagement in a communication intervention group. In: *World Down Syndrome Congress, 27th July 2018, Glasgow*. WDSC.

Harcourt, D., Perry, B. and Waller, T. 2011. *Researching young children's perspectives: Ethics and dilemmas of educational research with children*. London: Routledge.

Hoogsteen, L. and Woodgate, R.L. 2010. Can I play? A concept analysis of participation in children with disabilities. *Physical & Occupational Therapy in Pediatiatrics*, 30(4), pp. 325–339.

Imms, C., Granlund, M., Wilson, P.H., Steenburger, B., Rosenbaum, P. and Gordon, A. 2017. Participation - both a means and an end. A conceptual analysis of processes and outcomes in childhood disability. *Developmental Medicine & Child Neurology*, 59(1), pp. 16–25.

Kelly, B. 2007. Methodological issues for qualitative research with learning disabled children. *International Journal of Social Research Methodology*, 10(1), pp. 21–35.

King, G., Chiarello, L.A., Ideishi, R., D'Arrigo, R., Smart, E., Ziviani, J. and Pinto, M. 2020. The nature, value, and experience of engagement in pediatric rehabilitation: Perspectives of youth, caregivers, and service providers. *Developmental Neurorehabilitation*, 23(1), pp. 18–30.

King, M., Shields, N., Imms, C., Black, M. and Ardern, C. 2013. Participation of children with intellectual disability compared with typically developing children. *Research in Developmental Disabilities*, 34(5), pp. 1854–1862.

Law, M., Petrenchik, T., King, G. and Hurley, P. 2007. Perceived environmental barriers to recreational, community, and school participation for children and youth with physical disabilities. *Archives of Physical Medicine and Rehabilitation*, 88(12), pp. 1636–1642.

Leahy, R. and Carroll, C. 2021. How the perspectives of adolescents are realised in qualitative research. In: *Association of Speech and Language Therapists Biennial Conference, 9th September 2021, Virtual*. Irish Association of Speech and Language Therapists.

Lundqvist, J., Westling Allodi, M. and Siljehag, E. 2019. Values and needs of children with and without special educational needs in early school years: A study of young children's views on what matters to them. *Scandinavian Journal of Educational Research*, 63(6), pp. 951–967.

Lundy, L. 2018. In defence of tokenism? Implementing children's right to participate in collective decision-making. *Childhood*, 25(3), pp. 340–354.

Lyons, R., Carroll, C., Gallagher, A., Merrick, R. and Tancredi, H. 2022. Understanding the perspectives of children and young people with speech, language and communication needs: How qualitative research can inform practice. *International Journal of Speech-Language Pathology*, 24, pp. 547–557.

Lyons, R. and McAllister, L. 2019. *Qualitative research in communication disorders*. Guildford: J&R Press.

McCormack, J., Baker, E. and Crowe, K. 2018. The human right to communicate and our need to listen: Learning from people with a history of childhood communication disorder. *International Journal of Speech-Language Pathology*, 20(1), pp. 142–151.

McCormack, J., McLeod, S., Harrison, L.J. and Holliday, E.L. 2022. Drawing talking: Listening to children with speech sound disorders. *Language, Speech, and Hearing Services in Schools*, 53(3), pp. 713–731.

McCormack, J., McLeod, S., McAllister, L. and Harrison, L. 2010. My speech problem, your listening problem, and my frustration: The experience of living with childhood speech impairment. *Language, Speech and Hearing Services in Schools*, 41(4), pp. 379–392.

McLeod, S. 2018. Communication rights: Fundamental human rights for all. *International Journal of Speech-Language Pathology*, 20(1), pp. 3–11.

McNeilly, P., MacDonald, G. and Kelly, B. 2015. The participation of disabled children and young people: A social justice perspective. *Child Care in Practice*, 21(3), pp. 266–286.

Merrick, R., McLeod, S. and Carroll, C. 2019. Innovative methods. In: Lyons, R. and McAllister, L. eds. *Qualitative research in communication disorders: An introduction for students and clinicians*. Guildford: J&R Press, pp. 387–405.

Murphy J. 1997. *Talking Mats: A low-tech framework to help people with severe communication difficulties express their views*. Stirling: University of Stirling.

O'Loughlin, C., Carroll, C. and Caulfield, M. 2010/2011. 'Sowing the seeds': Exploring parents' experiences of an early intervention programme for children with down syndrome. *Journal of Clinical Speech and Language Studies*, 18, pp. 57–75.

O'Neill, M.T. and Moore, K.D. 2016. 'Keeping my mind strong': Enabling children to discuss and explore issues relating to their perceptions of positive mental health through the arts. *Journal of Research in Nursing*, 21(7), pp. 544–567.

O'Neil, M.E. and Palisano, R.J. 2000. Attitudes toward family-centered care and clinical decision making in early intervention among physical therapists. *Pediatric Physical Therapy*, 12, pp. 173–182.

Paige-Smith, A. and Rix, J. 2006. Parent's perceptions and children's experiences of early intervention – inclusive practice? *Journal of Research in Special Education Needs*, 6(2), pp. 92–98.

Pinto, A.I., Grande, C., Coelho, V., Castro, S., Granlund, M. and Björck-Åkesson, E. 2019. Beyond diagnosis: The relevance of social interactions for participation in inclusive preschool settings. *Developmental Neurorehabilitation*, 22(6), pp. 390–399.

Press, F., Bradley, B., Goodfellow, J., Harrison, L., McLeod, S., Sumsion, J., Elwick, S. and Stratigos, T. 2011. Listening to infants about what life is like in childcare: A mosaic approach. In: Roulstone, S. and McLeod, S. eds. *Listening to children and young people with speech, language and communication needs*. Guilford: J&R Press, pp. 241–249.

Psaila, E. 2017. Voices in the classroom: Exploring how the voice of the disabled child and the educational professionals are manifested in the classroom. *Malta Review of Educational Research*, 11(2), pp. 171–186.

Rosenbaum, P. and Gorter, J.W. 2012. The 'F-words' in childhood disability: I swear this is how we should think! *Child: Care, Health and Development*, 38(4), pp. 457–463.

Roulstone, S., Miskelly, C. and Simons, R. 2011. Making a film as a means of listening to young people. In: Roulstone, S. and Mcleod, S. eds. *Listening to children and young people with speech, language and communication needs*. Guildford: J&R Press, pp. 267–274.

Sapiets, S.J., Totsika, V. and Hastings, R.P. 2021. Factors influencing access to early intervention for families of children with developmental disabilities: A narrative review. *Journal of Applied Research in Intellectual Disabilities*, 34(3), pp. 695–711.

Singer, I., Klatte, I.S., Welbie, M., Cnossen, I.C. and Gerrits, E. 2020. A multidisciplinary Delphi Consensus study of communicative participation in young children with language disorders. *Journal of Speech, Language, and Hearing Research*, 63(6), pp. 1793–1806.

Tisdall, E.K.M. 2018. Applying human rights to children's participation in research. In: Twomey, M. and Carroll, C. eds. *Seen and heard: Participation, engagement and voice for children with disabilities*. Oxford: Peter Lang, pp. 17–38.

Twomey, M. and Carroll, C. 2018. *Seen and heard: Participation, engagement and voice for children with disabilities*. Oxford: Peter Lang.

Verdon, S., Melvin, K. and Cronin, A. 2021. Analysis of visual data. In: Lyons, R., et al. eds. *Diving deep into qualitative data analysis in communication disorders research*. Guildford: J&R Press, pp. 197–230.

World Health Organization. 2001. *ICF: International classification of functioning, disability and health*. Geneva: World Health Organization.

World Health Organization. 2007. *International Classification of Functioning, Disability and Health - Children and Youth Version*. Geneva: World Health Organization. [online] [Accessed 20 October 2022]. Available from: https://apps.who.int/iris/bitstream/handle/10665/43737/9789241547321_eng.pdf;jsessionid=6E89543F0BEB285531AF246999A4A07D?sequence=1

8

A MINORITY WITHIN THE FAMILY

Disabled Children and Parental Perceptions

Tessa-May Zirnsak

Introduction

The period after a child is diagnosed with an impairment is typically one of complex and negative emotions for parents. Parents engage in a process of grief (Padilla-Petry and Saladrigas-Tuà 2020, p. 5) that can continue into their child's adulthood (Fernández-Ávalos et al. 2021). Parents face struggles related to their child's impairment and disability – both in terms of their perceptions of the child's capabilities and in their experiences of trying to advocate for their child in disabling institutions (Cologon 2016). It has been established that broad social understandings of disability affect how parents experience their child's impairment (Padilla-Petry and Saladrigas-Tuà 2020; Runswick-Cole and Goodley 2018), which in turn informs the experience of the child in the context of their family.

Inclusive education expert Kathy Cologon (2016) found in her study that the family is a significant site for disabled people, as they 'experience disability within the context of the family and their communities'. Too often, disabled children are not completely accepted within their families. Disabled children have been described as 'misfitting' into their family community and may be left out of family activities (Stienstra 2015, pp. 55–57). Garland-Thomson (2014, n.p.) expresses that disabled people are 'like foreigners in their own families', meaning that the experience of a disabled person in the family is one marked by difference to their siblings, or to the non-disabled person they were expected to be.

Similarly to disabled children, lesbian, gay, bisexual, transgender, intersex and asexual (henceforth queer) children are often born to heterosexual parents who may have limited or harmful understandings of queer identity.

DOI: 10.4324/9781003102915-8

These parents, like some parents of disabled people, may be prejudiced. Queer communities have worked to overcome familial queerphobia and instead developed strategies for having mutual needs that would usually be met in biological families met instead within *chosen* families (Klesse 2018), marking a departure from the biosocial ties of the family.

The Politics of Disability and of Sexuality

The central aim of this chapter is to draw on queer theory to identify and discuss similarities in the family situation of disabled children and queer people. Queer theory has assisted the queer community to understand their own difference and to heal. This chapter approaches the problem of disabled children's place in the family through key ideological and methodological positions. It is worth making these positions clear before proceeding to analyse the situation of these children.

Growing interest in disability as a political category (Simplican 2015; Zirnsak 2021) and the construction of queer as a political category (Altman 2012; D'Cruz 2008) have meant that comparisons between the situation of members of these groups are possible. Both queer and disability communities are political communities, and as such, queer and disabled are political identities. These communities – like all communities of people with shared experiences and interests – house a variety of viewpoints and beliefs. Diversity of opinion and values creates a rich and vibrant culture and means that each individual cannot be reduced to a set of static beliefs based on their community membership alone. Similarly, parents of queer children or disabled children will have differing individual approaches to their child's minority status. This chapter discusses what researchers have illustrated to be the dominant responses and how they are formed.

Generally, the dominant constructions of disability fall into the categories of the social and medical models. Parents of disabled children may not have been exposed to the social model of disability. However, through the process of their child being diagnosed with an impairment, parents do have contact with medicalisation, or the medical model, of disability. According to Brisenden (1986, p. 20), 'the medical model of disability is one rooted in an undue emphasis on clinical diagnosis, the very nature of which is destined to lead to a partial and inhibiting view of the disabled individual'. The medical model supports the pessimistic attitude that 'the lives of people with disabilities are tragic' (Bloom and Miller 2011, p. 712), which mirrors the assumption within medicine that disabled bodies are defective and need to be cured (Brisenden 1986; Fisher and Goodley 2007). Under this model, there is the person to be cured and the person who does the curing, creating a narrative of authority where medical professionals are interpreted as having more legitimacy than disabled people (Shyman 2016). The medical model prevails as the dominant way to approach impairment in medical institutions. The impact is that, however well-meaning medical advice may be, parents are immediately interpolated into a medical model of disability when their child is diagnosed, without reference to other ways of understanding disability (Docherty et al. 2005; Finkelstein 1998).

The social model is a cornerstone of disability advocacy and posits that disabled people are more disabled by the inaccessibility of the world around them than they are by their impairment (Oliver 2013, p. 1024). The social model reframes impairment as not inherently negative, but as *manufactured* as negative by a hostile and disabling environment. By changing the environment, disability is lessened. In locating the problem of disability in the environment rather than in the individual, the social model of disability draws attention to how disability is a political designation, giving legitimacy to disability advocates' calls to improve environments for people with disabilities. It has been used as an activist framework for disability advocates who have chosen the social model as 'the foundation upon which disabled people [...] organise themselves collectively' (Oliver 1996, p. 39; see also Shakespeare 2014, p. 11).

While the medical model dominates in that, as noted above, it is often the first and only model for understanding disability that parents are exposed to, some parents do adopt progressive, social-model–informed understandings of disability. One of these parents is Sue Swenson (1993), the mother of Charlie, an adult with intellectual and physical disabilities. She has written about her experience of becoming an advocate following Charlie's diagnosis:

> It was a new idea to me that there was or ever had been a civil rights movement among people with disabilities. I don't remember how it happened, but slowly I became aware that I was no longer working on fixing Charlie so my family could 'go back' into the real world: now I was working on changing the attitudes of all those ordinary people, so they would see the value of communities which include people with disabilities and all people.
>
> *(Swenson 1993, p. 5)*

Swenson's experience of living with and loving her son has had the effect of altering her understanding of disability and helping her to locate and grow what she understands to be a civil rights movement. However, this chapter addresses the more dominant way that parents approach their child's disability status – through the medical model of disability (see for example Blum 2015; Davis and Manago 2016; Landsman 2005; Manago, Davis and Goar 2017).

Understanding disability as political, as the social model does, has resulted in significant scholarship in opposition to deficit-oriented and medicalised understandings of disability. Philosopher Eva Kittay (2009, p. 606) is the mother of a woman with 'severe intellectual disabilities'. She expresses that, in her relationship with her daughter, she learned that giving and receiving care is both part of what makes us human and a political question in a context whereby needing care is viewed as a deficit. Kittay characterises her relationship with disability to be a political one that impacts the way she experiences the world and particularly her relationship with her daughter.

The implications of understanding disabled people as a political community with disability-specific civil rights are twofold. On the one hand, it enables an understanding of impairment which is free from a medicalised understanding. On the other, it means that disability can be understood as culturally produced, while impairment is understood merely as 'something that makes you different' (Barnes 2016, p. 78). Disabled philosopher Elizabeth Barnes (2016, p. 88) has argued that physical impairment can 'sometimes be bad for you – depending on what … factors it is combined with' and can 'in different combinations, be good for you'. When the concept of impairment is understood without reference to a society that produces the barriers and prejudices inherent in disablism (Kumari Campbell 2008), impairment as a social category does not necessarily have a positive or negative value. The individual differences that constitute impairment can thus be considered as being value-neutral. By taking impairment as value-neutral, this chapter focuses wholly on the construction and politicisation of disability, in tandem with how queer theorists have understood the positioning of queer communities.

Queer Understandings of Acceptance and Tolerance

The queer theory framework applied to the context of the disability community in this chapter is queer theorist Dennis Altman's (2012) and novelist Sarah Schulman's (2009) work on acceptance as compared to tolerance. Altman and Schulman's works were selected because of their significance in queer theory (Cover 2013; Delatolla 2020; Milewski 2019; Walleser 2010) and because they outline a standard of human relations that can be easily transposed to the situation of the disability community.

Like queer advocates, disabled advocates want members of their community accepted into society – including their families – for who they are. Hence, it is worth outlining the differences between tolerance and acceptance and why this distinction matters. Altman (2012, p. 59) claims that 'tolerance is a gift extended by the superior to the inferior' insofar as it does not require the tolerator to change their opinion or to be open to the situation of the group they offer tolerance to. Tolerance, Altman (2012) argues, can exist at the same time as hostility, as it only requires that the tolerator does not openly protest the existence of the person or people group in some forums. This position instead allows the tolerator to maintain negative beliefs about the person or the social category in which they are placed, while still allowing that person to be in their social or professional sphere.

Acceptance occurs when people view the lives of others as of equal value to their own (Altman 2012). The implication is that the accepting person cannot stand by while members of the group are experiencing hostility, because the acceptor recognises that members of other groups are not fundamentally different from themselves. Schulman (2009) takes Altman's understanding of acceptance further to suggest that true acceptance is characterised by the unaffected group (1) refusing to partake in institutions that are not accessible to the stigmatised group (e.g., marriage) and (2) take the situation of the stigmatised group into account when making decisions (e.g., voting). Relatives would treat the person 'like full human beings' and commit their family's resources' to help the person and their community to access the rights and privileges prohibited to them (Schulman 2009, p. 2). However, heterosexual parents of queer children often do continue to enjoy rights afforded to heterosexual people that are not afforded to queer people (e.g., marriage, extended visits when one member of a heterosexual couple is hospitalised and equal access to reproductive healthcare), including their own child (Schulman 2009). Heterosexual parents usually do not recognise or challenge homophobia as a way that aspects of society are organised; and they often continue to participate in institutions or exercise rights that are not available to their child. While parents might outwardly be supportive of their child, they may inadvertently participate in a structure of homophobia. Parents may lack the social and cultural capital to address how human rights are applied unequally to heterosexuals and queer people. This, Schulman argues, is not consistent with true acceptance of their child – if the parents accepted their child for who they were, they would work to dismantle or boycott these institutions. Rather, these parents appear to be tolerating their child's queer identity. They are prepared to continue to have the child in their lives but inadvertently uphold systems that perpetuate inequality towards their child and the queer community more broadly. This is a standard of acceptance in the family that Schulman argues most queer people will never experience. Similarly, disabled people do not enjoy rights that their families enjoy, including the right to choice of housing, education, freedom from violence and freedom to live and work in the community (Diesfeld, Surgenor and Rychert 2020; People with Disability Australia 2018; Shakespeare 2014).

There are some functional differences between how Schulman's standard for queer acceptance in the family applies to queer and disabled communities, but the desire for acceptance and recognition is consistent across both the disability and queer communities. Many disabled people do not enjoy the standard of treatment Schulman outlines as necessary for the true acceptance for queer people in their own families. For example, families of disabled people may be more likely to feel the responsibility to protect a disabled relative. However, protection in families often comes at the expense of the person's autonomy (Brown 1999; Fyson and Kitson 2007). Family members of disabled people often do enjoy rights that the person does not have, including open-access employment, mainstream education and attendance at inaccessible venues. For family members to reject rights and privileges in solidarity with a disabled family member who cannot access them, as Schulman argues families of queer people should do, is almost unheard of. In the case of families where one child has a disability while their sibling/s do not, it is even further unheard of to restrict non-disabled children from the rights and privileges (e.g., attending an event that is inaccessible) their sibling does not have. This is likely because the barriers encountered by refusing to exercise rights and privileges unavailable to members of the disability community outweigh the benefit of standing in solidarity with the disability community.

Disabled Children and Medicine

Children's perceptions of their lives may be very different from the assumptions made by non-disabled people and institutions. Disabled children's understandings of themselves may challenge or disrupt medicalised understandings of disability, which often come to dominate their lives (Reinhardt and Robasse 2023). The medicalisation of disability is relevant to the family context because healthcare staff have a significant role in positioning how parents will interpret their child's disability in the future. Interactions with clinicians involved in diagnosis 'have a major, lasting influence on the parents' ability to cope with their child's condition' (Graungaard and Skov 2006, p. 296). This shared experience becomes a social phenomenon that impacts the disabled children of parents who engage with medical professionals.

Disabled children are not passive recipients of meaning from the world around them (Ba' 2021; Matthews 2007; Quennerstedt and Quennerstedt 2014), and this includes meaning ascribed by medical institutions. Adult researchers with learning disability (their terminology) have claimed that: 'it's time to stop it always being the professionals doing everything. We want people to listen to us; listen to us and learn from us' (Docherty et al. 2005, p. 31). These assertions by adults are applicable to the context of children given that they are informed by lived experience as a disabled child. Many disability activists insist that common therapies for 'curing' impairments constitute harms consistent at worst with abuse and at best with removal of autonomy (Devita-Raeburn 2016; Sequenzia 2015). For example, educator Robin Roscigno (2019) discusses the case of an 11-year-old boy who was harmed as the direct result of applied behavioural analysis (ABA), a type of 'therapy' targeted towards autistic children. The boy was to be punished for touching his hands in a self-stimulating, 'non-functional manner'. The method of punishment was to spray the boy in the face with water, lemon juice, or vinegar to disincentivise the behaviour. While it seems from Roscigno's reporting of the case study that the professionals designing and applying this 'treatment' did not suggest it out of a wish to harm the boy, being sprayed with water, lemon juice or vinegar is an unpleasant experience that may be experienced as harm to someone with a sensory disability.

A study by Sandoval-Norton, Shkedy and Shkedy (2021) argued that, because ABA therapy does not consider the structure and function of the minds of autistic people in favour of focussing on observable and measurable outcomes, 'one can only begin to imagine the unobserved psychological damages caused to the subjects of these failed experiments' (Sandoval-Norton, Shkedy and Shkedy 2021, p. 127). Disability advocate Sequenzia (2017) explains that common therapies such as intensive ABA are disguised as care and purported by medical institutions but in fact are 'still abuse' based on how it is experienced by autistic people. For example, autistic blogger Ira Kraemer (2021) has collated the published experiences of autistic people who experienced ABA therapy. One perspective, shared via Twitter, was:

> It's taken years of legitimate therapy to undo the trauma caused to me by ABA. I am beautifully autistic, and that is never something you should try to erase from a child. The only thing I got from ABA was crippling anxiety and self-hatred.

Therefore, a purely medical lens is inadequate to gain sufficient knowledge 'of what it is like to be a disabled person in a world run by non-disabled people' (Brisenden 1986, pp. 20–21) and, subsequently, to define what 'treatments' are necessary to assimilate people with disability into a non-disabled norm.

Disability advocates and theorists insist that 'our own opinions, as disabled people, on the subject of disability are not generally rewarded with the same validity as 'experts', particularly medical experts' (Brisenden 1986, p. 20). Members of the disability community critique medical institutions as a key governing actor in their lives (Docherty et al. 2005; Finkelstein 1998). Additionally, autism advocate Michelle Dawson (2006, n.p.) states that people with autism 'can only stay out of institutions by undergoing "medically necessary" [interventions], starting very early in life'. Disabled children themselves have challenged the authority of medicalised interpretations of disability in their lives (Goodley and Tregaskis 2006; Runswick-Cole and Goodley 2018; Stalker and Connors 2003). Jack Thomas, a tenth grader with autism living in the US has claimed: 'we don't have a disease, … so we can't be "cured"'. This is just the way we are' (Harmon 2004). There is a disconnection between how disabled people see themselves and how medical institutions and professionals position parents to view impairment.

The medicalisation of disability in the family has implications for whether the child has access to positive or value-neutral narratives of disability. Similarly, queer children born to cisgender heterosexual parents are also often alone in their family as the only member with a diverse sexual or gender identity. These children, Schulman (2009) argues, share experiences of having been treated badly by members of their families 'simply, but specifically', because of their queer identity (Schulman 2009, p. 1). Unlike racial minorities, who share their race status with at least one of their biological parents, queer and disabled children are alone in their minority identities in their families. Schulman argues that in being 'alone' in the families, without queer allies and mentors, they are vulnerable to mistreatment from their family members (Schulman 2009, p. 12), regardless of any good intentions family members may have.

Both disabled and queer children may be encouraged within the family and society more broadly to pass as cisgender, heterosexual and non-disabled. Schulman (2009) argues that, for queer children, the outcome of being able to pass as cisgender and/or heterosexual is that parents do not have to do the introspective work of challenging their own prejudice to have a relationship with their queer child. For example, queer studies academic Jennifer Miller (2019) argues that there is a trend in queer fiction aimed at children who are themselves queer or come from queer families to normalise homosexual identity as in essence the same as heterosexual identity – sending a message that queer people and families can be just like everyone else. Miller (2019, p. 1646) discusses *Asha's Mums*, *Daddy's Roommate*, *Molly's Family*, and *Heather Has Two Mommies* as examples of books where 'the modest conflict [between queer identity and heterosexual norms] is quickly resolved once the normalcy of gay and lesbian parented households is established', suggesting that 'familial norms are robust enough to be reproduced in a variety of forms'. Subsequently, queer identity is taught to children as an insignificant difference so long as queerness does not challenge the essence of heterosexual family forms and values.

Disabled people similarly experience visibility differently from non-disabled people. Like how queer identity is primarily targeted when it becomes visible, disabled people become visible when they exceed the expectations set for them by others. This is sometimes the case, even if the task is something that non-disabled people do in their lives (Déjean 2015). Claire Mitchell (International Day of People with Disability 2018) is one woman with an intellectual disability who has been considered noteworthy because she has a job. International Day of People with Disability (2018), the organisation that published her story, wrote that:

Despite the fact that there are 4.2 million people in Australia who have disability, less than half of 19 to 55-year-olds with disability are employed. Claire Mitchell is fighting to change those statistics. She's an Office Administration Assistant at Lady Cilento Children's Hospital School in Brisbane, a job she loves.

Mitchell's acceptance based on her employment reinforces what can be read as 'normal' (in other words, non-disabled) about her, rather than accepting her and other disabled people for who they are and the strengths they have regardless of their employment status. In other words, Mitchell's story does not invite non-disabled people to challenge their perceptions of what it means to have a disability but instead illustrates that disability is something that can be overcome. By being presented as engaging in paid employment, Mitchell becomes an example of overcoming disability to achieve a normative goal. However, many disabled people actively oppose narratives of overcoming impairment as measured by engagement in normative activities, like open employment. Instead, advocates call for unconditional acceptance of disability identity (see for example Barnes 2016; Chamberlin 1978). The unconditional acceptance that advocates call for begins at home, in the family.

Acceptance, Tolerance and Parents

Parents make sense of the situation of their disabled child in a variety of ways. Cologon (2016) investigated parent perspectives on the meaning of disability. She recruited 121 parents of at least one disabled child from Australia and conducted individual interviews with each to answer the following research questions: what do families in Australia, who have a child labelled 'disabled', understand the concept of 'disability' to mean, and what models of disability are reflected in the understandings of disability shared by the participants in this study? In this section, I draw on the findings of Cologon's study to discuss how parents demonstrate tolerance and/or acceptance according to Schulman (2009) and Altman's (2012) interpretations of these terms in the context of the queer community.

Parents within Cologon's (2016) study expressed nuanced and complex understandings of disability, which I discuss further in this section. Cologon (2016, n.p.) has briefly summarised that generally the parents in her study expressed:

[a] desire to reject the label of disability, and overt definitions of disability, viewing the notion as not having any meaning or value to themselves or their children. These parents preferred to focus on their child as a unique person with his/her own individual strengths and needs

This perspective of disability as something not relevant to their child contrasts with the social model of disability – that impairment is not inherently bad and, further, that disability is a feature of their identity that makes them who they are, that they can be proud of. Here, parents distance themselves and their child from the concept of disability and, subsequently, disability advocacy.

Medical literature continues to encourage parents and disabled people themselves to engage in therapies directed towards learning to behave normatively (Buchholz, Ferm and Holmgren 2017). The medical model is consistent with tolerance because of the base assumption in this model that the person is experiencing disability by virtue of their impairment, not because of a disabling society. Therefore, disabled people are understood as deviant. People who subscribe to a medical model of disability may not treat disabled people with overt hostility, but instead may hold ideals consistent with charity and pity. However, attitudes of pity are not in line with true acceptance of disabled people, regardless of their impairment (Hirschmann 2013; O'Driscoll 2016). Furthermore, as the previous section illustrated, disability activists maintain that some medicalised interventions for their disability cause them harm.

Cologon's (2016) study demonstrates that, while there are differences in opinion, some parents do hold disablist, normative understandings of 'normal' and have a desire for their child to meet that understanding. However, as identified earlier in this chapter, many parents do work to overcome aspects of the medical model of disability as it is relevant to their child (Fisher and Goodley 2007; Kittay 2009; Swenson 1993). Parents are capable of being reflexive about their experiences with their child's diagnosis of disability. They can and do change their perception of what it means to be disabled and can become critical of clinicians who characterise their child as abnormal. As time goes on, parents learn about their child and have experiences related to their disability that can shift their approach to their child's disability from a medical model perspective towards accepting their child for who they are (Fisher and Goodley 2007). Such an approach is consistent with how disability advocates see disability (Docherty et al. 2005; Harmon 2004; Young 2014).

Even if parents hold views broadly consistent with assimilation into non-disabled norms as a goal for their child, they are still able to see how their child contributes to their family and their community (Cologon 2016). Parents who want their child to be like non-disabled children may inadvertently devalue or overlook the contributions of their child to their families and communities. This demonstrates that the positioning of parents is complex. Parents can be *both* advocates for their child *and* hold problematic attitudes about their child's disability. For example, Bo, a father of a child with severe disabilities in Graungaard and Skov's (2006) study, expresses a complex view of disability when talking about his son. He claims:

> I don't see him as a sick little one, sitting in a wheelchair, and not able to do anything by himself. I see him as a little boy, running around, happy and well.
>
> *(Graungaard and Skov 2006, p. 303)*

Here, Bo expresses positive feelings about his son by positioning him as non-disabled. These feelings are positive; however, it would be more empowering to experience and express positive emotions about the child as a disabled person, rather than by ignoring the child's impairment as an inherent part of him.

Similarly to Bo, Rebecca, a mother of a disabled child in Fisher and Goodley's (2007, p. 71) study, expresses a complex perspective on disability as related to her child's diagnosis. She claimed that having a disabled child:

> really does detach you from life.... I wanted to take my baby out and show him off to the world. But, as much as he is absolutely beautiful, he's still got problems and he's not normal. It probably sounds totally self-centred. I wanted to take him to the supermarket and wanted him to be doing normal baby things.... But you feel very conscious about the way he is.... I can't stand to think of people thinking, 'what's up with that child?'... Some people aren't bothered about disability. As a child, I was scared of children with disabilities. If one of those special buses came past when I was little I'd be frightened. There's this whole stigma, isn't there? and then because Thomas is as he is, it makes me feel like a freak.... I know where people are coming from because I think like that myself. That's not very good is it?
>
> *(Fisher and Goodley 2007, p. 71)*

Rebecca expresses multiple and competing perspectives on disability and her child's identity in this section of the interview. She expresses love for her child ('he is absolutely beautiful'), while also maintaining concern that others see her child through a lens of prejudice (his disability 'makes me feel like a freak'). Simultaneously, she reflects on and challenges her own prejudices ('I was scared of children with disabilities'), while also expressing understanding of people who hold the attitudes that make her feel 'very conscious' of her son's disability, as she herself confesses to having held prejudiced views.

Given the complexity of Rebecca's position and her varying attitudes, it is little wonder then that parents invest 'in interventions that will help their children to achieve "their potential"' (Fisher and Goodley 2007, p. 71) and assimilate into non-disabled places. However, as demonstrated earlier in this chapter, these medicalised interventions can cause harm to disabled people. Here, there is a manufactured disconnection between the experiences of parents – who want their child to have a good life and may see medicalisation as a way to achieve that – and disabled people themselves who advocate against interventions that have harmed them.

Rebecca and Bo's experiences demonstrate that parents may construct nuanced understandings of their child as a disabled person that do not fit comfortably in the categories of social and medical models. Parents may employ medical model understandings of disability to deflect the stigma that their child faces (Manago et al. 2017). The employment of the medical model may be a way for parents to protect their child from stigma by framing their disability as something unwanted and out of the child's control. Parents are incentivised to engage with medicalised institutions, such as clinical allied health services in order to access services and support for disabled people.

Prescription to elements of a medical model of disability can be present even when parents are aware that it is social norms that manufacture stigma (Manago et al. 2017). The evidence of parents employing both social and medical models of disability suggests that individual parents do not prescribe to a single understanding of impairment, and subsequently both accept and tolerate their child as a disabled person. Rather than a particular ideology, parents are committed to reducing the stigma that their child faces. Deflecting stigma from their child can come at the expense of a disability rights movement or of full acceptance, for example, by drawing attention to their child's disability as a medical condition that the child cannot help. It may be difficult for parents to avoid disablist understandings of impairment due to limited contact with self-advocates and because of challenges articulating social model approaches to disability in situ.

Some parent advocates, like Sue Swenson (1993) and Eva Kittay (2009) as discussed earlier in this chapter, do engage in a process of attempting to fight disability stigma as it applies to all disabled people. However, parents also invoke the medical model of disability to mitigate stigma in one instance, while reinforcing regressive and outdated ideas about what it means to be a disabled person in another. As per studies that suggest that parents employ the medical model of disability to defend their child against disability stigma (Blum 2015; Davis and Manago 2016; Landsman 2005; Manago et al. 2017), it cannot be said that on the whole, parents view impairment as value-neutral – engagement with the medical model of disability prohibits this a priori. Schulman's concept of acceptance, as I have applied it to the context of disabled people, calls for family members to engage in a process of defending disability as a valid, value-neutral identity in almost all aspects of their own lives and hold accountable people who perpetuate negative attitudes towards disability. In this sense, Schulman's (2009) definition of acceptance calls for a profoundly deep commitment to a loved one with disability.

Radical Acceptance

In this section, Schulman's (2009) conceptualisation of acceptance is applied to some of the examples discussed earlier in this chapter. Subsequently, this section again returns to the situation of queer children.

Acceptance requires the challenging of beliefs in people who hold prejudicial views to be actualised. Accepting a person or people group means viewing this group as truly equal. The acceptor cannot see their own ways of living as superior or believe that they are more entitled to rights or privileges than others. In this sense, acceptance is radical, because it means that the acceptor must change their beliefs or resist broader cultural interpellation to achieve acceptance. They must see the ways in which queer people or disabled people are constructed as deviant or deficient and reject such a characterisation not only in words but also in actions. The tolerator, meanwhile, maintains the perspective that their way of being (e.g., able-bodied, neurotypical, cisgender, and straight) is superior to other ways of being and subsequently more deserving of rights and privileges than the people around them who are divergent. Schulman (2009, p. 48) follows Arendt's claim in *Eichmann in Jerusalem: A Report on the Banality of Evil* that homophobia is not exceptional – it, like anti-Semitism and disablism, is a part of the way societies are structured. In the same way, medicalisation of disability can be thought of as banal because the conceptualisations of impairment offered to parents when their child is being diagnosed are shaped by the standard operating procedures of large institutions. In doing their job, professionals in the medical system can only offer choices that conform to the operating logic of the institutions. Such conformation excludes the social model and the voices of disabled people because the inclusion of these differing perspectives on impairment is an intervention that the institutional logics that govern medicine are not structured to cater for.

The idea that disability is an adversity that can be overcome is a way that disability is tolerated, rather than accepted, in some societies and in some families (Larsson 2004). The belief that a disabled child is capable of at least partially overcoming their impairment means that parents do not have to challenge their deep-seated beliefs about disability. These beliefs include that disability is a bad thing that doctors are healers who have legitimate authority over disabled bodies and that disability is a medical condition, not a cultural or political category. This is similar to the situation of parents of queer children. As the discussion on representations of queer identity in children's books earlier in this chapter illustrates, queer children are also sent a message that queer identity is okay so long as it does not challenge a heteronormative norm. However, in actuality, disabled people and queer people alike make meaningful and vibrant contributions to society and to the lives of the people around them. In the context of disability, engagement with medical interventions is a personal decision that individuals and families make on behalf of disabled children. The intention of this chapter is not to argue that medical intervention is inherently wrong, but rather, that the belief that people with impairments inherently require intervention is in direct contradiction with what Altman (2012) and Schulman (2009) argue is acceptance.

Schulman's (2009) text complicates Mitchell's story. Schulman argues that families tolerate queer children so long as they do not challenge heteronormativity in the family. In other words, Schulman (2009) makes the case that when families do not accept the person as a full and equal person in spite of their queer identity, they are tolerated so long as they do not appear to be queer. For example, they may be permitted to live in the family home so long as they do not bring a same-sex partner home, or so long as they do not express discontent when their siblings are permitted or encouraged to have partners over when they are not (Schulman 2009; Reczek and Smith 2021; see also Nadal 2013). However, Mitchell is praised as a disabled person because she has assimilated into open employment. This is noteworthy, International Day of People with Disability (2018) argues, because of the low rate of employment among people with disability, particularly intellectual disability. It is Mitchell's exceptionality in holding this role that cultivates tolerance and mitigates social exclusion based on her disability status. Mitchell's story does not offer a challenge to ableism. It instead demonstrates that, with hard work and a special skill, disabled people can too be assimilated. Her exceptionality allows non-disabled people to tolerate disability because her narrative is one of a person overcoming their impairment, not one of a person being proud of their disability identity even when it is radical to do so. In other words, Mitchell's employment makes her disability status tolerable, because non-disabled people do not have to reframe how they see disability to celebrate Mitchell's achievement. Non-disabled people do not have to re-think the category of disability to celebrate their success. Mitchell's story is co-opted into a narrative that does not challenge non-disabled people's assumptions and beliefs about disability, echoing Schulman's (2009) argument that queer people are only tolerated so long as they do not challenge the heteronormativity of their family.

The evidence that medical intervention to lessen disability produces more good than broader socio-cultural inclusion of disabled people, starting in the family, is limited. Disability advocate Sequenzia (2015, n.p.) discusses the advertisement of

> medical discourses as a 'treatment' to make us 'better', to 'recover' us from the 'tragedy' of being neurodivergent, and 'experts' praise this as if it is not abuse, while parents fight for insurers to pay for such abuse.

Well-marketed treatment options which employ scientific-sounding jargon may be alluring to parents who feel obligated by societal framings to manage perceived problem behaviours (Mac Carthaigh 2020) but do little to assist parents to accept their child as a disabled person. For example:

> mothers may invest a huge amount of effort in accessing services aimed at addressing what they perceive as physical, emotional, intellectual and behavioural deficits and, while progress is often achieved, the failures and struggles involved in reaching the identified targets may undermine both mothers' and children's self-esteem
>
> *(Fisher and Goodley 2007, p. 71)*

Furthermore, 'many of these treatment options are not scientifically supported and may make life worse for autistic people' (Mac Carthaigh 2020, p. 52). These treatments and their popularity are evidence that parents of disabled people are not appropriately equipped to move from an outlook of tolerance of their child and their impairment, to acceptance of their child as a full, disabled person. By improving outlooks on disability available to parents, parents can be assisted in engaging with alternatives to medicalisation, consistent with the wishes of disability advocates as outlined in this chapter.

Conclusion

This chapter has demonstrated that disabled children share a precarious positioning within their family with queer children. Similarities between the situation of queer and disabled children become clear when disability identity, like queer identity, is interpreted as a political identity. Similarities between the positioning of queer and disabled children in their families present the opportunity for the disability rights movement to draw from the theory and gains that the queer community have developed to make sense of their role in society and in their families, and likewise, for the queer movement to learn from the resilience and strategies of disability advocates. There is more work that can be done to cultivate disability pride and support for disability identity in the family that is informed by the knowledge and gains of the queer community, the advocacy of people with disability and the social model.

Positioning disability as a political identity is significant as it opens a range of possibilities for how disabled children can be interpellated within the family. As such, the central topic of this chapter is significant to queer theory and disability studies and may be useful to parents and clinicians working with disabled people who are looking for new ways to see the disabled children in their lives. In the words of a mother of a disabled child in Fisher and Goodley's (2007, p. 73) study: 'this is how the world can be changed [...] we need to change people's thinking around disability'.

References

Altman, D. 2012. *Homosexual: Oppression and liberation*. Queensland, Australia: University of Queensland Press.

Ba', S. 2021. The critique of sociology of childhood: Human capital as the concrete 'social construction of childhood'. *Power and Education*, 31(2), pp. 73–87.

Barnes, E. 2016. *The minority body*. Oxford: Oxford University Press.

Bloom, A. and Miller, P. 2011. Blindsight: How we see disabilities in tort litigation. *Washington Law Review*, 86(4), pp. 709–753.

Blum, L. 2015. *Raising generation RX: Mothering kids with invisible disabilities in an age of inequality*. New York and London: New York University Press.

Brisenden, S. 1986. Independent living and the medical model of disability. In: Shakespeare, T. ed. *The disability reader*. London and New York: Cassell, pp. 20–27.

Brown, H. 1999. Abuse of people with learning disabilities: Layers of concern and analysis. In: Stanley, N., Manthorpe, J. and Penhale, B. eds. *Institutional abuse: Perspective across the life course*. London and New York: Routledge, pp. 89–109.

Buchholz, M., Ferm, U. and Holmgren, K. 2017. 'That is how I speak nowadays'- Experiences of remote communication among persons with communicative and cognitive disabilities. *Disability and Rehabilitation*, 40(12), pp. 1–12.

Chamberlin, J. 1978. *On our own: Patient controlled alternatives to the mental health system*. New York: Hawthorn Books.

Cologon, K. 2016. 'What is disability? It depends on whose shoes you are wearing': Parent understandings of the concept of disability, *Disability Studies Quarterly*, journal article [online]. [Accessed 26 December 2022]. Available from: https://dsq-sds.org/index.php/dsq/article/view/4448/4212

Cover, R. 2013. Conditions of living: Queer youth suicide, homonormative tolerance, and relative misery. *Journal of LGBT Youth*, 10(4), pp. 328–350.

D'Cruz, C. 2008. *Identity politics in deconstruction: Calculating with the incalculable*. Hampshire and Vermont: Ashgate.

Davis, L. and Manago, B. 2016. Motherhood and associative moral stigma: The moral double bind. *Stigma Health*, 1(2), pp. 72–86.

Dawson, M. 2006. Instant institutionalization, *the autism crisis*, blog post, 30 October, [online]. [Accessed 29 July 2022]. Available from: http://autismcrisis.blogspot.com.au/2006/10/instant-institutionalization.html

Delatolla, A. 2020. Sexuality as a standard of civilization: Historicizing (homo)colonial intersections of race, gender, and class. *International Studies Quarterly*, 64(1), pp. 148–158.

Devita-Raeburn, E. 2016. The controversy over autism's most common therapy, *Spectrum*, [online]. [Accessed 05 April 2022]. Available from: https://spectrumnews.org/features/deep-dive/controversy-autisms-common-therapy/

Déjean, B. 2015. Why we need more stories of disability that aren't about overcoming disability, *Disability Horizons*, blog post, 7 December, [online]. [Accessed on 02.08.2022]. Available from https://disabilityhorizons.com/2015/12/why-we-need-more-stories-of-disability-that-arent-about-overcoming-disability/

Diesfeld, K., Surgenor, L. and Rychert, M. 2020. Breaches to New Zealand's health and disability consumers' rights: Human rights review tribunal decisions, *Journal of Law and Medicine*, 27(3), pp. 679–692.

Docherty, D., Hughes, R., Philips, P., Corbett, D., Regan, B., Barber, A., Adams, M., Boxall, K., Kaplan, I. and Izzidien, S. 2005. This is what we think, in D. Goodley and G. Van Hove (eds.), *Another disability studies reader?*, Antwerpen-Apeldoorn: Garant, pp. 27–50.

Fernández-Ávalos, M., Pérez-Marfil, M., Ferrer-Cascales, R., Cruz-Quintana, F. and Fernández-Alcántara, M. 2021. Feeling of grief and loss in parental caregivers of adults diagnosed with intellectual disability, *Journal of Applied Research in Intellectual Disabilities*, 32, pp. 712–723.

Finkelstein, V. 1998. Emancipating disability studies, in T. Shakespeare (ed.), *The disability reader*, Cassel, London and New York, pp. 28–49.

Fisher, P. and Goodley, D. 2007. The linear medical model of disability: Mothers of disabled babies resist with counter-narratives, *Sociology of Health and Illness*, 29(1), pp. 66–81.

Fyson, R. and Kitson, D. 2007. Independence or protection – Does it have to be a choice? Reflections on the abuse of people with learning disabilities in Cornwall, *Critical Social Policy*, 27(3), pp. 426–436.

Garland-Thomson, R. 2014. The story of my work: How I became disabled, *Disability Studies Quarterly*, **34**(2), n.p.

Goodley, D. and Tregaskis, C. 2006. Storying disability and impairment: Retrospective accounts of disabled family life, *Qualitative Heath Research*, **16**(5), pp. 630–646.

Graungaard, A. and Skov, L. 2006. Why do we need a diagnosis? A qualitative study of parents' experiences, coping and needs, when the newborn child is severely disabled, *Child: Care, Health and Development*, **33**(3), pp. 296–307.

Harmon, A. 2004. How about no 'curing' us, some autistics are pleading, *New York Times*, news article, 20 December [online]. [Accessed on 05.08.2022]. Available from http://www.nytimes.com/2004/12/20/health/how-about-not-curing-us-some-autistics-are-pleading.html

Hirschmann, N. 2013. Queer/fear: Disability, sexuality, and the other, *Journal of Medical Humanities*, **34**, pp. 139–147.

International Day of People with Disability. 2018. Claire Mitchell, *International Day of People with Disability*, blog post, undated [online]. [Accessed 12.08.22]. Available from https://www.idpwd.com.au/claire-mitchell/

Kittay, E. 2009. The personal is philosophical is political: A philosopher and mother of a cognitively disabled person sends notes from the battlefield, *Metaphilosophy*, **40**(3–4), pp. 606–627.

Klesse, C. 2018. Polyamorous parenting: Stigma, social regulation, and queer bonds of resistance, *Sociological Research*, **24**(4), pp. 1–19.

Kraemer, I. 2021. Why ABA therapy is harmful to autistic people, *Autistic Science Person*, blog post, 19 June [online]. [Accessed 12.08.2022]. Available from https://autisticscienceperson.com/why-aba-therapy-is-harmful-to-autistic-people/

Kumari Campbell, F. 2008. Exploring internalized ableism using critical race theory, *Disability & Society*, **23**(2), pp. 151–162.

Landsman, G. 2005. Mothers and medical models of disability, *Journal of Medical Humanities*, **27**(2–3), pp. 121–139.

Larsson, M. 2004. Restoring the spirit: The rehabilitation of disabled soldiers in Australia after the Great War, *Health and History*, **6**(2), pp. 45–59.

Mac Carthaigh, S. 2020. Beyond biomedicine: Challenging conventional conceptualisations of autism spectrum conditions, *Disability & Society*, **35**(1), pp. 52–66.

Manago, B., Davis, J. and Goar, C. 2017. Discourse in action: Parents' use of medical and social models to resist disability stigma, *Social Science & Medicine*, **184**, pp. 169–177.

Matthews, S. 2007. A window on the 'New Sociology of Childhood', *Sociology Compass*, **1**(1), pp. 322–334.

Milewski, J. 2019. Privilege, access, shunning: Familial homophobia and its representations in the works of Sarah Schulman, *Polish Journal for American Studies*, **13**, pp. 57–71.

Miller, J. 2019. For the little queers: Imagining queerness in "new" queer children's literature, *Journal of Homosexuality*, **66**(12), pp. 1645–1670.

Nadal, K. 2013. *That's so gay! Microaggressions and the lesbian, gay, bisexual, and transgender community*, Washington D.C.: American Psychological Association.

O'Driscoll, D. 2016. We do not want your pity, *Learning Disability Practice*, **19**(8), p. 14.

Oliver, M. 1996. Defining impairment and disability: Issues at stake, in C. Barnes and G. Mercer (eds.), *Exploring the divide: Illness and disability*, Leeds: The Disability Press, pp. 39–54.

Oliver, M. 2013. The social model of disability: Thirty years on, *Disability & Society*, 28(7), pp. 1024–1026.

Padilla-Petry, P. and Saladrigas-Tuà, M. 2020. Autism in Spain: Parents between the medical model and social misunderstanding, *Disability & Society*, 37(3), pp. 1–22.

People with Disability Australia. 2018. Human rights violations, *People with Disability Australia*, industry article [online]. [Accessed 07.08.2022]. Available from https://pwd.org.au/resources/disability-info/student-section/human-rights-violations/

Quennerstedt, A. and Quennerstedt, M. 2014. Researching children's rights in education: Sociology of childhood encountering educational theory, *British Journal of Sociology of Education*, 35(1), pp. 115–132.

Reczek, R. and Smith, E. 2021. How LGBTQ adults maintain ties with rejecting parents: Theorizing "conflict work" as family work, *Journal of Marriage and Family*, 83(4), pp. 1134–1153.

Reinhardt, C. and Robasse, A. 2023. Framing does matter: How health professionals can empower disabled children and their families, in A. Beckett and A.M. Callus (eds.), *The international Routledge handbook of children's rights and disability*, London: Routledge, pp. 374–390.

Roscigno, R. 2019. Neuroqueerness as fugitive practice: Reading against the grain of applied behavioral analysis scholarship, *Educational Studies*, 55(4), pp. 405–419.

Runswick-Cole, K. and Goodley, D. 2018. The 'Disability Commons': Re-thinking mothering through disability, in K. Runswick-Cole, T. Curran and K. Liddiard (eds.), *The Palgrave handbook of disabled children's childhood studies*, London: Palgrave Macmillan, pp. 231–246.

Sandoval-Norton, A., Shkedy, G. and Shkedy, D. 2021. Long-term ABA therapy is abusive: a response to Gorycki, Ruppel, and Zane, *Advances in Neurodevelopmental Disorders*, 5, pp. 126–134.

Schulman, S. 2009. *Ties that bind: Familial homophobia and its consequences*, New York: New Press.

Sequenzia, A. 2015. My thoughts on ABA, *Autism Women's Network*, blog post [online]. [Accessed 02.08.2022]. Available from https://autismwomensnetwork.org/my-thoughts-on-aba/

Sequenzia, A. 2017. ABA providers making fun of autistic people, *Autism Women's Network*, blog post [online]. [Accessed 02.08.2022]. Available from https://autismwomensnetwork.org/aba-providers-making-fun-autistic-people/

Shakespeare, T. 2014. *Disability rights and wrongs revisited*, London and New York: Routledge.

Shyman, E. 2016. The reinforcement of ableism: Normality, the medical model of disability, and humanism in applied behaviour analysis and ASD, *Intellectual and Developmental Disabilities*, 54(5), pp. 366–376.

Simplican, S. 2015. *The capacity contract*, Minneapolis and London: University of Minnesota Press.

Stalker, K. and Connors, C. 2003. Communicating with disabled children, *Adoption and Fostering*, 27(1), pp. 26–35.

Stienstra, D. 2015. Trumping all? Disability and girlhood studies, *Girlhood Studies*, 8(2), pp. 54–70.

Swenson, S. 1993. Testimony to the Senate Subcommittee on Disability Policy Hearing Regarding Reauthorization of the Developmental Disabilities Assistance and Bill of Rights Act, *State Government of Minnesota*, 29 June.

Walleser, L. 2010. Ties that bind: Familial homophobia and its consequences, *Journal of American Culture*, **33**(2), pp. 163–164.

Young, S. 2014. I'm not your inspiration, thank you very much, *Ted Talk*, video [online]. [Accessed 02.08.2022]. Available from https://www.ted.com/talks/stella_young_i_m_not_your_inspiration_thank_you_very_much?language=en

Zirnsak, T. 2021. Contextualising distress: Understanding challenging behaviour as a product of resistance in the intellectual disability community, *Journal of Literary and Cultural Disability Studies*, **15**(3), pp. 269–286.

9

NATURE PLAY FOR DISABLED CHILDREN – *MUDDY PUDDLES FOR ALL?*

Angharad E. Beckett and Deborah Fenney

Introduction

This chapter considers nature play, a hot-topic in the world of child development and wellbeing. It is widely understood to be a type of unstructured play that happens outdoors and involves children engaging with natural elements such as plants, rocks and sand (Dankiw et al. 2020). It has famous supporters – Her Royal Highness, Catherine, Princess of Wales being a high-profile advocate.[1] The children's television character Peppa Pig is also fond of outdoor play and recommends[2] '(j)umping up and down in muddy puddles, Splish, splash, splosh, splish, splash'!

As adults concerned with climate change and the preservation of ecosystems and habitats, we both recognise that nature play is one important way in which children can gain an understanding of and appreciation for nature, which they will hopefully carry with them into adulthood. We are, however, concerned about equality of access to and inclusion in nature play for disabled children. The fact that insufficient attention has been given to this issue is the basis for our critique. Our aspiration is to stimulate *reflection* on the part of nature play advocates regarding this issue.

Disabled children's right to play in general is enshrined in Article 31 of the UN Convention on the Rights of the Child (CRC) and Article 30 of the UN Convention of the Rights of Persons with Disabilities. With regard to nature play in particular, General Comment 17, which focuses upon CRC Article 31, identifies lack of access to nature as a key challenge to be addressed in the realisation of children's right to play. Children require 'adequate access to green spaces' (CRC Committee 2013, 13). In our national context – the UK – disabled children's right to play, including to nature play, has been

DOI: 10.4324/9781003102915-9

recognised, to some degree, within the play policies (past and present) of England, Scotland, Wales and N.Ireland. To date, however, there has been insufficient monitoring of this issue to ensure that policy rhetoric translates into practice.

We approach this topic in two ways. First, we apply a barriers-mapping perspective, exploring what is known about barriers to nature play for disabled children. Second, we strike a series of 'notes of caution' regarding the articulation of nature play, highlighting in particular its colonisation by certain adult agendas ('adulteration') and ableist framing (however inadvertent). Our perspective is sociological, as opposed to the dominant perspectives within play studies which have tended, and continue to be those of the medical/biological and psy-sciences (Henricks 2020). Our perspective also reflects our background in disability studies. This means that:

a   Whilst we recognise that nature play and play in general have the potential to support children's development, this is not our primary concern. Instead, our focus is upon access to and inclusion in play *as a human right*, for *all* children and one that is important for their mental health and subjective wellbeing (Beckett 2022);

b   We oppose deficit-model approaches. This means that we are critical of play discourses or rhetorics (Sutton-Smith 1997) that over-emphasise 'progress' – in the case of disabled children, this translates as the power of play to 'normalise' (Beckett 2022). It also means that we are critical of approaches that articulate the so-called 'dysfunctional' play or non-functional play of children with particular impairments, comparing their play to that of the 'normal child' ('typical child') and to play judged to be 'functional' ('the typical or "correct" form of play'[3]);

c   We adopt a social relational understanding of disability, in alignment with the UN Convention on the Rights of Persons with Disabilities (2006 Art. 1). The latter states that 'disability results from the interaction between persons with impairments and attitudinal and environmental barriers that hinders their full and effective participation in society on an equal basis with others'. Accordingly, whilst not denying the effect of impairments on a child's play, we do not presume that these effects will always or necessarily be negative and we instead focus upon understanding the barriers to disabled children's play that exist beyond their minds and bodies, within a disabling social environment;

d   Finally, we follow Hodge and Runswick-Cole (2013) in recognising ableism within the framing of leisure and recreation for disabled children, arguing that this extends to articulations of nature play.

An immediate problem when seeking to investigate nature play is how to define 'nature', 'natural settings' and 'natural things'. There are competing understandings of each. In an interview with the *American Journal of Play* (AJP), leading advocates of nature play Richard Louv and Cheryl Charles took a flexible approach. Charles (in AJP 2011, 140) commented: 'Nature can be found in the cracks in sidewalks where a flower blooms, in the moss on a rock…'. Both recognised the difficulty in identifying entirely natural settings in our world today – there are so few truly untouched wildernesses left in the world. Many other proponents of nature play would go a little further than Louv and Charles, however, perceiving 'natural' spaces to be those that exhibit fewer elements of design, for example, woodland rather than a 'green' school playground, a sandy beach rather than a sandpit. Each of these spaces (woodland, beach) may be managed by humans, yet they are more wild than not.

We emphasise the latter point in order to clarify the parameters of this chapter. Herein, we do not consider the elements of school or other playgrounds that include natural elements or purpose-built forest/adventure playgrounds. Furthermore, whilst we make mention of Forest Schools, we will do so only briefly. Forest Schools, which began in Denmark in the 1950s (as 'Naturbørnehavens'), have spread across Scandinavia, the US, the UK, Australia and elsewhere. These schools are based upon 'friluftsliv' (outdoor life) as a deep-rooted philosophy. They incorporate play and playful activity, viewing outdoor play in the forest to be a 'way for children to…cultivate environmental awareness' and lay the foundations for a healthy lifestyle (Ärlemalm–Hagsér and Sandberg 2013, p. 43). Whilst limited, existing research into the impact of Forest Schools suggests that they can have a positive impact upon children's wellbeing. Taken together, this might suggest that we might consider them within our analysis. Nevertheless, the primary objective of Forest Schools is, or has increasingly become, *pedagogical*. Whilst the initial impetus/thinking behind them may have been more orientated towards play free of adult-agendas, the milieu in which they operate has pushed them to ensure that their activities 'fit within prerequisite classroom-based discourses' (Garden and Downes 2023, p. 334). It is for this reason – because they are primarily educational settings, rather than play settings – that we exclude them from our discussion.

Investigating Nature Play

Our approach was as follows: with regard to barriers-mapping, we undertook a scoping review (Grant and Booth 2009) of existing literature relating to disabled children's inclusion in/experience of nature play. Our method for identifying sources was dynamic and iterative, using multiple relevant search terms ('nature play', 'outdoor play', 'natural play', 'disability', 'disabilities', 'special needs', 'special educational needs', 'access' and 'inclusion'), Boolean operators and various search engines (Scopus, Proquest Central, Web of Science,

ERIC and Google Scholar). We also ran Google searches to find organisations promoting nature play or play for disabled children and for relevant reports. We focused upon English-language sources for practicality, inevitably resulting in some cultural bias. This may explain why the studies identified had a distinctly western-world view of 'natural settings' as areas with grass and trees. We uncovered no research reported in English acknowledging that, for many disabled children, such settings/spaces might be mountains, desert or tundra, for example, nor exploring the inclusion or exclusion of disabled children from nature play within such environments. Further reviews incorporating literature in other languages, and more research into nature play of/for disabled children inhabiting various landscapes, are clearly needed.

With regard to our 'notes of caution', we employed discourse analysis – by which we mean that we explored how knowledge about nature play, in general and for disabled children, is produced discursively, including via the use of rhetorical devices. Needless to say, we have not analysed every definition of nature play or everything ever written about this topic. Instead, we sought to gain a sense of the dominant discourse/s relating to nature play and how disabled children are positioned within these discourses. First, we considered a number of campaigns from Australia, Canada, the UK and the USA and associated resources which seek to promote nature play. We identified a popular device used by an array of organisations involved in this movement, namely posters or printable 'bucket lists' or lists of 'x number of things to do before you are x age' (Figure 9.1).

We considered these lists of activities and the extent to which they assume/ presuppose a particular type of child, embodiment and cognitive capacities (i.e., a child with particular abilities). Next, we spent time exploring the website of the Children and Nature Network (https://www.childrenandnature. org/). This influential organisation was co-founded in 2005 by Richard Louv, whose most famous contribution to the world of nature play is his book *Last Child in the Woods: Saving our Children from Nature-Deficit Disorder*.

Barriers to Nature Play

Inclusion in nature play for disabled children necessitates, but involves far more than, physical accessibility. In this section, we consider how disabled children's experiences of nature play are shaped by the interaction between children and their broader social environment. Nature – unmediated by humans (if such a thing exists) – is only one element of this environment, which also comprises human-built elements, attitudinal dimensions and social practices.

Our scoping review revealed that evidence is sparse in this area. Nevertheless, there is sufficient to conclude that disabled children do encounter barriers to nature play. In the UK, various reports from organisations such as children's charities, Play England, Natural England and the UK's Forestry

Commission highlight the importance of accessibility and taking into account disabled children's needs (e.g., Houston et al. 2006; Lester and Maudsley 2007; Shackell et al. 2008). It should be noted that their recommendations relate both to designated play spaces and to public outdoor and green spaces. Inspiring examples of inclusive play in natural environments are provided in some of these reports (e.g., Ludvigsen et al. 2005), demonstrating that disabled and non-disabled children can and do enjoy activities such as building campfires. These reports imply, however, that accessibility and inclusion are not the norm. Although many of these reports are now quite dated, more recent research suggests that at least here in the UK, little has changed. Horton (2017, p. 1170) investigated the experiences of families of disabled children visiting two outdoor/nature play-spaces in the UK and found that whilst parents wanted to support their child to experience nature place, and there were moments of joy and love experienced even in inaccessible spaces, as a result of their encounters with *multiple* socio-material barriers, these sites were perceived by parents to be 'hard work', characterised by 'barriers to fun' and as prompting feelings of 'sadness, dread and resignation'.

A logical and vital precursor to nature play for disabled children is of course access to natural environments. Various studies have identified barriers preventing or limiting access to the natural environment for disabled people (Burns et al. 2008; Countryside Agency 2005; Williams et al. 2004). Barriers include insufficient information about accessibility, inadequate personal and private transport, inaccessible facilities and staff attitudes at sites.

Curiously, disability studies have at times struggled to find a framework for the analysis of disabled people's experiences in this regard. For Shakespeare (2014, p. 36), the British social model of disability (which understands disability as a form of social oppression) 'falters' when seeking to understand the barriers disabled people face in relation to the natural environment, because it is 'hard to blame the natural environment on social arrangements'. However, US researcher Kafer (2013) disputes this understanding of the 'natural' environment as distinct from the human-built. She questions, as we do, how many of the 'wild spaces' where humans want or like to spend leisure time are really entirely wild. She states:

> the natural environment is also 'built': literally so in the case of trails and dams, metaphorically so in the sense of cultural constructions and deployments of 'nature', 'natural', and 'the environment'.
>
> *(Kafer 2013, p. 129)*

If the natural environment is understood to be socially constructed, then it can be understood, made or at least managed differently.

Caution is needed here, however. On the one hand, assuming that disabled people, including disabled children, prefer particular types of 'developed', easily accessible space and that this means that significant adaptations to the natural environment are required, is problematic. In fact, disabled people have been found to have very similar access preferences to non-disabled people regarding such spaces (McAvoy 2001). On the other hand, when adaptations *are* made to enable access to natural environments for disabled people, it is interesting how often they are considered to be problematic by those concerned with protecting nature. Kafer (2013) cites occasions when adaptations to ensure access for disabled people to the US wilderness were questioned (e.g., ramps into cabins), whereas adaptations to ensure access for non-disabled people (e.g., steps into cabins) were not. In the UK, as recently as 2019, over 3000 people signed a petition opposing the Lake District National Park Authority's decision to resurface four miles of countryside pathway with asphalt to improve accessibility. The following is an example comment by someone opposing this development:

> The Lake District National Park Authority's priorities, according to this piece: building a tarmac path through woods (damaging the very area it's meant to protect) & "inclusivity". A perfect example of how #Political-Correctness is destroying our #heritage and #culture. It's mad.
> *(December 2019 on Twitter, anonymised)*

Watching this 'row' (as the media described it) unfold, online, we were reminded of Kafer's (2013) observation that social arrangements are mapped onto natural environments. She suggests that we should examine the deployment of disability in popular discourses about nature and environmentalism and uncover the assumptions about 'able-bodiedness' infused within narratives around nature. We have adopted Kafer's analytical approach within this chapter, to consider nature *play*.

With regard to disabled children's experiences of accessing nature and being included in nature play activities, the attitudes and practices of adults can be enabling or disabling, just as in other aspects of life. For example, the attitudes of staff working at recreational sites that are managed natural environments, have been found to impact access, positively and negatively, for disabled children (Gleave 2010; Shackell et al. 2008). Where staff are aware of disabled children's access needs, their play has been enabled. Where staff hold deficit-model ideas about disability – emphasising and perhaps exaggerating the incapacities of disabled children – this can lead to restrictions upon children's play. Staff perceptions of risk figure highly here. In research conducted by Gleave (2010) for Play England, staff considered less supervised outdoor opportunities to be too risky for disabled children. In another study, Ludvigsen and colleagues (2005) found staff attempting to stop disabled children from engaging in messy activities such as kicking and throwing leaves. Apparently whilst Peppa Pig and friends might enjoy getting muddy and encourage other children to join in, this is not an appropriate activity for *disabled children*! We suggest that this attitude reflects a heightened perception of risk and level of control and surveillance of disabled children (Curran and Runswick-Cole 2013). A change of thinking is required amongst some staff working in outdoor contexts (Burns et al. 2008).

It is, however, not only staff attitudes at recreation sites that can limit access to nature play for disabled children. Parents can and do facilitate nature play for disabled children, but their perceptions of risk can also be problematic. Researchers have found that parents sometimes attribute additional vulnerability to their disabled children, with unintended negative consequences (Gleave 2010; Von Benzon 2011). Ludvigsen et al. (2005) describe a project emphasising free adventure play in natural settings. Parents of disabled children, who were initially positive about the idea, lost interest after hearing project details, perceiving the site to be 'unsafe'. Disabled children themselves report experiencing 'over-protection preventing their opportunities for creativity, risk and physical challenge – all essentials for play' (Andrews 2012, p. 114).

Furthermore, parents have been found to limit disabled children's access to nature play for fear of bullying (Gleave 2010; Horton 2017). We found no research exploring how peer attitudes may impact upon disabled children's nature play *directly*. Nevertheless, the impact of peer attitudes may be inferred from some studies. Robb et al. (1981) describe an inclusive tree-climbing exercise and state that involving teams of non-disabled and disabled children challenged the non-disabled children's assumptions about their disabled peers. They gained respect for the disabled children. This study implies the existence of disabling attitudes held by non-disabled children, requiring intervention. Whilst the Robb study was conducted many years ago, more recent research suggests that disabling attitudes held by non-disabled children are a persistent problem (Beckett 2015). Parents' concerns about their children encountering negative attitudes from peers are thus understandable. Challenging this may necessitate developing more initiatives wherein positive peer relations are encouraged, allaying parental concerns.

What Else Is 'at Play' in Relation to Disabled Children's Nature Play?

The short answer to this question is *ideology* – or various entangled ideologies. In this section, we unpack this statement. Over the past 15 years, concerns have been growing that *all* children's green time – their unstructured, free-play opportunities in natural settings has been reduced (Driessnack 2009). Concerns have been voiced about a 'backseat generation' (Karsten 2005) experiencing the natural environment only via a car window on their way to another adult-organised event within their overly-structured schedules; a 'couch potato' generation glued to electronic media and at risk of obesity (Hancox 2005); and a 'bubble wrap generation' (Malone 2007) suffering from 'paranoid parents' who fear for their safety in an environment perceived as hostile. Those of a more critical persuasion might observe that there is more than a soupçon of moral panic, fat-phobia and a particular type of Global North, middle-class, moralism evident within these discourses. Nevertheless, these concerns have captured the popular imagination, especially in the advanced capitalist world.

As previously mentioned, the writings of the journalist Richard Louv (2005) have been highly influential. It was Louv who coined the term 'nature deficit disorder' to describe the impact of childhood moving indoors. The consequences he claims are increased obesity, attention-deficit disorder, impaired social skills and declining mental health amongst our children. His evidence is largely anecdotal rather than research-based. Whilst he never intended the term 'nature deficit disorder' to be understood as a proper medical diagnosis – and it is certainly not an officially recognised condition – the idea that 'alienation from nature' has 'human costs' (AJP 2011, p. 138) caught on. There is now an extensive academic and non-academic body of literature focusing upon similar concerns. This forms part of a wider literature, too vast to summarise meaningfully here, suggesting that childhood is in crisis and that we need to be fostering free-range children as a matter of urgency.

According to its proponents, the benefits of nature play are as follows: it is claimed that when children engage with therapeutic landscapes (Brown and Bell 2007; see also 'Green Exercise' literature, for example, the edited collection by Barton et al. 2016) and nature play, this helps to improve their health and fitness (Beyer et al. 2014). Children's playful engagement with natural environments is said to stimulate all aspects of their development more readily than indoor environments, including physical development, attitudes and agency (Gill 2014; Milligan and Bingley 2007). Such environments allegedly prompt more diverse and creative play than purpose-built playgrounds (Fjørtoft and Sageie 2000) and nature play is said to enhance children's concentration and self-control (Wells 2000), motor skills (Fjørtoft 2004), language and collaborative skills (Moore and Wong 1997), cognitive skills (Wells 2000) and independence and autonomy (Freeman and Kearns 2015). Furthermore, natural settings are said to help to reduce bullying (Malone and Tranter 2003). It is also claimed that they instil a sense of awe and wonder and connection to the natural world (Cobb 1977). Regular contact with and play in natural environments during early childhood may help combat 'biophobia' (Vadala et al. 2007). Childhood experiences of playing in woodlands – or not – appear to relate to whether the natural environment is experienced positively or as intimidating by teenagers (Milligan and Bingley 2007) and whether children grow up to care about the environment.

There are also said to be benefits of engagement with nature for children who have particular impairments. Children who have ADHD are reported to experience reduced symptoms and improved concentration after taking part in 'green outdoor activities', based on ratings measured by their parents (Kuo and Faber Taylor 2004). There are also said to be benefits for autistic children, such as improved concentration or communication (Blakesley et al. 2013). Some literature has also considered how engagement with natural environments can be a vehicle for developing personal and social skills amongst children who have severe and complex learning difficulties (Pavey 2005) and improving relations between disabled and non-disabled children (Robb et al. 1981). How engagement with nature is defined within these studies varies, but play and playful activities are considered important and valuable.

This chapter does not test these claims about nature play – this would require a sustained program of empirical research. Instead, we strike notes of caution regarding the literature and research in this area, beginning with the concept of 'nature deficit disorder'. On one level, we are wary of this concept because we perceive it to be an example of 'narrative prosthesis'. Narrative prosthesis occurs when disability is used 'as a metaphorical signifier of so-cial...collapse' (Mitchell and Snyder 2001, p. 47) – in this case the collapse of an idealised childhood, of happy days playing in the woods. Louv (2005) is quite the repeat offender when it comes to narrative prosthesis, given that he defines it as a form of 'cultural autism'. Narrative prosthesis underlines the way in which disability is perceived to be a problem – an undesirable trait located within the individual – within many (perhaps most) cultures. Both Louv's use of the terms nature deficit disorder and cultural autism and the uncritical adoption and use of these terms by others are indicative of ableism, however inadvertent.

Furthermore, most probably due to his journalistic background, Louv tends to write in a rather emotive and hyperbolic style – a good example of this being the interview that he gave to the AJP, in which he claimed that there are 'huge psychological, physical, and spiritual risks in raising children under protective house arrest' (AJP 2011, p. 146). Such claims are not fully supported by independent studies. Faber Taylor and Kuo (2006) suggest that, in the absence of robust research evidence, the negative effects upon chil-dren's development of reduced time spent playing in natural settings remain largely an assumption rather than a fact. Childhood obesity – one of Louv's particular concerns – is a highly contested terrain. How it should be meas-ured and interpreted is a controversial issue within the scientific and medical communities (Flegal and Ogden 2010). For some critics, there are worrying ideological (fatphobic) foundations to the 'couch potatoes and tubby tots' crisis (Gard and Wright 2005). Lee and Maheswaran (2011) conclude that, on balance, evidence *is* generally supportive of the link between health and natural environments (albeit considering research involving adults rather than children). They emphasise, however, that this evidence is weak at best, with too much research being open to critique vis-à-vis inadequate research design and procedures not meeting basic standards of rigour.

There is also extensive literature problematising the broader crisis of childhood rhetoric to which many nature play advocates, Louv included, are prone. This rhetoric reflects social and political concerns about what children are and should be and says much about adult concerns about the future of the nation. A Google search reveals another invented syndrome– 'lazy child syndrome'[4] and a host of blogs and other web resources designed to help parents transform their lazy child into active and entrepreneurial children- and adults-of-the-future. Some of these recommend outdoor, nature play as a solution. We are reminded of disability studies' critiques of the construction of the ideal child and adolescent in neoliberal times, as a future citizen who possesses a particular and quite narrow set of abilities which include being self-sustaining, productive and entrepreneurial (Goodley et al. 2014; Slater 2015).

There are, however, additional problems with the crisis in childhood discourse. The 'loss of childhood' thesis, usually involving adult nostalgia regarding nature play, rests upon a concept of childhood that emerged with Romanticism. The supposed special relationship of children with nature has been thoroughly deconstructed (see Taylor 2011), as have adult constructions of childhood as long, blissful, carefree and always summer! As its critics point out, childhood has never been this for many children. This construct assumes childhood to involve 'the opportunity to play', 'neglecting to incorporate notions of toil, work or responsibility' (Muñoz 2009, p. 5). Other critics, including Lester and Maudsley (2007) and Valentine (1997), have demonstrated how this concept of childhood is gendered, White and adult-constructed – children's voices being largely absent. That disabled children are excluded from this construction, and their voices are largely absent is seldom noted, but therefore all the worthier of consideration.

To this line of critique, we would add that in Louv's writings, and those of many other nature play advocates, it is possible to identify not only romanticism about getting back to nature but also a certain frontier narrative, 'predicated on the cultural projection of the able-bodied hero' (Jordan 2012, para 1). Implicit within these constructions are assumptions about appropriate ways of engaging with natural environments and necessary embodiments. It is here, we suggest, that a disability studies critique is most urgently required and potentially most instructive. Louv's (2005) recollections of his childhood – the basis of his ideas about what has been 'lost' – emphasise physical abilities, particular sensory experiences and independence. This privileging of particular embodiments and embodied ways of interacting with nature in the articulation of nature play – unintentional though this may be – risks positioning disabled children, many of whom may not possess all of these 'necessary' abilities, as the 'Other' in relation to this type of play, effectively excluding them.

Implicit within many of these constructions of nature play are understandings of the natural environment's functionally significant properties (Kafer 2013). Many studies considering the benefits of nature (e.g., for health and wellbeing) use the concept of affordances, referring to aspects of an environment considered useful to a person (Gibson 1979). Although supposedly neutral, affordances are neither fully objective nor subjective and are often reified, with those for certain embodiments prioritised, whilst others are neglected (Gibson 1979). The types of physical activity and the environmental affordances highlighted in writings about nature play often assume and prioritise certain embodiments, for example, the ability to climb trees or hide in bushes (Fjortoft and Sageie 2000).

It is important to understand more closely the varied ways in which children engage with nature and the impact that diverse impairments might have upon their experiences. Trees and bushes may offer different affordances to different children. Assumptions that there is just one way to engage with natural environments, or that these environments bring the same benefits for all, are problematic. For example, natural settings that are restorative for some may be scary for others (Milligan and Bingley 2007). Furthermore, much research considering the experiences of nature play of children with particular impairments (e.g., ADHD or autism) and reporting positive benefits for these children has been small-scale and exploratory (see reviews by Gill 2014; Taylor and Kuo 2006). Firm conclusions cannot easily be drawn from such research. Many of these studies also rest upon parent/carer/teacher opinions rather than direct engagement with children. The views and voices of disabled children need to be at the heart of research.

Another note of caution relates to the prioritisation of the instrumental value of nature play for all children, but especially disabled children. Nature play may help children to acquire certain skills, knowledge, attitudes and 'abilities'. The intrinsic value of nature play, however, as an entertaining, fun or otherwise enjoyable activity, is seldom given top billing. The focus is upon health and/or learning 'benefits'.

Ironically, where the fun aspect of nature play is acknowledged, this is sometimes downplayed. Some studies suggest frivolous nature play for disabled children distracts from more important activities. Von Benzon (2010, p. 624), for example, critiques certain UK-based environmental organisations for 'emphasising recreation and failing to provide adequate educational opportunities' for disabled children, whilst Crosbie (2014), in a study of the work of the Calvert Trust (UK) – a provider of outdoor adventure holidays for disabled people, their families and friends – is critical of situations where disabled children are not encouraged to do anything other than play because of limiting perceptions of staff or workers. They are, he argues, being denied the wider benefits to be gained from outdoor *education.*

This focus upon health or educational outcomes reveals the dangers associated with what a well-known author in play studies, Sutton-Smith (1997), famously termed the 'play as progress' rhetoric. To date, play studies have been very largely shaped by the professional interests of psychologists and educational psychologists. Leading figures in these disciplines – e.g., Piaget and Vygotsky – emphasised the importance of play for child development. Whilst not denying this aspect of play, we suggest that one consequence of an over-focus on the connection between play and learning is the contamination of play aims and objects by adult agendas – a process that Else and Sturrock (1998) usefully termed 'adulteration'. Play is all too often viewed as the primary vehicle and indicator/measure of the development of a child and method by which science 'makes up people' as normal/abnormal, typical/atypical (Hacking 1986); a vehicle by which children can *chase normal* (McLaughlin et al. 2008); or even a way for children to exceed the norm, becoming a superchild (Kaščák and Pupala 2013).

For disabled children, these discourses have been 'magnified and read in particular ways' (Goodley and Runswick-Cole 2010, p. 500), reflecting or reinforcing a deficit understanding of disability. Not only are disabled children often presented as deficient in the abilities considered necessary for play and their play activities requiring adult intervention but also play has often become another 'mechanism for assessment, diagnosis and therapeutic intervention for atypically developing children' (Goodley and Runswick-Cole 2010, p. 500).

The critique developed by Goodley and Runswick-Cole implies a neoliberal re/purposing of the play as progress rhetoric. Play – including nature play – is at risk of being captured by neoliberal policy agendas that emphasise accountability and performance outcomes (Wood 2013). The identified outcomes most often relate to health and education and are about making children into future worker-citizens. Play has become a vehicle for training children to maintain their bodies and take responsibility for avoiding the 'chaos' of ill-health (Mitchell 2014). It has become a means for creating children 'full of potential', prepared for careers that require 'competitive, individualised, risk-embracing' beings, capable of 'exceeding themselves' (Kaščák and Pupala 2013, p. 320). This is worrying because neoliberalism provides an ecosystem that nourishes ableism (Goodley et al. 2014), for the valuing and promotion of certain abilities over others and problematising of perceived deviation from or lack of these abilities (Wolbring 2008).

Our analysis reveals that much of the discourse/s relating to nature play (academic and other) assumes that children either already possess, or have the potential to acquire, certain desirable abilities through play. Earlier, we mentioned the campaigns and resources that use the device of listing '50 things to do' (bucket list style or 'before you are age x'). Whilst some of the suggested activities are likely to be accessible to most – e.g., plant a seed and taste local honey – others assume a child has certain physical abilities, can see and hear, has the cognitive abilities to navigate or use a compass, is comfortable taking risks and has no sensory sensitivities. The following is an excerpt from a list published by the organisation 50thingstodo.org:

> go on a walk barefoot, run around in the rain, play conkers, climb a huge hill, try rock climbing, canoe down a river, build a raft
>   take risks, hide, run, jump, swing, balance, climb, sit, talk and have fun.[5]

We reproduce the National Trust's list of '50 things to do before you are 11 and three-quarters'[6] in full here:

a Climb a tree
2 Roll down a really big hill
3 Camp out in the wild
4 Build a den
5 Skim a stone
6 Run around in the rain
7 Fly a kite
8 Catch a fish with a net
9 Eat an apple straight from a tree
10 Play conkers
11 Go on a really long bike ride
12 Make a trail with sticks
13 Make a mud pie
14 Dam a stream
15 Play in the snow
16 Make a daisy chain
17 Set up a snail race
18 Create some wild art
19 Play pooh sticks
20 Jump over waves
21 Pick blackberries growing in the wild
22 Explore inside a tree
23 Visit a farm
24 Go on a walk barefoot
25 Make a grass trumpet
26 Hunt for fossils and bones
27 Go stargazing
28 Climb a huge hill

29 Explore a cave
30 Hold a scary beast
31 Hunt for bugs
32 Find some frogspawn
33 Catch a falling leaf
34 Track wild animals
35 Discover what's in a pond
36 Make a home for a wild animal
37 Check out the crazy creatures in a rock pool
38 Bring up a butterfly
39 Catch a crab
40 Go on a nature walk at night
41 Plant it, grow it, eat it
42 Go swimming in the sea
43 Build a raft
44 Go bird watching
45 Find your way with a map and compass
46 Try rock climbing
47 Cook on a campfire
48 Learn to ride a horse
49 Find a geocache
ax Canoe down a river

Whilst there are disabled children who would be able to do some or all of these activities, equally, there are those for whom such activities would prove difficult, perhaps impossible. Seldom (we have been unable to find any examples) is guidance provided regarding how these activities might be adapted to be accessible and inclusive. Even the Peppa Pig song from which we quote is entitled '*jumping* in muddy puddles' (our emphasis). This is a shame given that it would be possible to do the things encouraged by the song lyrics – splishing and splashing in puddles – in *many* ways, not just through the physical act of jumping!

That there is an imagined child embedded within many discussions regarding nature play – and this child is an 'ideal', defined in terms of ability preferences – is much in evidence on the Children and Nature Network's website, despite their more recent efforts to recognise diversity. For example, this web article warns that:

As we continue to decrease children's time and space to move and play outdoors, we are seeing a simultaneous rise in the number of children that are presenting with sensory deficits. ... children are walking around with underdeveloped vestibular (balance) systems ... and are generally clumsier than in years past. ... A child's neurological system is naturally designed to seek out the sensory input it needs ... to develop into a strong and capable individual ...into resilient and able-bodied people.[7]

No reference is made to children who have particular impairments. Presumably, the 'clumsy child' referenced here is a 'normally' clumsy child, not one who has, for example, been labelled dyspraxic. Such articulations of nature play and its functions effectively position disabled children as a source of uncertainty, perhaps even anxiety for adults (not only parents but also professionals in the field of child development).

Does outdoor play in natural settings help a child who has dyspraxia become less 'clumsy'? Should we hope that it *does*? Will they receive the *full* benefits envisaged here, i.e., will nature play help *them* to become strong, capable, resilient, able-bodied people? Or are the full benefits of this play only available/realisable for the child who has a 'normal' level of childhood 'clumsiness'? Is nature play part of the journey towards 'normal' for *all* children or only for *some*?

In this web article, people with 'sensory deficits' are positioned as the antithesis of being strong, capable, independent and resilient. This implies that there are abilities that we expect children to acquire if they are to go on to experience valuable living and valued lives. Such expectations can lead to the denial of rights to people with supposed 'ability-deficits' (Hutcheon and Wolbring 2013, p. 239). Principally, they can lead to a denial of their right to being accepted as they are, by self and others. We are reminded of Goodley's (2001, p. 225) call for more 'imaginative approaches' that 'embrace notions of distributed competence, ability, intelligence, capacity and "differently articulate"'.

The disproportionate focus upon play as a vehicle for the improvement of disabled children risks conveying a message to wider society and disabled children that they are unacceptable as they are – that they need to change. How this message reinforces wider disabling processes and practices and how it impacts disabled children's own subjectivities (undermining their psycho-emotional well-being) are questions worthy of consideration. We must remember, however, that disabled children are unlikely to be passive in the face of these processes and practices. We know, from wider research, that disabled children resist disabling discourses and, at times, reconstruct them to fit their experiences and priorities (Priestley 1998). It is therefore important to continue exploring both the impact of the constructions of nature play upon disabled children and how they negotiate these constructions.

Conclusion

Our chapter has identified a range of barriers preventing disabled children from accessing nature play, including, but going far beyond the physical.

Improved transport networks and investments in necessary infrastructure are required. Attitudinal barriers exist. Not all staff working at recreation sites, parents or non-disabled peers hold disabling attitudes, but where and when they do, these require challenging, suggesting a need for appropriate learning initiatives and family support.

Our discourse analysis revealed, however, that the main barrier to nature play for disabled children is the way that it is conceptualised. Assumptions about desirable embodiments and abilities infuse notions of nature play. This reflects the way in which children's play, in general, is at risk of colonisation by neoliberalism and ableism. Dominant articulations of nature play tell us much about the ability preferences of wider society, for independent/ autonomous, 'able-bodied' and 'able-minded' persons. This discursive framing of nature play is likely to have real effects, leading to the marginalisation of some children. It explains the prioritisation of the instrumental value of nature play over the intrinsic. Nature play may well have educational or other benefits for disabled children, but these are often over-emphasised. As another mechanism for their 'continual remediation' (Buchanan and Johnson 2009, p. 57) disabled children's play is all too often transformed into their work. Goodley and Runswick-Cole (2010) call for their play to be emancipated, an argument which is also highly pertinent vis-à-vis disabled children and nature play.

How might we move forward with research into disabled children's nature play, informed by these concerns? We suggest that we first need to understand the complex construction of their play; how it is constituted by the interrelations between play-activities (including the imagined player embedded within these), the material world (including the bodies of the players), the place where play occurs, the institutional structures that shape the game and activities of players and the impact of the wider culture with its conceptual frames (Taylor 2009).

Research also needs to find ways to enable disabled children to contribute fully to the shaping of research agendas, identifying that which gives quality to their lives (Watson 2012). We need to know whether nature play is important to disabled children and if it is, *how* and *why*? We need answers to these questions *in children's own terms*. Research also needs to recognise the heterogeneity of disabled children's experiences. Social class, gender, parental and family experiences, ethnicity and geographical location intersect with diverse impairments, leading to different experiences for different children. Finally, research needs to maintain an emphasis on disablement as a process in need of challenging. Whilst it is important to identify, as we began to do here, the ways in which disabled children may be excluded from nature play, we also need to find strategies that disrupt these processes. If these strategies are to be effective, disabled children need to be party to their development.

Notes

1 https://www.rhs.org.uk/gardens/wisley/garden-highlights/back-to-nature-garden (Accessed on 3rd June 2023).
2 Short extract from 'Jumping in Muddy Puddles' - a song from 'My First Album' (Peppa Pig). The composer is Julian Nott. The album was published in London, in 2019 by eOne Music.
3 See, for example: https://calliercenter.utdallas.edu/wp-content/uploads/2018/12/Play.pdf (Accessed on 16th May 2023).
4 Examples: https://www.greenspringsschool.com/lazy-child-syndrome/ and https://imwithholly.com/lazy-kids/ (Accessed on 16th May 2023).
5 https://www.50things.org.uk/activity-list.aspx; http://www.ywt.org.uk/discover-learn/pearson-park-wildlife-garden/natural-play (Accessed on 23rd August 2015).
6 As reproduced in the *Daily Mail* newspaper: https://www.dailymail.co.uk/news/article-3709212/Climb-tree-roll-big-hill-camp-wild-50-things-11-National-Trust-releases-bucket-spade-list-children.html (Accessed on 16th May 2023).
7 https://www.childrenandnature.org/2015/05/06/the-unsafe-child-less-outdoor-play-is-causing-more-harm-than-good/ (Accessed on 23rd August 2015).

References

AJP (American Journal of Play). 2011. Battling the nature deficit with nature play. An interview with Richard Louv and Cheryl Charles. *American Journal of Play*, 4 (2), pp. 137–149.

Andrews, M. 2012. *Exploring play for early childhood studies*. London: Sage (Learning Matters).

Ärlemalm-Hagsér, E. and Sandberg, A. 2013. Outdoor play in a Swedish preschool context. In: Knight, S. (Ed.) *International perspectives on forest school: natural spaces to play and learn*. London: Sage Publications Ltd, pp. 41–52.

Barton, J., Bragg, R., Wood, C. and Pretty, J. (Eds). 2016. *Green exercise. Linking nature, health and well-being*. Abingdon: Routledge.

Beckett, A.E. 2015. Non-disabled children's ideas about disability and disabled people. *British Journal of Sociology of Education*, 35 (6), pp. 856–875.

Beckett, A.E. 2022. 'But tell me, where do the children play?' Disabled children and the right to play. In: Tierney, R.J., Rizvi, F. and Erkican, K. (Eds.) *International encyclopedia of education* (Fourth Edition). Oxford: Elsevier, pp. 306–319.

Beyer, K.M., Kaltenbach, A., Szabo, A., Bogar, S., Nieto, F.J. and Malecki, K.M. 2014. Exposure to neighborhood green space and mental health: evidence from the survey of the health of Wisconsin. *International Journal of Environmental Resesearch and Public Health*, 11 (3), pp. 3453–72.

Blakesley, D., Rickinson, M. and Dillon, J. 2013. *Engaging children on the autistic spectrum with the natural environment: teacher insight study and evidence review*. publications.naturalengland.org.uk/file/5492760660410368 (Accessed on 20th October 2015).

Brown, T. and Bell, M. 2007. Off the couch and on the move: global public health and the medicalisation of nature. *Social Science & Medicine*, 64 (6), pp. 1343–1354.

Buchanan, M and Giovacco Johnson, T. 2009. A second look at the play of young children with disabilities. *American Journal of Play*, 2 (1), pp. 41–59.

Burns, N., Paterson, K. and Watson, N. 2008. Exploring disabled people's perceptions and use of forest recreation goods, facilities and services in Scotland, England

and Wales. [online] Available from: http://www.forestry.gov.uk/fr/infd-7psl75 [Accessed on 20th October 2015].

Cobb, E. 1977. *The ecology of imagination in childhood.* New York: Columbia University Press.

Committee on the Convention on the Rights of the Child. General comment no. 17 on the right of the child to rest, leisure, play, recreational activities, cultural life and the arts (Art. 31). 2013. [online] Available from: https://digitallibrary.un.org/record/778539 [Accessed on 8 September 2023]

Convention on the Rights of Persons with Disabilities and Optional Protocol. 2006. [online] Available from: www.un.org/disabilities/documents/convention/convoptprot-e.pdf [Accessed on 20 March 2023].

Countryside Agency. 2005. What about us? Diversity review evidence – part one. [online] Available from: http://publications.naturalengland.org.uk/publication/63060 [Accessed on 20th October 2015].

Crosbie, J.P.G. 2014. *The value of outdoor education for people with disabilities: an in-depth case study of the Calvert Trust.* PhD thesis, University of Edinburgh.

Curran, T. and Runswick-Cole, K. 2013. Concluding thoughts and future directions. In: Curran, T. and Runswick-Cole, K. (Eds.) *Disabled children's childhood studies.* Basingstoke: Palgrave MacMillan, pp. 196–199.

Dankiw, K.A., Tsiros, M.D., Baldock, K.L. and Kumar, S. 2020. The impacts of unstructured nature play on health in early childhood development: a systematic review. *PLOS ONE,* **15** (2), p. e0229006.

Driessnack, M. 2009. Children and nature-deficit disorder. *Journal for Specialists in Pediatric Nursing,* **14** (1), pp. 73–75.

Else, P. and Sturrock, G. 1998. The playground as therapeutic space: playwork as healing, paper presented at Play in a Changing Society: research, Design and Application, IPA/USA National Conference, Longmont, co, 17–21 June. [online] Available from: https://ipaewni.files.wordpress.com/2016/05/colorado-paper.pdf [Accessed on 18th March 2019].

Faber Taylor, A. and Kuo, F.E. 2006. Is contact with nature important for healthy child development? State of the evidence. In: Spencer, C. and Blades, M. (Eds.) *Children and their environments.* Cambridge: Cambridge University Press, pp. 124–140.

Fjørtoft, I. 2004. Landscape as playscape: the effects of natural environments on children's play and motor development. *Children, Youth and Environment,* **14** (2), pp. 21–44.

Fjortoft, I., and Sageie, J. 2000. The natural environment as a playground for children: landscape description and analyses of a natural playscape. *Landscape and Urban Planning,* **48** (1–2), pp. 83–97.

Flegal, K.M., and Ogden, C.L. 2010. High body mass index, overweight, and obesity in children: definitions, terminology, and interpretation. In: O'Dea, J.A. and Eriksen, M. (Eds.) *Childhood obesity prevention. International research, controversies and interventions.* Oxford: Oxford University Press, pp. 3–16.

Freeman, C. and Kearns, R. 2015. Childhoods under canvas: campgrounds as spaces of resistance to 'protective parenting'. *Childhood,* **22** (1), pp. 101–120.

Gard, M. and Wright, J. 2005. *The 'obesity' epidemic. Science, morality and ideology.* Abingdon: Routledge.

Garden, A. and Downes, G. 2023. A systematic review of forest schools literature in England. *Education 3–13,* **51** (2), pp. 320–33.

Gibson, J.J. 1979. *The ecological approach to visual perception.* Boston: Houghton Mifflin.

Gill, T. 2014. The benefits of children's engagement with nature: a systematic literature review. *Children, Youth and Environments,* **24** (2), pp. 10–34.

Gleave, J. 2010. *Making it our place: community views on children's play.* [online] Available from: http://socialwelfare.bl.uk/subject-areas/services-client-groups/children-young-people/playengland/making10.aspx [Accessed on 31 Mar 2015].

Goodley, D. 2001. 'Learning difficulties', the social model of disability and impairment: challenging epistemologies. *Disability and Society,* **16** (2), pp. 207–231.

Goodley, D., Lawthom, R. and Runswick-Cole, K. 2014. Dis/ability and austerity: beyond work and slow death. *Disability and Society,* **29** (6), pp. 980–984.

Goodley, D. and Runswick-Cole, K. 2010. Emancipating play: dis/abled children, development and deconstruction. *Disability and Society,* **25** (4), pp. 499–512.

Grant, M.J. and Booth, A. 2009. A typology of reviews: an analysis of 14 review types and associated methodologies. *Health Information and Libraries Journal,* **26** (2), pp. 91–108.

Hacking, I. 1986. Making up people. In: Heller, T.C., Sosna, M. and Wellbery, D.E. (Eds.) *Reconstructing individualism.* Stanford: Stanford University Press, pp. 222–236.

Hancox, B. 2005. Growing 'couch potatoes': television, computers and childhood obesity as a response to Gard (2004). *Childrenz Issues: Journal of the Children's Issues Centre,* **9** (1), pp. 32–36.

Henricks, T.S. 2020. Play studies. A brief history. *American Journal of Play,* **12** (2), pp. 117–155.

Hodge, N. and Runswick-Cole, K. 2013. 'They never pass me the ball': exposing ableism through the leisure experiences of disabled children, young people and their families. *Children's Geographies,* **11** (3), pp. 311–325.

Horton, J. 2017. Disabilities, urban natures and children's outdoor play. *Social & Cultural Geography,* **18** (8), pp. 1152–1174.

Houston, L., Worthington, R. and Harrop, P. 2006. Design guidance for play spaces. [online] Available from: http://www.forestry.gov.uk/forestry/INFD-7LSEHW [Accessed on 31 Mar 2015].

Hutcheon, E. and Wolbring, G. 2013. Deconstructing the resilience concept using and ableism lens: implications for people with diverse abilities. *Dilemata,* **5** (11), pp. 235–252.

Karsten, L. 2005. It all used to be better? Different generations on continuity and change in urban children's daily use of space. *Children's Geographies,* **3** (3), pp. 275–290.

Jordan, T. 2012 The myth of American ability: Cooper's Leatherstocking, the frontier tradition, and the making of the American canon. *Disability Studies Quarterly,* **32** (4). [online] Available from: http://dsq-sds.org/article/view/1739/3178 [Accessed on 3rd June 2023].

Kafer, A. 2013. *Feminist, queer, crip.* Bloomington: Indiana University Press.

Kaščák, O. and Pupala, B. 2013. Buttoning up the gold collar – the child in neoliberal visions of early education and care. *Human Affairs,* **23** (2), pp. 319–337.

Kuo, F.E., and Faber Taylor, A. 2004. A potential natural treatment for attention-deficit/hyperactivity disorder: evidence from a national study. *American Journal of Public Health,* **94** (9), pp. 1580–1586.

Lee, A.C.K. and Maheswaran, R. 2011. The health benefits of urban green spaces: a review of the evidence. *Journal of Public Health*, 33 (2), pp. 212–22.

Lester, S. and Maudsley, M. (2007). *Play, naturally - a review of children's natural play*. www.playengland.org.uk/media/130593/play-naturally.pdf [Accessed on 31 Mar 2015].

Louv, R. 2005. *Last child in the woods: saving our children from nature-deficit disorder*. New York: Algonquin Books.

Ludvigsen, A., Creegan, C. and Mills, H. 2005. Let's play together: play and inclusion - Evaluation of Better Play Round Three. [online] Available at: www.barnardos.org.uk/lets_play_together_report.pdf [Accessed on 31 Mar 2015].

Malone, K. 2007. The bubble-wrap generation: children growing up in walled gardens. *Environmental Education Research*, 13 (4), pp. 513–527.

Malone, K. and Tranter, P. 2003. Children's environmental learning and the use, design and management of schoolgrounds. *Children, Youth and Environments*, 13 (2), pp. 87–137.

McAvoy, L. 2001 Outdoors for everyone: opportunities that include people with disabilities. *Parks and Recreation*, 36 (8), pp. 24–36.

McLaughlin, J., Goodley, D., Clavering, E. and Fisher, P. 2008. *Families raising disabled children: enabling care and social justice*. Basingstoke: Palgrave MacMillan.

Milligan, C. and Bingley, A. 2007. Restorative places or scary spaces? The impact of woodland on the mental well-being of young adults. *Health and Place*, 13 (4), pp. 799–811.

Mitchell, D.T. 2014. Gay pasts and disability future(s) tense. Heteronormative trauma and parasitism in Midnight Cowboy. *Journal of Literary and Cultural Disability Studies*, 8 (1), pp. 1–16.

Mitchell, D.T. and Snyder, S.L. 2001. *Narrative prosthesis. Disability and the dependencies of discourse*. Ann Arbor: The University of Michigan Press.

Moore, R.C. and Wong, H.H. 1997. *Natural learning: rediscovering nature's way of teaching*. California: MIG Communications.

Muñoz, S.-A. 2009. Children in the outdoors – A literature review. [online] Available from: http://www.educationscotland.gov.uk/images/Children%20in%20the%20outdoors%20literature%20review_tcm4-597028.pdf [Accessed on 31 Mar 2015].

Pavey, B. 2005. *The forest school and inclusion: a project evaluation*. [online] Available from: www.leeds.ac.uk/educol/documents/161165.doc [Accessed on 23 Aug 2015].

Priestley, M. 1998. Childhood disability and disabled childhoods: agendas for research. *Childhood*, 5 (2), pp. 207–223.

Robb, G.M., Havens, M.D., Ku, B.J. and Whitman, J.P. 1981 *Special education in the natural environment: a resource guide in providing outdoor education, recreation and camping for children with disabilities*. [online] Available via eric.ed.gov [Accessed on 31 March 2015]

Shackell, A., Butler, N., Doyle, P. and Ball, D. 2008. *Design for play: a guide to creating successful play spaces*. [online] Available from: http://www.playengland.org.uk/resources/design-for-play.aspx [Accessed on 31 Mar 2015].

Shakespeare, T. 2014. *Disability rights and wrongs revisited*. Abingdon: Routledge.

Slater, J. 2015. *Youth and disability. A challenge to Mr Reasonable*. Abingdon: Routledge.

Sutton-Smith, B. 1997. *The ambiguity of play*. Cambridge, MA: Harvard University Press.

Taylor, A. 2011. Reconceptualizing the 'nature' of childhood. *Childhood*, **18** (4), pp. 420–433.

Taylor, T.L. 2009. The assemblage of play. *Games and Culture*, **4** (4), pp. 331–339.

Vadala, C.E., Bixler, R.D. and James, J.J. 2007. Childhood play and environmental interests: panacea or snake oil? *The Journal of Environmental Education*, **39** (1), pp. 3–18.

Valentine, G. 1997. A safe place to grow up? Parenting, perceptions of children's safety and the rural idyll. *Journal of Rural Studies*, **13** (2), pp. 137–145.

Von Benzon, N. 2010. Moving on from ramps? The utility of the social model of disability for facilitating experiences of nature for disabled children. *Disability and Society*, **25** (5), pp. 617–626.

Von Benzon, N. 2011. Who's afraid of the big bad woods? Fear and learning disabled children's access to local nature. *Local Environment*, **16** (10), pp. 1021–1040.

Watson, N. 2012. Theorising the lives of disabled children: how can disability theory help? *Children and Society*, **26** (3), pp. 192–202.

Wells, N.M. 2000. At home with nature: effects of 'greenness' on children's cognitive functioning. *Environment and Behavior*, **32** (6), pp. 775–795.

Williams, R., Vogelsong, H., Green, G. and Cordell, K. 2004. Outdoor recreation participation of people with mobility disabilities: selected results of the national survey of recreation and the environment. *Journal of Park and Recreation Administration*, **22** (2), pp. 85–100.

Wolbring, G. 2008. The politics of ableism. *Development*, **51** (no issue number), pp. 252–258.

Wood, E. 2013. *Play, learning and the early childhood curriculum*. London: Sage.

10

DISABLED CHILDREN'S RECREATIONAL USES OF DIGITAL TECHNOLOGIES IN THE CONTEXT OF CHILDREN'S DIGITAL RIGHTS

Sue Cranmer

Introduction

Disabled children and young people's everyday lives are frequently challenged by the prejudice that exists within society towards them. Moreover, disabled children's voices are often missing within key debates that affect their lives and directly impact their experiences and aspirations. A notable example is the lack of research that exists about disabled children's uses of digital technologies. Computers, laptops, mobile devices and the internet have had a profound impact on children's lives over the last two decades. They became especially important during the COVID-19 pandemic with the need to 'stay at home' and the associated shift of education to remote learning. Yet, while a comprehensive evidence base has been developed about children and young people's uses of digital technologies, particularly in high-income countries, there is limited research that specifically examines how disabled children and young people use such technologies (Söderström, 2009a; Passey, 2013; Lundy et al., 2019; Cranmer, 2020a, 2020b). This is surprising given that mobile devices are especially useful for disabled children due to the general attributes of devices and convergence with assistive technologies through in-built accessibility features. The ability to zoom in and read text aloud, for example, enables disabled children to use mainstream technologies without the adaptation provided by specialist assistive technologies, such as magnification and screen reader software installed on computers and laptops.

The research about disabled children's uses of digital technologies that does exist is often focussed around online safety and suggests that disabled children are more at risk online (Chadwick et al. 2017; Livingstone et al., 2017; UNICEF, 2017; Kowalski and Toth, 2018; Cavallini and Cavallini, 2021).

DOI: 10.4324/9781003102915-10

These studies are well-intentioned and essential to support disabled children to develop strategies to prevent online risk. Nevertheless, they often inadvertently reinforce deficit models of disability and characteristically render disabled children vulnerable by focussing on the potential harms of being online without setting these risks within the context of disabled children's positive experiences. This is in contrast to extensive research about non-disabled children that provides balanced accounts of the opportunities as well as the risks that children experience online. Research that does aim to provide a more holistic picture of disabled children's online activities is carried out by only a small number of researchers, which include studies by Alper (2017); Alper and Goggin (2017); Ellis and Goggin (2017); Ellis, Goggin and Kent (2020); Kaur and Saukko (2022); Kaur, Saukko and Lumsden (2018); Lidström and Hemmingsson (2014); Lundy et al. (2019); Söderström (2009a, 2009b, 2013); and Tsaliki and Kontogianni (2014).

There has been a determined drive within disability studies to challenge perspectives that frame children and young people as somehow deficient and to assume that disability and disadvantage are direct outcomes of impairment (Cameron, 2014, p. 33). Curran and Runswick-Cole emphasise that research about disabled children should not unquestioningly conflate 'impairment, inequality and abuse' and instead should:

> begin with the concerns of disabled children, young people, their families and allies; this means that it takes the voices of disabled children and young people very seriously; it does not compare disabled children's childhood with 'normal' childhoods, but values all childhoods equally.
> *(Curran and Runswick-Cole, 2014, p. 1617)*

Taking these perspectives on board, this chapter focuses specifically on out-of-school recreational experiences with digital technologies to explore the opportunities and challenges that disabled children encounter with these technologies to complement formal learning perspectives reported previously (see Cranmer, 2017, 2020a, 2020b). Differences between formal, informal and non-formal learning are complex and widely debated (Sefton-Green, 2004, 2013) and are outside of the scope of this chapter. Informal learning is understood here, relatively straightforwardly, as taking place outside of school. Informal learning activities are typically considered unplanned, unassessed and unaccredited (Tusting, 2003); they may go unrecognised, be undervalued and occur as part of family and community life (Eshach, 2007).

Recreational activities are hugely important in children's lives. Yet, as noted earlier, there remains limited research that considers how disabled children use digital technologies to support hobbies, games, sports and socialising. In light of this gap, the questions addressed in this chapter are:

- How do disabled children access and experience recreational uses of digital technologies out of school?

- What factors enable or constrain disabled children's recreational uses of digital technologies out of school?
- How developed are disabled children's digital skills and competencies including online risk and safety to support recreational uses of digital technologies out of school?

Disabled children with vision impairment are the focus of this chapter as there is evidence that adults with vision impairment encounter more barriers online than other impairment groups (Disability Rights Commission, 2004). This finding suggests the importance of considering whether disabled children with vision impairment can access the same opportunities for learning when online as their non-disabled peers.

Disabled children's experiences need to be considered in relation to the recent landmark shift in human rights legislation, most notably the United Nations Convention on the Rights of the Child (UNCRC) General Comment No. 25 (United Nations Committee on the Rights of the Child (UNCRC), 2021). This Comment crucially extends children's rights to the digital environment and provides an important lens for reflecting on the situation of disabled children. Children's digital rights legislation is explained in the next section.

Human and Children's Digital Rights

Human rights legislation, particularly the 1989 UNCRC (1989) and the 2006 UN Convention on the Rights of Persons with Disabilities (2006) has been a key driver for upholding disabled children and adults' rights. The articles of the UNCRC set out the following entitlements:

- the 'right to provision (of resources necessary for survival and development to their full potential);
- the right to protection (from a wide array of threats);
- the right to participation (to enable children to engage and play an active part in a society)' (Chernyavskaya, 2015).

Importantly, children's rights were extended to the digital environment in 2021 with the introduction of the UNCRC General Comment No. 25 (UNCRC, 2021). This means that all 196 signatories to the Convention will now have to formally report on children's digital rights based on four recommendations:

- No child should be discriminated against or digitally excluded.
- The best interests of the child should guide the development of online provision.
- Children should be protected from risks to their 'life, survival and development'.

- Digital technologies should enable children to express opinions and provide their views on the matters that relate to them.

A key aspect of the legislation is that all children have entitlement to 'culture, recreation and play.' (UNCRC, 2021)

The General Comment is far-reaching. While it covers the more obvious digital technologies that children use, such as computers and mobile devices, it also seeks to ensure children's rights in relation to other technologies that children use or are impacted on by others' uses now and in the future. These include assistive technologies; automated processing (software that analyses data and bases decisions on algorithms); behavioural targeting (analysis of users' online activity in order to target them with advertising or other content); risks associated with content, contact (using online services), conduct (behaviour by other users or peers) and contract risks (inappropriate exposure to commercial relationships and pressures that could cause potential harm to users) (5Rights Foundation, 2021). Commercial products, for example, frequently designed for adults then used by children to connect to friends and family, may have aspects that 'adversely impact the child's experience or violate their rights' (5Rights Foundation, 2021, p. 3). Algorithms are being widely used to collect large amounts of data from children, often not in their own interests, and constitute surveillance and other attacks on their right to privacy (Lupton and Williamson, 2017). These issues show how the General Comment is potentially a game-changer for upholding children's digital rights.

Importantly, disabled children's rights are specifically set out in the General Comment, emphasising that:

> The digital environment opens new avenues for children with disabilities to engage in social relationships with their peers, access information and participate in public decision-making processes. States parties should pursue those avenues and take steps to prevent the creation of new barriers and to remove existing barriers faced by children with disabilities in relation to the digital environment.
>
> *(UNCRC, 2021, p. 15)*

The General Comment also states that there are particular challenges that apply when ensuring disabled children's rights:

- Barriers (e.g., content in inaccessible formats).
- Limited access to assistive technologies.
- Prohibited uses of digital devices in schools and other environments.
- Provision of the skills and knowledge needed to use digital technologies effectively.

- Technological innovations designed for children with different types of disabilities.
- All digital products and services designed for universal accessibility (e.g., without the need for adaptation).
- Involvement of children in the 'design and delivery of policies, products and services' that affect their digital rights.
- Identification and removal by states parties of the increased risks of 'cyberaggression and sexual exploitation and abuse'; that disabled children may be exposed to.
- Opposing the prejudice that disabled children encounter that can lead to 'overprotection or exclusion'.
- afety information, protective strategies and public information, services and forums' to be provided in accessible formats. (UNCRC, 2021, p. 15)

Clearly, having rights is not the same as exercising them and research has a crucial part to play in ensuring that disabled children's rights are respected. Indeed, the involvement of children in matters that relate to them is a central aspect of children's rights legislation. This chapter contributes to the agenda through exploration of disabled children's uses and experiences of recreational uses of digital technologies including the opportunities and challenges encountered in the digital environment in view of the General Comment.

Children and Young People with Vision Impairment's Experiences of Digital Learning

In what follows, I draw upon the findings of the 'Understanding how children and young people with vision impairment experience digital technologies for learning' project (Cranmer, 2017) to explore disabled children's recreational uses of digital technologies and the opportunities and challenges that disabled children encounter online. This participatory, qualitative study explored disabled children's uses and experiences of digital technologies for formal and informal learning inside and outside school settings. Findings reported here about recreational activities are drawn from the wider project results (see Cranmer, 2017 for full report). Interviews were carried out with disabled young people, subject teachers, qualified teachers of children with vision impairment and teaching assistants. The focus of this chapter is based mainly on discussions with disabled young people. Ongoing discussions with participants ensured the development of inclusive and appropriate data collection tools, methods, analyses and reporting. Seven young people aged between 13 and 17 were recruited in three secondary schools via the VI-forum (c), which offers support for teachers of vision-impaired students (RNIB, 2019). The young people were engaged in semi-structured interviews to hear about their uses and experiences of digital technologies in and out of school (Table 10.1).

TABLE 10.1 Description of sample of young people (with pseudonyms)

Child	Age	Gender	School
Fern	14	Girl	A
Rachel	14	Girl	A
Nigel	13	Boy	B
Laura	16	Girl	B
Jem	17	Boy	B
Simon	17	Boy	B
Siobhan	14	Girl	C

Interviews were transcribed and carefully read to identify common themes in line with grounded approaches (Charmaz, 2006). A coding framework was developed and refined to categorise the data into themes using NVivo analysis software. The interviews were carried out pre-pandemic; data relating to the disabled young people's recreational uses was re-analysed and reported during the summer of 2021. The discussion section was generated by clustering the key findings from the thematic analysis under each of the four main recommendations of the General Comment No. 25 while bringing in relevant examples of the specific challenges for ensuring disabled children's rights listed in the General Comment (UNCRC, 2021, p. 15) set out earlier in the chapter. This method allowed the research questions to be answered while reflecting on the recommendations in the General Comment in light of these results.

Recreational Uses of Digital Technologies

Access, Hobbies and Social Media to Connect with Peers

The availability of digital technologies is a precursor to their use. In common with many children in the Global North, this group of young people own or have access to a range of technologies that include computers, laptops and tablet computers such as the Apple iPad or Microsoft Surface, mobile phones and combined music/games/web browsing devices such as the iPod touch). While, most children in the UK do have access to the internet (99% of 0–17 year olds, Ofcom, 2022), this is in contrast to children in low-income countries who may experience digital poverty and exclusion (UNICEF and International Telecommunication Union, 2020).

Children with access often consider these devices essential to their lives (Bond, 2014), and it was the same for the young people who took part in the study. Laura, for example, said of her tablet: 'I feel like it's my own personal thing that I can't live without sort of thing.'

School policies had influenced out-of-school access for some of the participants. Nigel, for instance, was provided with a tablet through a parent-funded scheme. Out of school, he was able to use the tablet as he wished, including the ability to download apps. However, he said that some of the apps got blocked when he brought the tablet into school, due to safeguarding measures in school. This showed how mobile devices can operate differently in different settings, creating a device with changing characteristics in and out of school that participants negotiate on a daily basis. Within the same school, Simon and Jem, both in the sixth form, were provided with tablets through an alternative scheme specifically due to their vision impairment, but not allowed to take them home. For out-of-school recreational uses, Jem, for instance, relied instead on his own mobile phone and iPod Touch, separating these from schoolwork and using them instead for 'more social' uses such as calling and texting friends and using Facebook.

Unsurprisingly, there was variation in how much the young people used these technologies. Fern said that she used her tablet for five hours every evening after school, while Nigel said he used the tablet less than his friends did as he goes swimming every evening. The young people clearly liked using mobile devices out of school, rather than desktop and laptop computers. Reasons included ease of use, being lighter and more portable, being faster to turn on, reliable and being versatile, for instance, having detachable keyboards. Nigel explained how he used his tablet in the car, on the train and in aeroplanes:

> Well I might not use it on a bus, just because of the tight space sometimes, but I use it on trains and I use it on aeroplanes and I use it in the car when we're going somewhere.

For this group of young people, inbuilt accessibility settings on mobile devices were useful given their vision impairment. These were said to be important for zooming in and enlarging what is on screen, listening to text and changing contrasting colours and font sizes. Nigel also commented that the tablet was small enough that he could 'bring it close to my eyes and it doesn't really weigh more.' Fern said she liked the touchscreen because she sometimes struggles to find the mouse when using a laptop, 'the mouse blends into the background. With a touchscreen you can just like touch it.' Siobhan, who has very little sight, relies often on the voiceover option on her mobile phone and iPod Touch. When describing recreational uses of digital technologies, the young people expressed a clear preference for using mobile devices rather than computers with assistive technology with the exception of Laura who said that she preferred to use the laptop with Supernova (magnification software) rather than her tablet for magnifying lyrics during choir practice.

The young people identified a wide range of benefits to their uses of digital technologies for out-of-school recreational and social activities. This included finding mobile devices helpful for fitting in while using the same technologies as friends. Laura, for example, described the benefits of using her tablet to support independence and sense of belonging:

> I like it because it's more independent for me. I feel like just an ordinary person when I'm using it, because I like to be a tiny bit different, but I don't like to be so much different that everyone treats me differently. Um, I like to be just like a normal girl sort of thing in the mix, which I quite like. And having a tablet and my friends have tablets as well, it just makes me feel like I'm one of them basically.

Similarly, Siobhan was keen to emphasise that her engagement with mobile devices was no different to other teenagers.'

> Definitely, because that's how I access the internet with my phone and tablet. I use my phone like any other teenager would. So texting, Facebook, that's what I like, You Tube.

Even so, Siobhan, unusual among the participants in having no vision, used a colour detector app on her mobile phone to help her to choose matching clothes for going out when there was nobody at home to ask. She said:

> Yeh, I basically just know what goes with what. For me a colour's just a tag, it doesn't really mean anything but I know that blue, a light colour wouldn't really go well with a dark colour. Um, yeh I don't know, I just know, I think just from people talking and, er that's an ugly colour, and that doesn't go with that. So my wardrobe's just filled with jeans. Jeans go with everything, that's what I think anyway.

The interviews showed the diverse ways that uses of digital technologies enable this group of young people to enhance their hobbies and interests, for instance, music and sport. Siobhan was particularly engaged in listening to and composing music. A keen guitarist, she described how she uses Garage Band to lay down tracks:

> So then I'd record what I'm singing and then play it back and then, just to make sure it's ok. And then I could, um. I'd go on to track and in the tracks I could listen to what I've just done, record something else and use an overlay to um, put them together and then create a song with it.

Sport also emerged from the interviews as a keen pursuit for the young people in terms of spectating and taking part. The interviews highlighted the diverse ways that uses of digital technologies complement young people's sporting activities. Nigel said that he liked to play with the Fifa App on his tablet and on the Xbox. He is also a competitive swimmer and uses a tablet to record and improve his swimming as recounted here:

> Like playing games. I like to play on the Fifa app that you can get, football app, and I also tend to like recording my swimming and then noticing the points and things.

Other participants liked to play games on their mobile devices too. Fern, for instance, said that she played on the Angry Birds app.

Laura is a keen (guided) skier and completes an online diary showing her progress to share with her coach as follows:

> On line I have to, because I'm like a ski racer, so I have to do like a training diary online and that's always good because I can zoom in on what I've written, so I can spellcheck and do whatever, which is really good.

These examples highlight how the use of digital technologies can enhance sporting activities. Importantly, these accounts also challenge the negative assumptions often made about the sporting abilities and mobility of young people with vision impairment.

The use of social media was popular amongst participants for keeping in touch. Typical choices were Facebook, YouTube and Instagram with Fern and Simon occasionally viewing Twitter. Facebook was said to be useful for keeping in touch with friends and family either close by or further afield, organising meet-ups and sharing achievements. Siobhan talked of how Facebook enabled her to keep in touch with friends made at 'residentials for the blind' through texting, Facebook and Skype. Siobhan expresses pride in her vision impairment within this context and, therefore, the importance of social media for maintaining these relationships:

> Yeh. I mean I laughed at one of my friends for falling down the stairs and I was like, I shouldn't have laughed at you, but then he laughed at me when I walked into a door, so we're even. We're not really supportive. Um, when I was at a college, I was so happy for being the blindest. I was the blindest out of all the students and I thought it was really ironic being the blindest on a blind residential. (Siobhan)
> That made you proud? (Sue)
> Yeh. (Siobhan)

Less typically, Simon, uses Facebook to promote sport as part of a scheme attached to a local football team where he volunteers on a council run scheme to support 'children who have difficulties':

> My role is to promote the programme so I use Facebook and stuff to get people involved. I haven't actually put it on Twitter yet but I predominantly use Facebook to try and just get people involved really. Try and get more people signed up because it is, it's a good programme.

These examples show how the young people benefit from the uses of digital technologies to enhance their everyday lives. Many of these digital activities are typical of other children within the same age group, such as supporting hobbies and interests and using social media to keep in touch. Other uses are distinct to this group of disabled children such as regular use of the inbuilt accessibility settings on mobile devices, describing how mobile devices help them to fit in and use Apps to choose what clothes to wear. Participants also talked about the issues they encountered using digital technologies. For example, Fern said that uses of apps on her tablet, particularly to draw, were constrained by data limitations. Siobhan described how she was learning to use Sibelius (a music composition programme) on the laptop. However, she was struggling to link this to the assistive technologies needed. This suggested the importance of having both the skills and competencies needed for the effective and safe use of digital technologies, as discussed in the next section, alongside raising questions about the compatibility and accessibility of products such as Sibelius.

Digital Skills and Competencies Including Online Risk and Safety

The interviews with the young people suggested that they were broadly positive about the level of their own digital skills and competencies. Skills had often been developed through trial and error on their own and with help from parents, siblings, teachers and teaching assistants and hardware company representatives. Mostly, the young people said that they had the skills they needed to do what they wanted and needed to or could access additional support where needed. Possession of such skills and competencies is important given that a lack of skills and competencies can create barriers to online participation. Laura and Jem's responses suggested that their skills and confidence had grown alongside developments in technology that had made mobile devices easier to use than previous technologies. Laura said:

> Yeh. I do, I'm not really struggling to do much at the moment but it's just a lot easier …

Jem explained how he had been nervous about using digital technologies when he was younger, given issues with magnification. That meant that his skills lagged behind his peers by 'a couple of years' though he was catching up now as technology had become easier to use:

Any reason why you were apprehensive? (Sue)

Um, maybe because they were difficult to enlarge. Because talking like ten years ago where it, so knowledge, tablets didn't really exist and it was a lot less advanced than it is now. So maybe it was that, um but yeh sort of more recently I've sort of got more used to it and it's not really a problem.

A key skill, often needed by the young people, was searching for and selecting key information online. The interviews suggested competence in using keywords to carry out internet searches though unsurprisingly there was variation in skill. Simon, for example, named 'Google Advanced' as the search engine he uses to find 'exactly what you're looking for.' Laura said that she would search, then compare and gather the information from the different websites:

Yeh, um I would search for the keywords obviously and then obviously like 100 odd websites come up. I just literally go onto different websites, see which information is similar, what they have in common basically and put them in my own words basically.

Whereas Laura appears to carefully evaluate what she finds, other youngsters are less careful. Jem said: 'Um, mm, er well I do use Wikipedia quite a bit. You're not really supposed to but…' Similarly, Siobhan commented that she selected websites by preference rather than careful evaluation of what she found: 'I guess I'd have to see if it's a reliable source and all that stuff. I'm not really bothered if it's reliable. If I like it, I'll believe it.'

Rachel said that she relied on her mother's support with searching, which suggested that her own skills were underdeveloped. She said that her mother suggested keywords to type, while she would discuss with her which sites might be reliable. She mainly used Wikipedia. The other youngsters' comments suggested that they carried out searches independently, though some relied on other members of their families for support with technology more widely. Fern, for example, said that she would ask her mother or her brother for help when she encountered a problem; her brother was the most helpful because he is a 'techie,' studying technology at college. Siobhan likewise found her brother's help useful. Jem and Laura both said that their fathers would help. Jem said this was particularly useful given the lag in his skills, described here: 'Yeh, I'd say um I probably didn't know er as much about computers as like the average person my age, um but fortunately my dad's all right, so.' Nigel, exceptionally among this group, said both his parents help out. Simon explained that his skills were now beyond those of his parents as he had grown up with technology. He said:

> This may sound really big-headed, I don't think they're as good as me, in the sense that I guess because they're older, they haven't. I've kind of grown up with technology because of the generation I am, so I just think that's probably why.

In common with other young people, Simon had developed his skills and competencies with digital technologies by starting young and 'picking[ing] things up as you go along.' Jem similarly said he had learnt through 'trial and error' and familiarity with mobile devices at home: 'Um, just trial and error really. Um so my dad has a tablet so I sort of er, and I've got a tablet so I know the sort of Apple like design.'

Likewise, Siobhan described how she approached learning to use technology:

> I think I can learn if I put my mind to it. It can be a bit challenging at first but then anything seems hard when you're trying to learn it. And when you get the hang of it, it's easy.

Some of the youngsters did mention that they had received support in schools to develop their skills and competencies from teaching assistants who were 'brilliant at technology,' specialist teachers of vision impairment or information technology, or for using assistive technology, representatives from particular companies. Supporting the young people appeared to be ad hoc rather than a comprehensive school programme to ensure they had the skills and competencies needed to move forward with technology.

Generally, the young people appeared satisfied with what they were able to do with technology. Any frustrations noted tended to be mundane. Fern, for example, described how she got exasperated when she forgot how to do something. Jem talked about his impatience when having to wait for 'loading and things like that.' Jem and Simon had struggled to send and save large documents such as textbooks. Simon said:

> But I guess that's where emails and Dropbox and things like that come into useful. Sometimes it's a bit fiddly say if you've got for argument's sake a textbook that you're trying to put on a tablet, sometime if the file size is too big, it's not an issue, it's just a bit [...]. You have to either, or if it's a perfect size you can just email it and then save it to iBooks or if you can't you have to upload it to Dropbox and share it.

Simon and others also talked of computers crashing; losing work or error messages that fail to make sense.

An important aspect of disabled children's uses of digital technologies is negotiating risk and staying safe online given the need to ensure that all children have strategies to stay safe online. Among this group of youngsters, there were accounts relating to content, contact and conduct risks but these were fairly mundane rather than upsetting. Indeed, they appeared to be taken for granted by this group. For example, Laura explained that she occasionally encounters 'the odd thing,' such as bullying, as 'a normal part of life.' She had strategies in place for rationalising these experiences based on the understanding that disability can attract negativity. Laura explained this:

> If you've got slight difference um and not one of the, I was going to say ordinary people, but yeh if you have got visual impairment, I did used to get, I did used to get bullied quite a lot but I just, I very much think positively about most things. I say things happen for a reason and if I get bullied, I don't mind, because it's who I am, I'm not going to change who I am just because someone doesn't like it.

Laura also said that these incidents made her tougher and 'in some ways ready for the workplace' where everything will not be 'all happy, all sweet' all of the time. Others talked of ableist comments (Campbell, 2009). Siobhan had encountered and reported an example of this on Facebook:

> There was once someone that made a comment on disabled people and it was just a Facebook page and I was like. I just thought, well it's not really acceptable, I might as well report it, but it's not directed at me.

Other participants played down the threat of bullying. Simon described how bullying in the school was unusual and reinforced through blocking software:

> Obviously there's the odd case of there will be somebody sees it as their kind of thrill to do it but generally the school does stamp down on it hard, there's kind of like a no tolerance policy. Um and with the systems they have at school, they have all the firewalls and everything in place to make sure everybody's protected in that sort of respect.

On the whole, the young people considered that they were equipped to handle risk for the most part. There were suggestions in the interviews that schools had been helpful in supporting young people to develop strategies to stay safe online, thereby sustaining their digital activities both inside and outside of school. Jem, for example, said that his understanding of risk was informed by the school and his parents: 'Yeh, school are pretty clued on to stuff like that so over the years and obviously my mum and dad are conscious of things like that so.'

Many of the strategies that the young people had developed related to their uses of social media, particularly Facebook. Approaches included only talking to people online that had been met first off-line; not chatting to people in online games; not announcing where they were going to; and not meeting up with people first met online. Fern, for instance, was careful about who she would accept as a friend on Facebook:

> On like Facebook I would like, if someone asked for my friend request I would like click on them and then I'd click on their friends and then click on mutual friends, see who like, and if I have like a load of friends in common with them, I would add them because I would know [...], or that they go to my school.

Fern also said that if she decided to meet someone first met online, she would always take a friend along with her.

The impression given in the interviews overall was that negotiating online risk appeared commonplace. The youngsters were aware of a range of potential risks online and reasonably successful in avoiding them or having strategies in place to protect themselves when risks, such as bullying or ableist comments, were encountered.

This group of young people were broadly positive about their digital skills and competencies including having strategies to avoid and negotiate online risk. General skills and those related to risk had been developed by trial and error alongside both school and familial support. Mobile devices were said to be easier to use than the computers and laptops with assistive technologies previously relied on. Most of the young people were able to carry out independent internet searches though their commitment to evaluating information carefully varied across the group. Technical issues such as losing work caused occasional frustration but all the children had support from siblings and parents at home. Risks encountered included bullying and seeing ableist comments online but these were infrequent, well managed by the young people and, as reported, did not appear to cause undue distress. School and parental support in terms of developing the young people's strategies for avoiding risk was clearly beneficial alongside school clampdowns on bullying. These research findings above will be considered in light of the General Comment No. 25.

Disabled Children's Digital Rights

The research findings will be discussed in light of the four key recommendations of the General Comment No. 25 in order to respond to the research questions in relation to the General Comment and highlight examples where further research is needed to ensure disabled children's digital rights.

No Child Should Be Discriminated Against or Digitally Excluded

Digital inclusion is critical to disabled children's uses of digital technologies. The results of this study show why this is important. Participants in this study have access to a range of up-to-date technologies provided either at home, school or a mixture of both. Many of the participants consider digital technologies to be indispensable, especially mobile devices, and reported the many and varied benefits that they are able to engage in through having access. These included uses on the move given their portability, in cars, on trains and in aeroplanes, expounding the 'mobility' aspect of their potential. Devices are said by the youngsters to be easier to use than traditional technologies, lighter and multifunctional. Convergence with specialist assistive technologies through the inbuilt accessibility settings is hugely important to this group allowing them to belong and fit in with their peers; enhance hobbies and interests; enrich creativity; play games, and in one case, match clothes through the use of a colour detector app. They enable young people to easily keep in touch with friends and family and to share achievements.

These benefits show why access is so important for disabled young people. Even so, there were inequalities within this group that impacted uses with some of the young people not allowed to use mobile devices provided by schools outside of school. Other participants experienced data constraints, especially within schools. This is within a group of young people who reside within a high-income country and could be considered relatively privileged within the global context. This is often not the case for disabled youngsters in low-income countries. During the pandemic, in December 2020 when many children were locked out of schools and reliant on remote learning, UNICEF reported that two-thirds of young people aged 25 years or less did not have access to the internet at home (UNICEF and International Telecommunication Union, 2020). In West and Central Africa, for example, only 5% of young people have internet access at home compared with the global average of 33%. This means that children's access – including disabled children's access – to many of the benefits reported above can be limited or non-existent.

Furthermore, within high-income countries where access is generally good, governments are increasingly regulating the uses of mobile devices in schools (Burden et al., 2019). This can have negative consequences for disabled children, foreseen within the General Comment as 'prohibited uses of digital devices in schools and other environments.' These regulations can erode access for some children and undermine the potential benefits available to young people who rely on school provision of digital technologies for both in- and out-of-school activities and the development of skills and knowledge.

The Best Interests of the Child Should Guide Development of Online Provision

This recommendation is necessarily far-reaching and presents a huge challenge given the overtly commercial orientation of the internet. A key area of concern for disabled children in this regard is accessibility. Indeed the General Comment notes that 'inaccessible formats' can present a barrier specifically for disabled children 'through software design, inaccessible websites, services and applications, lack of adaptations, or financial difficulties' (5Rights Foundation, 2021, p. 38). While participants in this study were benefiting from the inbuilt accessibility settings on their mobile devices to zoom and magnify, change colour contrasts and font sizes to access recreational activities out of school, it is possible that accessible design from the outset could have prevented the need for some of these workarounds and improved their everyday online experiences. Moreover, these workarounds require disabled young people to acquire and use additional digital skills and competencies when compared to their peers or rely on other people's support.

Children Should Be Protected from Risks to Their Life, Survival and Development

Protection from risk is clearly an important component of children's digital rights. In terms of the results from the current study, of particular relevance for disabled children are the challenges of: 'Provision of the skills and knowledge needed to use the digital technologies effectively' and 'opposing the prejudice that disabled children encounter that can lead to 'overprotection or exclusion.'

The skills and knowledge needed by children are the topic of widespread and ongoing global debate. The UNESCO (2018) framework of reference on digital literacy skills, for instance, categorises 'Competence Areas' as: fundamentals of hardware and software; information and data literacy; communication and collaboration; digital content creation; safety; problem-solving; and career-related competencies. However, there have been calls for a more 'critical digital literacy' that goes beyond this in seeking to openly challenge the political and commercial drivers present within many initiatives introduced to develop digital skills (Pötzsch, 2019). Furthermore, Pötzsch argues that preparation for young people's 'future lives requires a widest possible contextualization of technology, including issues of exploitation, commodification, and degradation in digital capitalism' (p. 221). In contrast, the participants in this group expressed their skills and knowledge somewhat more narrowly but in positive terms. They were able to carry out the activities they wanted and needed to, in ways that were often developed through trial and error. Few frustrations or barriers were mentioned and all had helpful support from parents, siblings and schools when needed, essential to overcome the barriers they encountered. Uses of digital technologies were also said to have been made less demanding for mobile devices, given their ease of use and inbuilt accessibility settings. While most of the participants were readily able to search online and identify useful information, some were reluctant to carefully compare and evaluate what they found. This is of concern given the substantial amount of misinformation found online. Perhaps supporting disabled children to develop their knowledge of the 'digital capitalism' underpinning much internet content would support more critical approaches to their uses.

In relation to online risk and safety, for the most part, it appeared that the disabled youngsters were avoiding risk through using strategies to stay safe online, such as not meeting up physically with people who first met online or taking a friend along. On the one hand, online bullying was said to be uncommon, reinforced by blocking software in schools and no tolerance policies. On the other hand, there were examples of the youngsters encountering it occasionally along with ableist comments, either directed at them or other people. While participants were clearly able to rationalise these, they are of wider concern given the increase in online hate noted in previous studies. The 'Net Children Go Mobile: UK Report' (Livingstone et al., 2014), for instance, noted a sharp increase in UK children seeing hate messages that attack particular groups or individuals. It is clear from this that safety interventions in schools not only need to be taught inclusively in ways that include all children but need to be current in order to address disabled children's emergent experiences and concerns.

Digital Technologies Should Enable Children to Express Opinions and Provide Their Views on the Matters That Relate to Them

Clearly, the study reported here contributes to the recommendation that children's views are taken account of 'about matters that affect them including on how to enhance the opportunities the digital environment affords' (5Rights Foundation, 2021, p. 8). While there is limited research about disabled children's online activities, further studies are crucial for understanding and challenging the barriers that undermine their rights to enable them to contribute to the debates that impact their lives. The research that does exist is mainly in high-income countries, and this presents an enormous challenge to develop a comprehensive global evidence base comparable to that which has emerged for non-disabled children. The need for this is highlighted by this study where there are clear indicators of the need for more research about particular facets of use. For example, the increased shift to ban mobile devices in schools (Burden et al., 2019) will negatively impact access in and out of school. This is an important issue for all children but especially disabled children and young people whose access to the same technologies as their peers and, consequently, sense of belonging may be eroded. Disabled children's perspectives matter and policy-makers could usefully take note of their views. Similarly, disabled children, like disabled adults, need to be able to draw on accessible content that does not require them to develop worka-rounds. There needs to be more research that aims to understand and develop disabled children's online skills and competencies, perhaps further support-ing children's criticality and knowledge of 'digital capitalism.' Disabled chil-dren need to be included in initiatives to challenge the endemic ableism in society which means that they are at particular risk of being targeted by hate messages.

In summary, it is crucial that disabled children are supported to share their views on all online issues that affect them and have opportunities to challenge assumptions and misconceptions about them that lead to prejudice. Clearly, research and other fora that allow for disabled children's views to be heard is a key priority for informing and underpinning the much-needed and wel-comed recommendations within the General Comment.

Conclusions

This chapter has contributed to understanding the 'new avenues' that some disabled children are using digital technologies to 'engage in [to develop] social relationships with their peers, access information and participate in public decision-making processes' (UNCRC, 2021, p. 15). Drawing on par-ticipatory, qualitative research with children with vision impairment, the opportunities and barriers that potentially manifest when disabled children carry out activities for digital recreation were illustrated, and then considered in relation to the groundbreaking General Comment No. 25 that seeks to protect children's digital rights. The results highlighted are:

- the importance of enabling disabled children's digital inclusion in order that they can participate in recreational activities online while raising con-cerns about the high numbers of children, including disabled children, who are currently excluded due to lack of access;
- the importance of online accessibility and the barriers presented to disa-bled children and young people through inaccessible design formats;
- the importance of disabled young people's digital skills and competencies and how additional skills are needed to overcome the barriers alongside familial and school support; the need for disabled children to develop a stronger critical awareness of what they find online to negotiate hate and the inherent capitalist orientation of the digital environment.

Crucially, the study highlighted the urgent need for more research that can provide an audience for disabled children's views and concerns that can impact policy and practice in order to challenge the barriers that potentially undermine their digital rights.

Acknowledgements

My appreciation goes to the disabled young people and teachers who kindly participated in this project.

References

5Rights Foundation. 2021. 'Explanatory notes. General comment no. 25 (2021) on children's rights in relation to the digital environment'. [online] [Accessed on 6.1.2023]. Available from: https://5rightsfoundation.com/uploads/ExplanatoryNotes_UNCRCGC25.pdf

Alper, M. 2017. *Giving voice: mobile communication, disability, and inequality.* Cambridge, MA: MIT Press.

Alper, M. and Goggin, G. 2017. Digital technology and rights in the lives of children with disabilities. *New Media & Society*, 19(5), pp. 726–740.

Bond, E. 2014. *Childhood, mobile technologies and everyday experiences.* Basingstoke: Palgrave.

Burden, K., Kearney, M., Schuck, S. and Hall, T. 2019. Investigating the use of innovative mobile pedagogies for school-aged students: a systematic literature review. *Computers & Education*, 138, pp. 83–100.

Cameron, C. 2014. *Inclusion. Disability studies: a student's guide.* London: Sage.

Campbell, F.K. 2009. *Contours of ableism.* Basingstoke: Palgrave Macmillan.

Cavallini, M. C. and Cavallini, F. 2021. Online risks in children with special educational needs: an exploratory study. *Journal of Clinical and Developmental Psychology*, 3(1), pp. 58–68.

Chadwick, D.D., Quinn, S. and Fullwood, C. 2017. Perceptions of the risks and benefits of Internet access and use by people with intellectual disabilities. *British Journal of Learning Disabilities*, 45(1), pp. 21–31.

Charmaz, K. 2006. *Constructing grounded theory: a practical guide through qualitative analysis.* London: Sage.

Chernyavskaya, A. 2015. 'Children's Rights in the Digital Age' LSE Blog. [online] [Accessed on 6.1.2023]. Available at: https://www.lse.ac.uk/media-and-communications/events/past-events/childrens-rights-in-the-digital-age

Convention on the Rights of the Child. 1989. [online] [Accessed on 6.1.2023]. Available from https://www.ohchr.org/en/professionalinterest/pages/crc.aspx

Convention on the Rights of Persons with Disabilities and Optional Protocol 2006. [online]. [Accessed on 6.1.2023]. Available from https://www.un.org/disabilities/documents/convention/convoptprot-e.pdf

Cranmer, S. 2017. *Disabled children and young people's uses and experiences of digital technologies for learning.* Lancaster, UK: Lancaster University. [online] [Accessed on 6.1.2023]. Available from: https://eprints.lancs.ac.uk/id/eprint/88991/4/Disabled_children_final_report_30.11.17.pdf.

Cranmer, S. 2020a. Disabled children's evolving digital use practices to support formal learning: a missed opportunity for inclusion. *British Journal of Educational Technology*, 51(2), pp. 315–330.

Cranmer, S. 2020b. *Disabled children and digital technologies: learning in the context of inclusive education.* London: Bloomsbury Academic.

Curran, T. and Runswick-Cole, K. 2014. Disabled children's childhood studies: a distinct approach? *Disability & Society,* 29(10), pp. 1617–1630.

Disability Rights Commission. 2004. *Web access and inclusion for disabled people: a formal investigation conducted by disability rights commission.* London: TSO. [Accessed on 11.1.2023] https://www.city.ac.uk/__data/assets/pdf_file/0004/72670/DRC_Report.pdf

Ellis, K. and Goggin, G. 2017. *Disability and the media.* London: Palgrave Macmillan.

Ellis, K., Goggin, G. and Kent, M., 2020. Disability, children, and the invention of digital media. In Green, L., Holloway, D., Stevenson, K., Leaver, T. and Haddon, L. eds. *The Routledge companion to digital media and children* (1st ed., pp. 358–367). Routledge: New York.

Eshach, H. 2007. Bridging in-school and out-of-school learning: formal, non-formal, and informal education. *Journal of Science Education and Technology,* 16(2), pp. 171–190.

Kaur, H. and Saukko, P. 2022. Social access: role of digital media in social relations of young people with disabilities. *New Media & Society,* 24(2), pp. 420–436.

Kaur, H., Saukko, P. and Lumsden, K. 2018. Rhythms of moving in and between digital media: a study on video diaries of young people with physical disabilities. *Mobilities,* 13(3), pp. 397–410.

Kowalski, R.M. and Toth, A. 2018. Cyberbullying among youth with and without disabilities. *Journal of Child & Adolescent Trauma,* 11(1), pp. 7–15.

Lidström, H. and Hemmingsson, H. 2014. Children and youths with disabilities–a part of the digital generation? *World Federation of Occupational Therapists Bulletin,* 69(1), pp. 19–23.

Livingstone, S., Haddon, L., Vincent, J., Mascheroni, G. and Ólafsson, K. 2014. Net children go mobile: the UK report. London: London School of Economics and Political Science. [online] [Accessed on 6.1.2023]. Available at: https://eprints.lse.ac.uk/57598/1/__lse.ac.uk_storage_LIBRARY_Secondary_libfile_shared_repository_Content_EU%20Kids%20Online_EU_KIids_Online_Net_Children_go.pdf.

Livingstone, S., Davidson, J., Bryce, J., Batool, S., Haughton, C. and Nandi, A. 2017. Children's online activities, risks and safety. A literature review by the UKCCIS evidence group. London: UKCCIS. [online] [Accessed on 6.1.2023]. Available from https://www.gov.uk/government/publications/childrens-online-activities-risks-and-safety-a-literature-review-by-the-ukccis-evidence-group.

Lundy, L., Byrne, B., Templeton, M. and Lansdown, G. 2019. 'Two clicks forward and one back'. Council of Europe. Strasbourg, France.

Lupton, D. and Williamson, B. 2017. The datafied child: the dataveillance of children and implications for their rights. *New Media & Society,* 19(5), pp. 780–794.

Ofcom. 2022. Children and parents: media use and attitudes report 2022. [Accessed on 16.1.2023]. Available from: https://www.ofcom.org.uk/__data/assets/pdf_file/0024/234609/childrens-media-use-and-attitudes-report-2022.pdf

Passey, D. 2013. *Inclusive technology enhanced learning: overcoming cognitive, physical, emotional and geographic challenges.* New York: Routledge.

Pötzsch, H. 2019. Critical digital literacy: technology in education beyond issues of user competence and labour-market qualifications. *tripleC: Communication, Capitalism & Critique,* 17, pp. 221–240.

RNIB. 2019. Get support from your VI Forum online community. [online] [Accessed on 6.1.2023]. Available from: https://siforums.org.uk/4-the-vi-forum.

Sefton-Green, J. 2004. *Literature review on informal learning with technology outside school*. Bristol: Futurelab. [online] [Accessed on 6.1.2023]. Available from: https://www.nfer.ac.uk/publications/FUTL72/FUTL72.pdf.

Sefton-Green, J. 2013. *Learning at not-school: a review of study, theory, and advocacy for education in non-formal settings*. Cambridge, MA: Massachusetts Institute of Technology (MIT).

Söderström, S. 2009a. Offline social ties and online use of computers: a study of disabled youth and their use of ICT advances. *New Media & Society*, 11(5), pp. 709–27.

Söderström, S. 2009b. The significance of ICT in disabled youth's identity negotiations. *Scandinavian Journal of Disability Research*, 11(2), pp.131–144.

Söderström, S. 2013. Digital differentiation in young people's internet use—eliminating or reproducing disability stereotypes. *Future Internet*, 5(2), pp. 190–204.

Tsaliki, L. and Kontogianni, S. 2014. Bridging the disability divide? Young children's and teenager's with disability internet experiences in Greece. *Journal of Children and Media*, 8(2), pp. 146–162.

Tusting, K. 2003. *A review of theories of informal learning*. London: NRDC. [online] [Accessed on 6.1.2023]. Available from: https://dera.ioe.ac.uk/22486/1/doc_2768.pdf.

UNESCO. 2018. *A global framework of reference on digital literacy skills for indicator 4.4.2*. Quebec, Canada: UNESCO Institute for Statistics. [online] [Accessed on 6.1.2023]. Available from: http://uis.unesco.org/sites/default/files/documents/ip51-global-framework-reference-digital-literacy-skills-2018-en.pdf.

UNICEF. 2017. The state of the world's children 2017: children in a digital world. New York, US. [online] [Accessed on 6.1.2023]. Available from https://www.unicef.org/media/48601/file.

UNICEF and International Telecommunication Union. 2020. 'How many children and young people have internet access at home? Estimating digital connectivity during the COVID-19 pandemic'. UNICEF, New York, 2020. [online] [Accessed on 6.1.2023]. Available from https://data.unicef.org/resources/children-and-young-people-internet-access-at-home-during-covid19/

United Nations Committee on the Rights of the Child. 2021. General comment No. 25 (2021) on children's rights in relation to the digital environment. [online] [Accessed on 6.1.2023]. Available from: https://5rightsfoundation.com/our-work/childrens-rights/uncrc-general-comment.html.

11

THE INDIVIDUAL EDUCATION PROGRAMME

Who Knows Best?

Anne-Marie Callus and Georgette Bajada

Introduction

We invite the reader to imagine this: a group of adults are sitting around a table discussing the individual educational programme (IEP) of a disabled child. Let's say that it's a boy with cerebral palsy called Tom who attends a Year 6 class in a mainstream primary school. The meeting is taking place in the school and present is Tom's teacher, his learning support educator and the inclusion coordinator, who is chairing the meeting. They have invited Tom's speech therapist and physiotherapist to the meeting, and, after discussing amongst themselves, they will also ask Tom's parents to join them and give their input. All of these adults will have the opportunity to have their say about Tom, even if not everyone's input will be valued equally.

There will remain one glaring omission – *Tom himself*.

If we take the above picture as representative of an IEP meeting, then we can consider the missing piece in the centre to be Tom's voice. Everyone seems to be eager to put their piece in the middle. Nobody seems to think about asking Tom to do that. This scenario is played out many times over for disabled children, whether it's a Tom or Harriet, whether they are in a mainstream primary or secondary or even a special school, whether the child has a physical, sensory, intellectual or other type of disability, whether they are older or younger children. The feature that IEP meetings have in common is the production of a plan that determines the direction that the education of the disabled child in question will take for the next year. The most common thing missing in these meetings is the child themselves.

Tom's very presence in a mainstream school is a story of inclusion, of an education system that accepts its responsibility to attend to his individual

DOI: 10.4324/9781003102915-11

educational needs and those of other disabled children, of educators and other professionals who find the time to sit around a table to discuss the specific educational needs of one particular student and to agree on what they need to do to attend to those needs. This chapter first provides the historical and policy background that enabled inclusive education to happen in many countries and, by extension, for Tom's IEP meeting to take place. It then provides an overview of the situation regarding inclusive education according to official reports and the research literature. This overview highlights the gaps that exist in ensuring that inclusive education is realised fully.

Recommendations for change that emerge from the literature are also presented. We argue that the most significant change that is required is acknowledging the important insights that are gained when children's voices are utilised as key instruments, helping to overcome the persistent limitations of IEP meetings like Tom's and the failure to fully achieve inclusive education more widely. This change is important because, ultimately, Tom's story and that of countless other disabled children, is also one of exclusion. He is being excluded from decisions that affect him, with adults presuming to know best what is beneficial for him and other disabled students.

Historical Developments in the Education of Disabled Children

The documented history of disability is relatively recent. Although to different degrees in various countries, it portrays a story of struggle for inclusion and social justice, with attempts to undo the effects of discourses of retribution, shame, pity, charity, angelic metaphors, divine healing, ridicule, deficit, incapability, abnormality, segregation, institutional care, medical fixes, welfare benefits recipients and special education, amongst others. Before the 1960s, there were sporadic events of groups of disabled people organising protests and demanding better life conditions, as recorded by Campbell and Oliver (1996). However, as these authors and others (including Driedger (1989) and Fleischer and Zames (2013)) describe in detail, it was from the 1960s onwards that the disabled people's movement really took off and reached the critical mass needed for change to happen. Eventually, disabled people's efforts to reconceptualise disability from a social model and rights' standpoint (Lawson and Beckett 2021) began to have an impact on disabled children's education, which was historically based on segregation in special schools.

Education has been widely accepted as a basic right since the Universal Declaration on Human Rights (1948). The right to education is also acknowledged in the United Nations Convention on the Rights of the Child (1989), with disabled children's right to be integrated within the education system. This was followed by the World Declaration on Education for All (1990) from the conference held in Jamtien, Thailand, in which the idea to eliminate what it calls 'educational disparities' between students was emphasised. Moreover, although not directly related to disability or education, Article 13 of the United Nations' International Covenant on Economic, Social and Cultural Rights (1966) also binds signatories to consider everyone's right to education and seek 'full development of the human personality and the sense of its dignity, while strengthening human rights respect and fundamental freedoms' (Article 13.1).

However, it was the signing of the UNESCO Salamanca Statement and Framework for Action in Special Needs Education in 1994 that effectively paved the way towards the adoption of inclusive education systems around the world. This important milestone prioritised inclusive education practices over special education and policies which embrace inclusive education for all children, irrespective of their characteristics and needs. Ainscow et al. (2019) remarks that, in itself, the Salamanca Statement served as an education justification for all children to attend school together – a social justification in that schools will be the basis to a non-discriminatory society and ultimately an economic justification, the argument being that special education is more costly than educating all children together.

As Ainscow et al. (2019) also argue, the framework reaffirmed each child's right to education and set the standards for inclusive schools to shift the focus from fitting the disabled child to the system to adapting the system to cater for the uniqueness of each child. It thereby endorsed the fact that regular schools, with the proposed inclusive approach, are the most effective means to achieve meaningful inclusion for each child. Furthermore, it proposed that the child remains the nucleus of the educational system and called for the educational systems to change direction towards flexibility in the school management and teaching approaches to accommodate the diversity of children. Most importantly, the Salamanca Framework for Action laid the groundwork for the signatories' legislation and policies to be based on inclusive education principles, although it was non-binding. The legacy of the Salamanca Statement was restated 25 years later in what is referred to as the Cali Commitment to Equity and Inclusion in Education (2019). While reaffirming the inclusion principles of the Salamanca Statement, the Cali Commitment includes the adherence to the intersectional aspect incorporated in exclusion, the understanding of evolving societies and a changing world, as well as the significance of the voices of children and youth in decisions related to education and the future.

Globally, there have been significant developments at a national level as well. In 1990, the Americans with Disabilities Act became the first anti-discrimination disability legislation at a national level. It paved the way for, among others, stronger legislation in the area of education in the United States through the Individuals with Disabilities Education Act (1990). As Bérubè (2016, p. 136) remarks,

the Individuals with Disabilities Education Act (IDEA) … was passed in 1975, but only in the 1990s did 'the least restrictive environment' become, for most children with disabilities, something other than the special education classroom.

In other countries, it was the anti-discrimination legislation itself that provided for the right to inclusive education – for example, the Equal Opportunities (Persons with Disability) Act (2000) in Malta.

Internationally, the most recent significant achievement for disabled persons' rights is the legally binding UN Convention on the Rights of Persons with Disability (2006). Article 24 of this Convention directly refers to the right for inclusive education of disabled persons and binds ratifying states to realise disabled persons' right to inclusive education 'without discrimination and on the basis of equal opportunity' by aiming at actualising disabled persons' human potential, their holistic development and their meaningful participation in a free society. Abiding by the requirements of Article 24 entails unrestricted accessibility to the general education system throughout life on an equal basis with others, the provision of individualised reasonable accommodation and specific disability-related support.

The international commitment towards inclusive education was reinforced in the 2030 Agenda for Sustainable Development's proposed 'shared blueprint' to protect the planet and eliminate inequalities. Goal 4 aims to 'ensure inclusive and equitable quality education and promote lifelong learning opportunities for all' through legislation and actions which encompass rightful education to each student. A framework for action and further international commitment towards Goal 4 were discussed in the Incheon Declaration (2015) and Oslo Declaration (2015). In Incheon, participating organisations and state delegates reaffirmed the significance of education for holistic development and pledged to promote rightful, equitable, inclusive, quality and lifelong education (UNESCO, 2016). Then, the Oslo Summit on Education for Development built on the Incheon Declaration by pledging to transform commitment to prioritise education into action by governments' implementation of related effective policies and funding of resources (Norwegian Ministry of Foreign Affairs 2015).

The Current State of Inclusive Education

Considering that it is almost three decades after the signing of the Salamanca Statement, with 185 countries having ratified the UN CRPD and anti-discrimination disability legislation – covering education among other life domains – having been enacted in around 120 different (UN Department of Economic and Social Affairs 2022), one may think that inclusive education policies and practices have now become well established and are, as it were, the default mode in which education is delivered. Unfortunately, the picture that emerges from various reports and official documentation tells a different story.

First of all, children with disabilities are over-represented in the population of those who are not in education. As reported by UNESCO (2022), globally there are between 93 million and 150 million children living with a disability – 80% of whom live in developing countries. Children and youth with sensory, physical, or learning disabilities are two-and-a-half times more likely than their peers to never go to school. Where disability intersects with other barriers, such as gender, poverty, or geographical remoteness, the risk of exclusion is greater still.

The exclusion of many disabled children from education is also lamented by the UN Special Rapporteur (2021) who speaks of 'underinclusive educational systems' (para. 75) and the Committee on the Rights of Persons with Disabilities (2016) in the General Comment on the Right to Inclusive Education. The Committee notes that, where disabled children do go to school, they do not necessarily attend the same schools as their non-disabled peers. This lack of progress is attributed to a lack of understanding of the human rights model of disability; the persistence of discrimination against disabled people; lack of awareness about the benefits of inclusive education; lack of data and research to ensure accountability; lack of will, knowledge and resources to implement inclusive education; and lack of legal remedies for redress of violations to the right to inclusive education.

The *Report on Inclusive Education in European Schools* (Schola Europaea 2018) reported that in Europe, not all students with disabilities receive the reasonable accommodation needed to enjoy their right to inclusive quality education in European schools in line with the Convention and that schools still discriminate between disabled and non-disabled students. It also mentioned that European schools are not fully accessible to children with disabilities nor do they provide for inclusive, quality education. This was also recently evident in the European Agency for Special Needs and Inclusive Education (2020) report, which states that children with disabilities are still considered highly vulnerable to being out of school or leave schooling earlier than their peers, mainly due to ineffective inclusive systems. To compound matters, children with disabilities tend to be invisible in absenteeism data due to related statistical arrangements within the countries. A situation of lack of inclusion of disabled children in mainstream education systems is reported by Rieser (2012) with regard to Commonwealth countries.

Perspectives from Research

Despite these disheartening reports, progress can also be said to have been registered. A review of the research literature shows that there have been improvements and many disabled children – some of whom are now adults – have benefitted and continue to benefit from being educated alongside their non-disabled peers in inclusive schools and classrooms which cater for their individual educational needs. But sadly, this statement does not apply for each and every disabled child.

Van Mieghem et al. (2020) carried out a meta-review of 26 systematic reviews of such studies, most of which were carried out in the first two decades of the 21st century. The results of this meta-review are significant given the number of research studies that it encompasses. The main themes identified relate to attitude (general beliefs about inclusion and attitudes of teachers, parents and peers); the professional development of teachers with regards to inclusive education; enhancing practices (additional support for teachers and for students with disabilities; and social and academic participation of these students); and directions for research (establishing the definition of inclusive education being used); conducting research that responds to current issues; collaborating with practitioners; and supporting schools to act on research recommendations.

Varied Understandings of Inclusive Education

Some of the research literature, for example, the article by Göransson and Nilholm (2014), highlights the different ways that inclusive education is understood by practitioners and operationalised by researchers. Waitoller and Artiles (2013, p. 321) comment that inclusion has become a buzzword even while '[t]he notion of inclusive education ... is highly contested'. They point out that it can be understood broadly as a means of ensuring equity for all students in schools or more narrowly to refer to focusing 'on the academic outcomes of students with disabilities'. Indeed, Bartolo (2010) and Thomas (2013) explain how inclusive education originated as a practice to make regular schools inclusive of students with disabilities but was eventually widened to encompass other students who are at risk of exclusion from the mainstream.

This widening is certainly welcome, and the scope of inclusive education being utilised by specific practitioners, policy makers or researchers is quite easy to ascertain. What is more difficult to establish is what each person understands by inclusion. Bartolo (2010) draws attention to the distinction between 'integration' and 'inclusion', with the former referring to students with disabilities being placed in mainstream schools as long as they can adjust to the prevailing educational system and the latter referring to adjustments made to that system to ensure that individual educational needs are catered for. This distinction is the crux of inclusive education and, arguably, it is the extent to which it is understood, adopted, and put into effect that determines the effectiveness of the inclusion experienced by students with disabilities.

Consequently, the attitudes of teachers and other professionals directly involved in education play a significant part in the effectiveness of inclusive education. Results from different studies about the attitudes of educators towards the inclusion of students with disabilities in their classrooms evince a variety of mindsets. In research with Finnish mainstream and special school teachers and with school principals, Saloviita (2020) concludes that mainstream teachers were the most negative about inclusion, regardless of their age, gender, and the training they had received. On the other hand, research in Ghana by Butakor, Ampadu and Suleiman (2020) showed a tendency for male and older teachers to be less positive about inclusive education.

Inclusion can also be accepted in principle by teachers who then qualify the extent to which they think it can be implemented in practice, as seen, for example, in the research with Irish teachers by Young, McNamara and Coughlan (2017). Scepticism about the practicality of including all children with disabilities in mainstream classrooms is partly motivated by what are perceived to be the insurmountable obstacles of catering for the needs of students with severe cognitive impairment, with profound and multiple disabilities and those with behaviour of concern. Miyauchi's (2020) systematic review of research about the inclusion of students with visual impairment shows that they are likely to enjoy a high level of inclusion academically (although not always in social activities). The trend for students with physical or sensory impairments to be more easily accepted in mainstream classrooms than those with intellectual disability or challenging behaviour also emerges in research by Colley (2020), Dell'Anna et al. (2020), Krischler and Pit-ten Cate (2020), Rieser (2012) and Yeo et al. (2016).

Inclusion may thus be understood as being possible for some but not all disabled students. This interpretation highlights the importance of seeking to understand how inclusive education is conceptualised, especially by educators, given that the most significant document on the right to inclusive education, Article 24 of the UNCRPD, presumes that it is a right to be enjoyed by *all* disabled students without exception.

Inclusive education, therefore, entails unlearning the way that education has been done for years, if not for decades, especially when disabled students have traditionally been segregated (Slee 2013). Since educational systems vary from one country to another – and sometimes even in the same country – the culture in which each particular system is embedded also needs to be taken into account, as shown for instance by Moberg et al. (2020) in their research with Finnish and Japanese teachers. Moreover, the changes wrought by inclusive education can range from radical overhauls in approaches to education to adjustments made to educational practices that will very often have been in place for a long time. In fact, some of the studies included in Waitoller and Artilles' (2013, p. 325) systematic review focus on how inclusive education is considered 'as an ongoing and systemic process of changing school cultures to inform practices that facilitate access, participation, and learning for students with diverse abilities'.

The different factors that impinge on the ways in which inclusive education is conceptualised make it difficult to reach a shared understanding of what it is about. Added to these external factors are the different positions from which students, parents and educators approach the task of inclusion as well as their personal attitudes.

Teachers' Attitudes Towards the Inclusion of Students with Disabilities

Teachers' beliefs and attitudes are affected by practice and affect practice. As seen in the research by Saloviita (2020), the day-to-day practical experience of including disabled children in the mainstream classroom can affect whether teachers view such inclusion positively or not. In turn, as argued by Woodcock (2021) in research about the inclusion of students with specific learning difficulties (SpLD) in British schools, the predispositions with each teacher enter the inclusive classroom can impact how that teacher – and by extension their students – experience the adjustments needed to make inclusion a reality. Woodcock (2021, p. 121) writes thus:

> Teachers who believed that inclusive education is an effective way to teach all students were more positive and encouraging in the feedback, and held lower expectations of future failure toward students with SpLD. Moreover, they were also more positive with their feedback and felt less frustration toward students without SpLD than their colleagues who did not believe in inclusive education for all. The success of inclusive education for all can be determined from the teachers' beliefs about inclusive education and their behavior and reaction to the classroom context.

Consequently, one of the keys to successful inclusion may be the unlearning of what has been established through a segregationist system in which disabled students – especially those who need modification of the curriculum, educational material and pedagogical approaches – have for a long time been placed in special schools. In his argument for a re-thinking of how inclusive education is done, Thomas (2013, p. 486) argues that

> [t]he future contribution of inclusive education hinges on its ability to retreat from histories of identify-assess diagnose-help and to examine the ways in which schools enable community and encourage students' belief in themselves as members of such community.

Thomas's remark can be extended to general beliefs about the place of disabled persons in society. The inclusion of disabled students in mainstream education can be seen as the advent of disability politics and the demands of the disabled person's movement in the classroom. If, according to Dewey's (1956, p. 18) dictum, the school has 'a chance to be a miniature community, an embryonic society', then the inclusive school has the opportunity to contribute towards the creation of a society which is capable of adapting itself for disabled persons, at the same time as preparing disabled students to be a part of mainstream society. In fact, the UN Committee on the Rights of Persons with Disabilities (2016) has highlighted how the process of inclusive education is key to fairer societies and a fairer world.

The attitude of teachers towards inclusion as a concept can be considered both a cause and an effect of the inclusion of disabled students in mainstream classrooms. A predisposition towards the value of inclusion motivates teachers to seek ways in which to make this inclusion happen. In turn, putting inclusion into effect can engender positive attitudes towards inclusion in the classroom and beyond. Sheehy et al. (2019) found that Indonesian teachers in inclusive schools adopted a social constructivist and favourable standpoint towards the inclusion of students with intellectual disabilities. Consequently, in the same way that attitudes can affect experience, experience can also affect attitudes. Therefore, seeking changes in attitudes is not enough on its own. For teachers to have a positive experience of putting inclusive education into effect, they need access to the requisite resources, training and support.

Teacher Training, Resourcing and Support

Woodcock (2021) argues that teachers' attitudes can be influenced by the training, support and resources that they have access to. In his review of the implementation of inclusive education in Commonwealth countries, Rieser (2012) repeatedly refers to these three components of inclusion, thus highlighting their importance. The importance of teacher training also emerges from Kurniawati et al.'s (2014) review of research about the topic. On a conceptual level, training can be a means of introducing teachers to the crucial difference between integration and inclusion, discussed above. For example, Al Shoura and Ahmad's (2020) research in Jordan indicates that pre-service training can inculcate positive attitudes towards the inclusion of students with severe or profound and multiple intellectual disabilities. On a practical level, it can equip teachers with the know-how to respond to disabled students' individual educational needs.

This training can also help equip teachers with the skills necessary to work in multidisciplinary teams, which are an important component of inclusive education (Waitoller and Artiles 2013). This teamwork is necessary if the impairment-related needs of disabled students are to be met, especially when students need one-to-one support, require technical support, for example, through braille or sign language or need interventions which teachers cannot reasonably be expected to be able to know how to administer on their own. These varied needs call for differentiated and individualised teaching. Lindner and Schwab (2020) carried out a systematic review of research about this type of teaching. Among others, they identify collaborative practices and teamwork as being very important.

The multidisciplinary approach to inclusive education can also have the added benefit of ensuring that teachers are adequately supported to deal with the requirements of making inclusive education a reality. In fact, Bartolo (2015) discusses the role of the school psychologist in providing support in the inclusive classroom. Likewise, other professionals can also be a source of support. In Woodcock's (2021) research, support for teachers emerges as an important component of effective inclusive education policies and practices.

Another aspect of supporting teachers in inclusive classrooms concerns resourcing. In Lindner and Schwab's (2020) systematic review as well as in other research cited above, the availability or lack of resources is identified as a factor that impinges heavily on the effectiveness of inclusion. Similar findings emerge in research by Tiwari, Das and Sharma (2015) in India and in the systematic review of research about inclusive education in low-to-middle-income countries by Mendoza and Heymann (2022). An issue related to resourcing is that of class sizes as noted by Su, Guo and Wang (2020) regarding inclusive education in China.

Recommendations for Achieving Tangible Inclusion in Education

As can be seen from the above review of official reports and research articles, the factors that impede inclusive education from being fully realised for all disabled children have been thoroughly diagnosed. There are also enough recommendations that can serve as guidance for this realisation to be brought about.

The General Comment on Article 24 by the UN Committee on the Rights of Persons with Disabilities (2016) includes sets out strategies for States to actuate effective inclusive education, namely, a whole-government commitment to inclusive education, the implementation of legislation which supports international human rights standards, access for disabled people to challenge discrimination, enabling disabled persons' transitions from institutions to the community, early intervention support, an efficient data system related to disability, allocation of useful financial and human resource to reach inclusive education aims, teacher training and support, monitoring progress in inclusive education with the involvement of disabled persons' themselves and working in partnership with disabled persons and their families.

Additionally, the *Report on Inclusive Education in the European Schools* (2018) gives recommendations on 12 key issues it deems crucial for effective inclusive education, namely, human resources, qualification and training of teaching and non-teaching staff, budgetary allocations, built environment accessibility, information and communication accessibility, teaching material, personalised support, teaching methods and smooth transitions between schools and in other systems, adaptability regarding curriculum, assessment and examination procedures, applicable certification of capacities and attainment, legal redress, and monitoring, quality assurance and evaluation.

The supranational documents and declarations mentioned above also refer to the significance of students' voices within the implementation of educational practices. In 2007, the member states of the European Agency for Development in Special Needs Education invited 'young people with special educational needs' to reflect and discuss inclusive education, to propose the best related practices in a European Hearing, conclusions of which have been established as the Lisbon Declaration (European Agency for Special Needs and Inclusive Education 2007). Among others, the young people agreed on their fundamental human rights, namely, rights to be respected, not to be discriminated against, treated equally, having opportunities on an equal basis as everyone, to be supported as necessary, make own decisions and choices, be heard, live independently and society's awareness and acknowledgement of their rights. With regards to education, the young people expressed their views on potential improvements such as the acknowledgement of diverse needs that individual persons encounter, individual support and adapted resources, providing meaningful subjects life skills and counselling and raising awareness about disability. They gave importance to the freedom to choose where to be educated, with the right conditions. Finally, the young people affirmed:

> We are the ones to build our future. We need to remove barriers inside ourselves and inside other people without disabilities. We have to grow beyond our disability – then the world will accept us in a better way.

Following the Lisbon Declaration, the European Agency for Development in Special Needs Education (2011) issued a report entitled 'Key Principles for Promoting Quality in Inclusive Education: Recommendations for Practice'. The first principle, 'Responding to learners' voices', calls for empowering students to fully participate in 'all discussions and decisions regarding their education and plans for the future' (p. 13), such as in assessments, the learning process, plans of their learning, support to overcome learning barriers, relevant, meaningful and personalised outcomes and evaluation in the curriculum. The other principles cover the active participation of learners in the life of their schools and community, positive attitudes from teachers towards all learners and towards collaborating with other colleagues, the importance for teachers to develop the skills they need to meet learners' diverse needs, school leadership that values diversity and encourages collaboration and access to interdisciplinary support for schools.

It is clear from these various sets of recommendations that inclusive education is something that can only be achieved collaboratively. Consequently, what is needed is a collaboration that brings on board various actors who need to work in a transdisciplinary manner: teachers, teaching assistants, school leaders, allied health professionals and others whose work directly or indirectly impinges on education. But that is not enough. The participation of disabled children and their parents or other primary caregivers is equally important. As adults, the latter may find a place around the discussion table with relative ease, although not always and not automatically. As children, the former need to have their place around the table facilitated. It is to the reasons why the disabled child's place around the table is important that we now turn our focus to.

The Disabled Child's Voice in Inclusive Education

There is a growing body of literature which evinces that disabled children's viewpoints are instrumental in decision- and policy-making. Indeed, when given the opportunity to participate in research related to them, children bespeak self-determination and ingenuity (Bajada, Callus and Borg 2021). As Dimitrellou and Male (2020) write, disabled children participating in inclusive education research can be influential in school improvement, teaching and learning, school reform and inclusive practice. For instance, Dimitrellou and Male's (2020) study with disabled students in England depicts the negative mainstream secondary school experience of disabled students, which according to the participating students, this experience will improve upon effective behaviour management strategies and good-natured educators. Those views are consistent with the sentiments of the participating students with SEBD of Leeuw et al.'s (2019) research, who maintain that while they preferred to attend mainstream schools, they would like their voice to be included within educational practices and that their suggestions regarding their social experiences are noted. Correspondingly, the participants (girls with autism) of Goodall and MacKenzie's study (2019) impart that in contrast to actuality, students with autism need teachers who listen attentively to them, understand the difficulties and problems they encounter because of their sensory and socialisation issues and support them accordingly. Another study which highlights the importance of adhering to disabled students' voices is that of Psaila (2017) which notably outlines the contrasting perceptions of the educators and the student. As she puts it, 'whereas the child projects a message of normalcy and equality with peers, the education professionals still place emphasis on disabling discourse' (Psaila 2017, p. 171). Pazey et al.'s (2017) research centres around the voice of a black, disabled student whose determination allures him to lead advocacy for educational reform decisions within his ineffectual school in Texas. Similarly, Opie et al.'s (2017) study in

Australia brings out the resilience that their participant with vision impairment has built following the awareness and understanding of his disability. This enabled him to feel a sense of belonging in the classroom along with his peers. Rouvali and Riga (2021) carried out their research in Greece, with a young student with autism about her individual learning plan. Together with her, and through alternative communication means, they explored her views and wishes regarding her learning experience at school, as well as specific needs that she herself identified with the adults' support. In following the implementation of this plan, the researchers conclude that their collaboration with the student resulted in positive progress holistically.

The widening of inclusive education, noted above, to refer not only to disabled children but also to other children who are at risk of exclusion from rigid educational systems is telling. It speaks of the realisation that children should not be expected to fit into preordained educational systems and that it is the systems themselves that need to adapt so that all children can fit into them. However, the extent to which educational systems have been transformed into truly inclusive ones remains a matter of debate.

As far as disabled children are concerned, the earlier review of official reports and research literature, as well as the recommendations made, strongly indicate that – almost three decades after the signing of the Salamanca Statement – the expectation for them to fit into pre-existing systems persists. This is not to deny the many changes that have been brought into effect. Let us return to the scenario that we started this chapter with. As noted earlier, the fact that Tom attends a mainstream school and the fact that various professionals are sitting round that table discussing his IEP are concrete signs of all the efforts over the past decades to make education systems tangibly inclusive and to attend to individual children's educational needs. However, a purely professional perspective on Tom's (or any other disabled child's) inclusion – however transdisciplinary that perspective may be – risks focusing only on the impairment side of Tom's disability. It risks, therefore, creating exclusion despite intentions to the contrary due to a lack of awareness of the power that professionals exert through their dominant position, a power that includes imposing their own knowledge. As Graham and Slee (2008) have remarked, no matter how euphonious the talk about inclusion is, it remains entrusted to those in the inner circle, while rarely focusing on identifying the dominating power relations that produce exclusion, and thus can in itself throw a veil over or endorse exclusion.

Professional knowledge, however important it is (and it is, of course, very important), is neither omniscient nor omnipotent. It needs to be complemented by the knowledge that emerges from the lived experience of disability. Awareness of the importance of this experiential knowledge (Borkman 1976) is arguably the single-most important legacy of the disabled people's movement. It was from this knowledge that the social model distinction between biological impairment and socially created barriers arose. Heeding to that distinction in inclusive educational settings means taking into account the disabling barriers that each disabled child meets within their lives. Otherwise, the term 'inclusion' continues to be related to practices which contradict its intended outcomes, as Byrne (2022) notes.

Inclusive education requires educators, and other professionals directly or indirectly involved in education, to not only be aware of the distinction but also to actively identify disabling barriers and seek ways of removing them. Disabling barriers can be very clearly evident – lack of physical accessibility and lack of access to printed material to take just two examples. They can also be subtle – for instance, lack of adaptations to the curriculum and lack of differentiated teaching methods that lead educators to conclude a particular disabled child's place is not in a mainstream classroom. Added to that is the question of how each disabled child experiences inclusion and the extent to which arrangements that are put in place are perceived as effective by each child. Without the child's experiential perspective, educators and other professionals can only assume what barriers the child is encountering and how effective the remedies to remove those barriers are. They may even miss out on the barriers that they are inadvertently creating themselves.

The odds of disabling children making their voice heard are stacked high against them. The forces that enable adults to control the lives of children are probably as old as humanity itself. Human beings are an altricial species, with the human baby being born with a yet-to-be-fully-developed brain. This means that human children are highly dependent on adults for their continued development. Children, therefore, are generally regarded as dependent beings whose full development is yet to be attained. Disabled children often risk being seen as even more dependent since their developmental trajectories tend to be different from those of so-called typically developing children. Being altricial also means that human development takes place in a particular social context, which is inevitably different for each and every child. No social context is neutral, and, for disabled children, it also includes disabling barriers. Social context is also not a fixed reality that can be measured and described accurately. It is, rather, knowable through the experiences of those directly involved in it. Additionally, it is not monolithic but multifarious in nature. Its complexity can be seen in the ecological system devised by Bronfenbrenner (1979) which comprises the microsystem, mesosystem, exosystem, macrosystem and chronosystem and the effects they have on each other and the development of the child.

When a disabled child starts their educational journey, it is most probably their parents (or other adults entrusted with their day-to-day care) who know most about how the child has experienced their social context so far. The importance of their input into their child's IEP can be seen as being in inverse proportion to the child's age. This view is correct to some extent. One cannot expect a five-year-old child about to start their schooling to engage as meaningfully in discussions about their own inclusion as a 16-year-old student considering their post-secondary options. However, regardless of how obvious the difference between two students at each end of the compulsory schooling system is, there is no clear cut-off point between these two polarities. The same goes for the clear differences in the input that can be provided by children with different types of impairment, especially when the impairment affects cognitive and communication skills. The capacity for a disabled child to participate meaningfully in decision-making processes about their education develops and, just like any other aspect of human development, it develops in a specific social context (Baraldi and Cockburn 2018).

Letting Tom in on his own IEP discussion has two beneficial and intertwined effects. It affords Tom the opportunity to share his experiential knowledge and for his educators and other professionals to learn from it. It also enables him to gain skills and develop his capacity to share this knowledge. Conversely, keeping him out of this and other discussions concerning his education also means keeping him in a subservient position and ironically excluding him from the very process that is supposed to facilitate his inclusion.

That said, Tom's inclusion in his IEP meeting is not a magic wand that will ensure his full and automatic inclusion. It can, however, be a very significant step towards ensuring that educational systems take account of the way that disabled children experience inclusion. That step is important because, ultimately, inclusive education is not only about having the right legislation, policies and systems in place. These are certainly the bedrock on which inclusive education can be built and realised. Its realisation is brought about by taking into account the individual needs of each and every disabled child, and the IEP is an essential tool in the process (Pierangelo and Guiliani 2007). After all, the IEP is an *individual* education programme, and not including the individual concerned directly in its development and implementation cannot bode well for its effectiveness.

Conclusion

The direct and active involvement of disabled children in their own IEP meetings does not take away any of the importance of the role of educators themselves. The power imbalance between them and the disabled students (and indeed all other students) in their classroom inevitably remains. But the educators' disposition towards inclusion and their actions can and needs to be shaped by the input of disabled students themselves, an input that comes directly from the lived experience of disability as a socially created phenomenon. If the various pieces of soft and binding legislation on inclusive education, such as those mentioned earlier in this chapter, were informed by the disabled people's movement and therefore also their experience of living in a disabling society, their implementation also needs to be informed by that experience.

References

Ainscow, M., Slee, R. and Best, M. 2019. Editorial: the Salamanca Statement: 25 years on. *International Journal of Inclusive Education* 23(7–8), pp. 671–676.

Al Shoura, H.M. and Ahmad, A.C. 2020. Inclusive education for students with severe or profound and multiple learning difficulties: identification of influencing factors and challenges. *South African Journal of Education* 40(2), pp. S1–S9.

Bajada, G., Callus, A. and Borg, K. 2021. Unpretentious education: a Foucaultian study of inclusive education in Malta. *Disability & Society* 37(8), pp. 1247–1271.

Baraldi, C. and Cockburn, T. ed. 2018. *Theorising childhood. Studies in childhood and youth*. London: Palgrave Macmillan.

Bartolo, P.A. 2010. The process of teacher education for inclusion: the Maltese experience. *Journal of Research in Special Educational Needs* 10, pp. 139–148.

Bartolo, P.A. 2015. The role of psychologists in inclusive settings. In Da Fonte, M.A. and Capizzi, A.M. eds. *Working with teaching assistants and other support staff for inclusive education*. Yorkshire: Emerald Group Publishing Limited, pp. 49–63.

Bérubè, M. 2016. *Life as Jamie knows it: an exceptional child grows up*. Boston: Beacon Press.

Borkman, T. 1976. Experiential knowledge: a new concept for the analysis of self-help groups. *Social Service Review* 50(3), pp. 445–456.

Bronfenbrenner, U. 1979. *The ecology of human development: experiments by nature and design*. Cambridge, MA: Harvard University Press.

Butakor, P.K., Ampadu, E. and Suleiman, S.J. 2020. Analysis of Ghanaian teachers' attitudes toward inclusive education. *International Journal of Inclusive Education* 24(11), pp. 1237–1252.

Byrne, B. 2022. How inclusive is the right to inclusive education? An assessment of the UN convention on the rights of persons with disabilities' concluding observations. *International Journal of Inclusive Education* 26(3), pp. 301–318.

Cali Commitment to Equity and Inclusion in Education. 2019. [online]. [Accessed on 18.10.2022]. Available from: https://unesdoc.unesco.org/ark:/48223/pf0000370910

Campbell, J. and Oliver, M. 1996. *Disability politics: understanding our past, changing our future*. London: Routledge.

Colley, A. 2020. To what extent have learners with severe, profound and multiple learning difficulties been excluded from the policy and practice of inclusive education? *International Journal of Inclusive Education* 24(7), pp. 721–738.

Convention on the Rights of the Child. 1989. [online] [Accessed on 18.10.2022]. Available from: https://www.ohchr.org/en/professionalinterest/pages/crc.aspx

Convention on the Rights of Persons with Disabilities and Optional Protocol. 2006. [online]. [Accessed on 18.10.2022]. Available from: https://www.un.org/disabilities/documents/convention/convoptprot-e.pdf

Dell'Anna, S., Pellegrini, M., Ianes, D. and Vivanet, G., 2020. Learning, social, and psychological outcomes of students with moderate, severe, and complex disabilities in inclusive education: a systematic review. *International Journal of Disability, Development and Education* 69(6), pp. 1–17.

Dewey, J. 1956. *The school and the curriculum and the child and society*. Chicago: Phoenix Books.

Dimitrellou, E. and Male, D. 2020. Understanding what makes a positive school experience for pupils with SEND: can their voices inform inclusive practice? *Journal of Research in Special Educational Needs* 20(2), pp. 87–96.

Driedger, D. 1989. *The last civil rights movement: Disabled Peoples' International.* London: Hurst and Company.

Equal Opportunities (Persons with Disability) Act. 2000. Malta. [online] [Accessed on 24.10.2022]. Available from: https://legislation.mt/eli/cap/413/eng/pdf

European Agency for Development in Special Needs Education. 2011. Key principles for promoting quality in inclusive education: recommendations for practice. [online] [Accessed on 24.10.2022]. Available from: https://www.european-agency. org/sites/default/files/Key-Principles-2011-EN.pdf

European Agency for Special Needs and Inclusive Education. 2007. Lisbon Declaration: young people's views on inclusive education. [online] [Accessed on 24.10.2022]. Available from: https://www.european-agency.org/sites/default/files/lisbon-declaration-young-people2019s-views-on-inclusive-education_declaration_en.pdf

European Agency for Special Needs and Inclusive Education. 2020. Out-of-school learners: background information report. [online] [Accessed on 18.10.2022]. Available from: https://www.european-agency.org/sites/default/files/EASIE_Out-of-School_Learners_Background_Information_Report.pdf

Fleischer, D.Z. and Zames, F. 2013. *The disability rights movement: from charity to confrontation.* Toronto: CNIB.

Goodall, C. and MacKenzie, A. 2019. What about my voice? Autistic young girls' experiences of mainstream school. *European Journal of Special Needs Education* 34(4), pp. 499–513.

Göransson, K. and Nilholm, C. 2014. Conceptual diversities and empirical shortcomings–a critical analysis of research on inclusive education. *European Journal of Special Needs Education* 29(3), pp. 265–280.

Graham, L.J. and Slee, R. 2008. An illusory interiority: interrogating the discourse/s of inclusion. *Educational Philosophy and Theory* 40(2), pp. 277–293.

International Covenant on Economic, Social and Cultural Rights. 1966. [online] [Accessed on 18.10.2022]. Available from: https://www.ohchr.org/en/instruments-mechanisms/instruments/international-covenant-economic-social-and-cultural-rights

Individuals with Disabilities Education Act. 1990. United States. [online] [Accessed on 18.10.2022]. Available from: https://sites.ed.gov/idea/statuteregulations/

Krischler, M. and Pit-ten Cate, I.M. 2020. Inclusive education in Luxembourg: implicit and explicit attitudes toward inclusion and students with special educational needs. *International Journal of Inclusive Education* 24(6), pp. 597–615.

Kurniawati, F., De Boer, A.A., Minnaert, A.E.M.G. and Mangunsong, F. 2014. Characteristics of primary teacher training programmes on inclusion: a literature focus. *Educational Research* 56(3), pp. 310–326.

Lawson, A. and Beckett, A.E. 2021. The social and human rights models of disability: towards a complementarity thesis. *The International Journal of Human Rights* 25(2), pp. 348–379.

Leeuw, R.R.D., Boer, A.A.D. and Minnaert, A. 2019. *Student voices on social exclusion in general primary schools.* [online] [Accessed on 18.10.2022]. Available from: https://www.doabooks.org/doab?func=fulltext&uiLanguage=en&rid=33420

Lindner, K.T. and Schwab, S. 2020. Differentiation and individualisation in inclusive education: a systematic review and narrative synthesis. *International Journal of Inclusive Education* pp.1–21.

Mendoza, M. and Heymann, J. 2022. Implementation of inclusive education: a systematic review of studies of inclusive education interventions in low- and lower-middle-income countries. *International Journal of Disability, Development, and Education*, Ahead-of-print(Ahead-of-print), pp. 1–18.

Miyauchi, H. 2020. A systematic review on inclusive education of students with visual impairment. *Education Sciences* **10**(11), p. 346.

Moberg, S., Muta, E., Korenaga, K., Kuorelahti, M. and Savolainen, H. 2020. Struggling for inclusive education in Japan and Finland: teachers' attitudes towards inclusive education. *European Journal of Special Needs Education* **35**(1), pp. 100–114.

Norwegien Ministry of Foreign Affairs. 2015. The Oslo Declaration Paper presented at the *Oslo Education Summit*. [online] [Accessed on 18.10.2022]. Available from: https://www.regjeringen.no/globalassets/departementene/ud/dokumenter/oslo-statement.pdf

Opie, J., Southcott, J. and Deppeler, J. 2017. 'It helps if you are a loud person': listening to the voice of a school student with a vision impairment. *Qualitative Report* **22**(9), pp. 2369–2384.

Pazey, B., Cole, H. and Spikes, D. 2017. A single voice in the crowd: a case study of one student's determination to challenge top down school reform. *Teachers College Record (1970)* **119**(9), pp. 1–37.

Pierangelo, R. and Guiliani, G.A. 2007. *Understanding, developing and writing effective IEPs*. Thousand Oaks, CA: Corwin Press.

Psaila, E. 2017. Voices in the classroom: exploring how the voice of the disabled child and the educational professionals are manifested in the classroom. *Malta Review of Educational Research* **11**(2), pp. 171–186.

Rieser, R. 2012. *Implementing inclusive education: a Commonwealth guide to implementing Article 24 of the UN Convention on the Rights of Persons with Disabilities*. 2nd ed. London: Commonwealth Secretariat.

Rouvali, A. and Riga, V. 2021. Listening to the voice of a pupil with autism spectrum condition in the educational design of a mainstream early years setting. *Education 3-13* **49**(4), pp. 464–480.

Salamanca Statement and Framework for Action in Special Needs Education. 1994. [online] [Accessed on 18.10.2022]. Available from: https://unesdoc.unesco.org/ark:/48223/pf0000098427

Saloviita, T. 2020. Teachers' changing attitudes and preferences around inclusive education. *International Journal of Disability, Development and Education* **69**, pp. 1841–1858.

Schola Europaea. 2018. *Report on Inclusive Education in the European Schools*. [online] [Accessed on 18.10.2022] Available from: https://www.eursc.eu/Documents/2018-09-D-28-en-4.pdf

Sheehy, K., Budiyanto, Kaye, H. and Rofiah, K. 2019. Indonesian teachers' epistemological beliefs and inclusive education. *Journal of Intellectual Disabilities* **23**(1), pp. 39–56.

Slee, R. 2013. How do we make inclusive education happen when exclusion is a political predisposition? *International Journal of Inclusive Education* **17**(8), pp. 895–907.

Su, X., Guo, J. and Wang, X. 2020. Different stakeholders' perspectives on inclusive education in China: parents of children with ASD, parents of typically developing children, and classroom teachers. *International Journal of Inclusive Education* **24**(9), pp. 948–963.

Thomas, G. 2013. A review of thinking and research about inclusive education policy, with suggestions for a new kind of inclusive thinking. *British Educational Research Journal* 39(3), pp. 473–490.

Tiwari, A., Das, A. and Sharma, M. 2015. Inclusive education a 'rhetoric' or 'reality'? Teachers' perspectives and beliefs. *Teaching and Teacher Education* 52, pp. 128–136.

UN Committee on the Rights of Persons with Disabilities. 2016. General Comment No. 4 (2016) on the Right to Inclusive Education. [online] [Accessed on 18.10.2022]. Available from: https://documents-dds-ny.un.org/doc/UNDOC/GEN/G16/263/00/PDF/G1626300.pdf?OpenElement

UN Department of Economic and Social Affairs. 2022. Disability Laws and Acts by Country/Area. [online] [Accessed on 18.10.2022]. Available from: https://www.un.org/development/desa/disabilities/disability-laws-and-acts-by-country-area.html

UN Special Rapporteur on Disability. 2021. Report of the Special Rapporteur on the rights of persons with disabilities. [online] [Accessed on 18.10.2022]. Available from: https://documents-dds-ny.un.org/doc/UNDOC/GEN/G21/012/14/PDF/G2101214.pdf?OpenElement

UNESCO. 2016. *Education 2030. Incheon Declaration and Framework for Action for the Implementation of Sustainable Development Goal 4.* UNESCO.

UNESCO. 2022. What you need to know about inclusive education. [online] [Accessed on 18.10.2022]. Available from: https://www.unesco.org/en/education/inclusion/need-know

United Nations. *Transforming our world: the 2030 Agenda for Sustainable Development.* Available from: https://documents-dds-ny.un.org/doc/UNDOC/GEN/N15/291/89/PDF/N1529189.pdf?OpenElement.

Universal Declaration of Human Rights. 1948 [online] [Accessed on 18.10.2022]. Available from: https://www.ohchr.org/en/udhr/documents/udhr_translations/eng.pdf

Van Mieghem, A., Verschueren, K., Petry, K. and Struyf, E. 2020. An analysis of research on inclusive education: a systematic search and meta review. *International Journal of Inclusive Education* 24(6), pp. 675–689.

Waitoller, F. and Artiles, A. 2013. A decade of professional development research for Inclusive education: a critical review and notes for a research program. *Review of Educational Research* 83(3), pp. 319–356.

Woodcock, S. 2021. Teachers' beliefs in inclusive education and the attributional responses toward students with and without specific learning difficulties. *Dyslexia* 27(1), pp. 110–125.

World Declaration on Education for All. 1990. [online] [Accessed on 18.10.2022]. Available from: https://unesdoc.unesco.org/ark:/48223/pf0000127583

Yeo, L.S., Chong, W.H., Neihart, M.F. and Huan, V.S. 2016. Teachers' experience with inclusive education in Singapore. *Asia Pacific Journal of Education* 36(sup1), pp. 69–83.

Young, K., McNamara, P.M. and Coughlan, B. 2017. Authentic inclusion-utopian thinking?–Irish post-primary teachers' perspectives of inclusive education. *Teaching and Teacher Education* 68, pp. 1–11.

12

DIGITAL PARTICIPATION AND COMPETENCIES FOR YOUNG PEOPLE WITH INTELLECTUAL OR DEVELOPMENTAL DISABILITIES

Sue Caton, Kristin Alfredsson Ågren
and Parimala Raghavendra

Introduction

The internet, social media and online gaming are now a universal part of childhood as much as they are of adulthood. Much of our engagement with the world today is happening through the internet (Livingstone, Mascheroni and Staksrud, 2018). In 2020, the EU Kids Online study reported on findings from a survey of 21,964 children aged 9–16 from 19 European countries and found that there was a substantial increase in smartphone-using children compared to the EU Kids Online Survey in 2010 (Smahel et al., 2020). Across the EU, young people aged 15–16 are more likely to use smartphones daily compared with younger children. Watching videos, listening to music, communicating with friends and family, visiting a social networking site and playing online games are common daily activities (Smahel et al., 2020). There are, however, differences in access and use across countries in the EU. For example, in France, 65% of children access the internet through smartphones several times each day or at least once per day compared to 89% in Lithuania. There is also varying daily use of tablets with 14% in Poland compared to 43% in Malta (Smahel et al., 2020). Worldwide, there are inequalities in access to digital technology with some regions such as the USA, Canada and Australia matching the picture in the EU, while almost three-quarters of adults have never been online in the 46 least-developed countries (ITU, 2021; Smahel et al., 2020).

Digital participation is a complex concept to define as the context, intensity and perceived value of participation can be so varied (Literat et al., 2018). For simplicity, we have adopted a broad definition of participation to encompass taking part in any online activities, including leisure activities and

DOI: 10.4324/9781003102915-12

managing activities in everyday life such as studying, working and taking part in community-based activities. Digital participation requires digital competencies. We use the term digital competencies where other authors have used the terms digital skills or digital literacy, but as a concept, whichever term is used, the daily experience for digital users is 'far more than knowing how to use the tools; it's about understanding how to access, organise, evaluate, use, and share digitally produced or available information, safely, legally and creatively' (Lewis, 2014, p. 34).

In line with this development, the Committee on the Rights of the Child (2021) includes guidance that children's rights apply in the digital world to the same extent as in the offline world in its General Comment No. 25. It highlights digital competencies as being important for young people to gain today, because the digital environment is becoming increasingly important across most aspects of young people's lives. This has been highlighted during the COVID-19 crisis, as societal functions such as education and health have relied upon digital technologies (Chadwick et al., 2022).

Many commonly acknowledged transitions through life now require digital participation. For young people, the transition towards adult life might mean that digital participation and, therefore, the development of digital competencies are important. Digital participation that supports the transition towards adult life could mean being able to independently purchase a new t-shirt from an online shop, developing and fostering friendships and taking part in shared online activities for entertainment or finding information.

Young People with Intellectual or Developmental Disabilities

A proportion of young people with intellectual or developmental disabilities are part of the digital transformation, engaging with internet use, owning smartphones, taking part in social media, watching YouTube and engaging in online gaming (Alfredsson Ågren, Kjellberg and Hemmingsson, 2020a). However, participation can also be limited, with some young people with intellectual or developmental disabilities taking part in passive activities (such as reading social media posts but not commenting or reacting) and often alone (Raghavendra et al., 2015). Research by Alfredsson Ågren et al. (2020a) also shows that young people with intellectual or developmental disabilities are not undertaking Internet activities to the same extent as young people without intellectual disability, except for playing online games. The lesser participation of young people with disabilities in the online world might, therefore, be a barrier to the transition into independent adults. There are, of course, risks associated with being online, but the benefits are especially important in relation to young people with intellectual or developmental disabilities in terms of facilitating agency, autonomy and control (Alper and Goggin, 2017).

In this chapter, we identify and discuss research that has taken place globally with young people with intellectual or developmental disabilities around digital participation and digital competencies that allow participation in everyday life and society through internet and social media use. We will specifically be utilising findings from our own research projects in the UK, Sweden and Australia. The scope of the research that we focus on for this chapter is around internet and social media use, for seeking information, entertainment and enhancing social connections and building social networks.

Why Is Digital Participation Important?

Digital participation matters for young people because the opportunities for social connection, developing identity and a sense of belonging are particularly important for this age group as they move towards a developing independence (Small, Raghavan and Pawson, 2013). As young people transition into adulthood, they are expected to develop an increasing degree of independence, to manage money, to enter into romantic relationships and to have their own points of view, pastimes, preferences and tastes. The digital world has the potential to support this transition through connectedness, opportunities for independence and enjoyment (Caton and Chapman, 2016; Molin, Sorbring and Löfgren Mårtensson, 2017).

Young people with disabilities are known to be more commonly socially isolated (Raghavendra et al., 2011, 2012). The causes of this social isolation are multidimensional but include segregated education, schooling at geographically disperse locations, caution and protectiveness on the part of parents, carers and teachers. With this in mind, participation in digital communities can be seen to have potential for increased social connections and supporting young people in their developing sense of self (Raghavendra et al., 2013a, 2013b, 2018). However, it is important for young people to have opportunities for connecting in person in physical communities which could reduce the risk of further isolation and strengthen their offline connections online and vice versa.

The EU Kids Online report found that the majority of children say they find it easier to be themselves online at least sometimes (Smahel et al., 2020). In 2012, the US agency Common Sense Media produced a report entitled 'Social Media, Social Life; How Teens View Their Digital Lives' which stated that more than a quarter of teens say that using their social networking sites makes them feel less shy and more outgoing. While online connections are sometimes considered 'less' than real-life connections, it is important to remember that online social connections are connections with other young people. As Bex Lewis pointed out, 'The online world is not a "virtual world". There are real people behind the keyboards at either end of any online activity' (Lewis, 2014, p. 32).

How Are Young People with Intellectual or Developmental Disabilities Using the Internet and Social Media?

The research we have introduced has shown how some young people with intellectual or developmental disabilities are actively enjoying smartphone and internet use. We now move to examining in more detail the possibilities and benefits associated with digitalisation, highlighting the specific difficulties it may bring to young people with disabilities (Alper and Goggin, 2017). Detailed knowledge is required to target and implement resources and enable digital inclusion (Raghavendra et al., 2013a, 2015, 2018), as it has been found that some young people with intellectual or developmental disabilities may find it difficult to realise their rights in contemporary digital society (Alper and Goggin, 2017).

A significant difference was found in the online activity *searching for information*, which was performed by 20% of young people with intellectual disabilities compared with 84% among young people without intellectual disabilities (Alfredsson Ågren et al., 2020a). This is worrying and of importance since information can be viewed as the first step towards participation in everyday life and making informed decisions (Goodman et al., 2008).

A small-scale study demonstrated that young people with intellectual disabilities have comparable access to social media but have smaller social network sizes than their non-disabled peers with online acquaintances providing an additional way to contact existing acquaintances but few new relationships being forged (White and Forrester-Jones, 2020). Participants with intellectual disabilities interacted with a significantly lower percentage of their social contacts using social media than their typically developing counterparts suggesting social media use differed between the two groups (White and Forrester-Jones, 2020). In contrast to White and Forrester-Jones's study, Alfredsson Ågren et al. (2020a) found that young people with intellectual disabilities did not have access to and use the internet to the same extent as young people in general, except for having tablets and playing online games.

Exploring internet use is a fast-moving area of research and as such it can be a challenge for researchers to keep current in terms of social media use of young people with disabilities. As pointed out by Bayor et al. (2018), research remains incomplete on the nature of participation across popular social media, and there is little understanding of how different social media sites fulfil different participation interests and understanding their participation in social media holds potential for developing wider digital competencies. Bayor et al.'s (2018) research with young people found that social media use varied between platforms: all participants used YouTube for entertainment, some participated in Facebook to stay connected with family, whereas Snapchat and Instagram were used for playful interaction with strangers.

Challenges of Using the Internet and Social Media for Young People with Intellectual or Developmental Disabilities

As seen in the previous section, there are potential benefits to digital participation for young people with intellectual or developmental disabilities, but in this section, we explore the challenges that are preventing full participation.

Possibly the most significant challenge for full participation in the digital world is demonstrated by the research that has shown that the real and virtual worlds mirror each other, and most young people socialise online with offline friends (e.g. Livingstone and Bober, 2003; Madell and Muncer, 2005; Valentine and Holloway, 2002). If young people with intellectual or developmental disabilities have restricted social lives offline (Caton and Landman, 2022; Raghavendra et al., 2011, 2012), it could be that their online worlds would be similarly restricted. Indeed, parents of young people with disabilities living in rural areas of Australia identified that their children had limited social networks offline which was a barrier to expanding their social networks online (Raghavendra et al., 2018). Whether this issue can be widened to other areas of life/online lives such as shopping or information seeking is still unclear.

However, other challenges also exist for young people with intellectual or developmental disabilities that are potentially actionable and have every possibility for improvement to allow for greater participation. Examples of these types of challenges are:

- Accessibility: In Sweden, a survey among young people with intellectual disabilities showed that having studied at special schools correlated with the lowest proportions having access to internet-enabled devices (Johansson, Gulliksen and Gustavsson, 2020). Research by Alfredsson Ågren, Kjellberg and Hemmingsson (2020b) has also shown that challenges exist around remembering passwords, codes to access the devices and lacking sustainable internet connections, updates to software and apps.
- Literacy: Specific reading and writing difficulties may affect literacy skills that can be difficult to overcome in the digital environment when one interacts online (Alfredsson Ågren et al., 2020b; Borgström, Daneback and Molin, 2019; Raghavendra et al., 2015, 2018).
- Financial restrictions: Despite costs associated with digital participation coming down, barriers still exist in terms of both purchasing of devices and ongoing costs of internet access and mobile phone data (Alfredsson Ågren et al., 2020b).
- Online risk: The risks associated with being online for young people are well documented. From a young age, young people today are taught about stranger danger online as well as offline and parents are acutely aware of risks online around cyberbullying, grooming and inappropriate content.

A number of studies have discussed risks of being online for people with intellectual disabilities of all age groups such as cyberbullying, financial and sexual exploitation and unwanted messages (Bannon et al., 2015; Holmes and O'Loughlin, 2012; Molin et al., 2015; Norman and Sallafranque-St-Louis, 2016). It has been suggested that people with intellectual disabilities who lack understanding of risks, engaged in more risk-taking behaviour (Bannon et al., 2015).

- Perceptions of risk: Concerns about internet use are prevalent amongst family members, carers or supporters of young people with intellectual disabilities (Ramsten et al., 2019). The views of family members, professionals and paid carers in terms of risk are also important because, as Chadwick (2019) points out, these perceptions can lead to gatekeeping restrictions. Studies have shown that perceptions of parents of young people, and teachers, are that young people with intellectual disabilities are more at risk on the internet compared to young people in general (Molin et al., 2017). However, parents are more open to the benefits of internet use in relation to paid support staff, who are more evidently expressing the risks. It is likely that the expectation that young people with intellectual or developmental disabilities could be vulnerable and should be protected feeds into what Wall (2008) identifies as prevailing myths about internet use such as that it is unsafe and that users cannot be trusted and need to be protected from themselves.

- Digital competencies of parents: Parents of young people without disabilities have reported feeling challenged in their competencies needed to provide support (Livingstone and Byrne, 2018). It follows that this is likely to be the same for parents of young people with intellectual or developmental disabilities. Raghavendra et al. (2013a, 2013b, 2015, 2018) observed that some parents of young people with disabilities living in metropolitan and rural areas of Australia did not feel confident in using the internet and social media and needed support with their digital competencies before supporting their children.

This list (while not exhaustive) demonstrates the numerous barriers faced by young people with intellectual or developmental disabilities in being able to tap in to the previously mentioned potential benefits associated with the online world. While accessibility may be partly related to financial restrictions, the perception of others of risks with internet use may be linked with the finding of parents feeling challenged and not confident enough in their own digital competencies to be able to provide digital support to their children with intellectual and developmental disabilities. A final significant challenge to explore, that is faced by young people with intellectual or developmental disabilities in full digital participation, is that of acquiring the necessary digital competencies themselves. This may be one way to improve safe digital participation and make young people with intellectual or developmental disabilities more aware of online risks they may come across and also provide more resilience to online risks.

Developing Digital Competencies in Young People with Intellectual or Developmental Disabilities

The challenge that we want to focus on in more detail is that of developing digital competencies for young people with intellectual or developmental disabilities. Research by Alfredsson Ågren et al. (2020b) shows that sometimes young people do not have the digital competencies needed to benefit from and keep safe within this potentially beneficial arena with opportunities for connections with friends and families, access to leisure and recreation, education and employment.

The previously mentioned EU Kids online report (Smahel et al., 2020) found that, when older children without disabilities were asked to report on their competencies, most young people aged 12–16 scored highly on operational and social skills. Information, navigation skills and creative skills were found to be uneven across EU countries with lower skill level in Switzerland, Germany, Spain, Italy and France (Smahel et al., 2020). In Bayor et al.'s (2018) study, a number of digital competencies were revealed that highlighted online activities that participants could successfully do without challenges. These competencies included awareness of safety concerns, desire and interest in learning and developing new skills and social media participation interests. Identifying these competencies can be useful for further work on how to leverage participation strengths in further skills development. Digital competencies are employed as a concept with the EU (Carretero Gomez, Vuorikari and Punie, 2017). It comprises five necessary competencies to achieve digital participation: information and data literacy, communication and collaboration using the internet, creating digital content, internet safety and problem-solving (Carretero Gomez et al., 2017).

Supports for Developing Digital Competencies

The complexities around the mirroring of real life and online lives mean that some aspects of online lives will always be challenging for young people with disabilities while those challenges continue to exist in wider offline society. An example is problem-solving that has been identified as a digital competence being specifically difficult to handle due to the rapid changes in the digital environment (Alfredsson Ågren et al., 2020b), even though handling rapid changes is a challenge offline as well due to deficits in intellectual and adaptive functioning (American Psychiatric Association, 2013). However, as discussed, some of the challenges that prevent wider participation for young people with intellectual or developmental disabilities can be addressed through tailored training and support for developing digital competencies. Research by Raghavendra and colleagues (2018) and Caton and Landman (2022) has shown that young people with intellectual or developmental disabilities do benefit from targeted support. Furthermore, a need for problem-focused coping strategies and advocating for a perspective of positive risk-taking is highlighted (Borgström, 2023).

Research Focus

To provide some examples of ways that researchers have focused on the importance of developing digital competencies for people with intellectual or developmental disabilities, we have drawn on our own research work in Sweden (Research Focus 1), the UK (Research Focus 2), and Australia (Research Focus 3).

Research Focus 1: Comparing Perceptions of Online Risks

In Sweden, Alfredsson Ågren, Kjellberg and Hemmingsson (2020c) carried out a comparative cross-sectional study of parents' perceptions of the opportunities and risks with the internet for their young people with and without intellectual disabilities. The research showed that parents of young people with intellectual disabilities see greater opportunities with the internet for their adolescents compared to parents of young people in general. Furthermore, a significantly lower proportion of parents of young people with intellectual disabilities have concerns about online risks. For example, in the case of bullying, 46% of parents of young people with intellectual disabilities have concerns about their adolescent being bullied, compared to 63% in the reference group of parents to young people in general ($p = 0.003$). Another example is 39% of parents having concerns about their adolescents being approached by adults seeking sexual contact, compared to 56% in the reference group ($p = 0.002$).

An even lower proportion of all parents perceived that any incidents had occurred in line with online risks, for example, only 12% of parents of young people with intellectual disabilities perceived this and 16% in the reference group. The lesser concerns of online risks among parents of young people with intellectual disabilities may be due to the finding that a significantly lower proportion of young people with intellectual disabilities use a smartphone (26% fewer compared to the reference group ($p < 0.001$)) and about 50% do not have access to social media. However, the young people in both groups spend most of their time engaged in internet activities in comparison with other leisure activities (Alfredsson Ågren et al., 2020c). Other qualitative research from Sweden has shown that parents of young people with intellectual disabilities rank the positive aspects of using the internet to pro-mote social connections higher than they worry about the risks for their child (Molin, Sorbring and Löfgren-Mårtenson, 2015).

Positive risk-taking may be a useful approach in allowing the development of digital competencies (Alfredsson Ågren et al., 2020c; Borgström, 2023). Young people with intellectual disabilities have described an awareness of risks in their internet use, and that they are taking risks if the outcome may be worth it (Molin et al., 2017). However, higher precautions have been re-ported, for example, personal information is not revealed online to the same extent as young people in general do (Alfredsson Ågren et al., 2020a).

Research Focus 2: Learning Internet Safety Skills

Caton and Landman's (2022) research used interviews and focus groups to explore what young people (age 11–20) with intellectual disabilities, their parents and teachers thought about internet safety, extremism and online radicalisation. The young people in the study were active internet users who used the internet every day. The young people were confident about online safety but had a preference for accessing the internet in a location where they had privacy as explained by one of the college students who said:

> I feel a bit like award if I do it around everyone because I don't really want them to see what I am doing if you know what I mean. (Libby, college student)

Parents in the study highlighted how internet use for their children with intel-lectual or developmental disabilities had specific benefits, such as it being an attractive way to spend free time after school and a place where social barriers could be minimised. However, the parents in the study were concerned about the risks associated with internet use and expressed strong concerns about the safety of the young people online, saying that when they were engrossed in social media or gaming, safety rules were quickly forgotten or ignored: 'they know the rules around internet safety but when they're in that moment, when they're on that game, it's different'. Parents also identified a difficulty in that they did not always possess the digital competencies themselves to be able to fully supervise and support the safety of the children. An important finding in this research was that there was a gap between the young people's online safety knowledge and their parents' perceptions of their online safety knowledge and behaviour.

The young people in the study took part in a peer education project that aimed to develop digital competencies around internet safety and specifically about risks of online radicalisation and extremism. The training included group discussions around online and 'real' life, bullying and supportive online behaviours as well as hearing from guest speakers with expertise on grooming and extremism. Following participation in the project, the students understood possible links between grooming and online radicalisation and their teachers increased their understanding of the importance of digital engagement for their students, as can be seen from the following quotations:

> It's helped me understand a bit more about how it can affect people and how easy it is for them to be able to like infiltrate certain groups of people and turn them evil.
>
> *(Luke, college student)*

> people tell you that this is right and they are trying to tell you to be, like, religious or something like that and then they're saying things that's wrong and you just believe it.
>
> *(Katie, school student)*

> And some of the discussions that we had in the [project] meetings were incredibly honest and illuminating. I mean, I've worked with autistic young people for a long time but what they were saying about how important it is to feel that sense of belonging and to be part of a community – and how – when you can be anyone you want online. And for them that's an incredible positive, because nobody judges you – they don't feel they're judged.
>
> *(Joanne, school teacher).*

Increasing teacher understanding is important because this research has also highlighted a discrepancy between the views of young people with intellectual disabilities and their parents and/or professionals who work to support them. A greater understanding of the importance of the digital world for young people by their teachers is likely to mean that any internet safety training provided within schools would take place with a positive risk-taking approach allowing the young people to benefit from online connections.

Research Focus 3: Home-based Training to Support Social Media Use

Raghavendra et al. (2013a, 2013b, 2015, 2018) and Grace et al. (2014) have investigated the effectiveness of home-based training on social media use and cyber safety on enhancing the social networks and reducing loneliness of young people with disabilities. Their research focused on building operational and social skills around Internet use, communication and collaboration and internet safety and problem-solving. Eighteen young people with developmental disabilities or acquired brain injury living in the city of Adelaide and 17 young people with intellectual or developmental disabilities living in rural areas of Australia between 10 and 18 years received tailored training. The young people set up their own social media use goals (e.g., 'I want to learn how to upload photos on Facebook to share with my family and friends'; 'I want to learn to use Skype so that I can talk with my grandma who lives in another state'). The training was individualised, led by the young people with a focus on what they wanted to be able to do. The one-on-one training with appropriate assistive technology concentrated on addressing *their* goals. Training focused on teaching the young person and their parents about cyber safety and provided training materials including visual supports and hands-on training and practice to use the internet, software and the computer. A variety of quantitative tools were administered to collect data before and after the training: (a) self-rated perception of performance on each goal and satisfaction with their performance was measured using the Canadian Occupational Performance Measure (Law et al., 2005), (b) Goal Attainment Scaling (Kiresuk and Sherman, 1968) was used to measure the attainment of digital competency goals, (c) perceived loneliness using Asher's Loneliness Scale (Asher, Hymel and Renshaw, 1984) and (d) number of online and offline people they communicated with using the Circles of Communication Partners (Blackstone and Hunt Berg, 2012).

The young people and their families were provided with individualised cyber safety training before the intervention commenced. Some participants initially expressed concern talking to new people online, but many felt safer and confident from the online safety information provided by researchers. Parents felt that this approach was more useful as the information came from the researchers rather than the family. The young people may have responded more positively to researchers as they were not their family and the information was presented step-by-step using visual representations (pictures and drawings). The training and support used person-centred approaches, focusing on what the young person wanted to learn. The findings showed that majority of the participants attained their goals and learnt social media skills:

> I was friends with them [school peers] and didn't really talk to them much outside of school or sport, or whatever, and found them on Facebook or they found me and then we got chatting on the instant messaging on that and it's helped me connect with more friends, (John, 14 years old).

There was an increase in the number of people that they connected with online even though it was predominantly with family and pre-existing friends. Twenty of 35 participants did not connect with anyone online before the intervention and connected with one to over 50 people after the intervention.

The use of assistive technology to convert text to speech and speech to text reduced literacy barriers and helped young people with disabilities to interact more effectively with other social media users. Interviews with the young people with disabilities and their family indicated that the former benefited from and valued the personalised support provided at home, strengthening of existing relationships: 'now I've got Facebook I can talk with my sisters and I couldn't do that before', Jane, aged 16; and feeling confident and independent to use social media. These benefits were also reported in a sub-group of 13 young people who had severe communication difficulties. Additionally, parents had observed improved literacy, communication and conversational skills and changes in the speech intelligibility of their children with communication difficulties. Parents also commented that this was an age-appropriate activity: 'she's not a child anymore and it's important that… this has been a positive adult, a major growing step', mother of a 15-year-old. This acknowledgement of transition to adulthood may have also been due to the individualised nature of training and support provided at home using the young person's or family's computer and communication technology and the family may have felt safe. The researchers built rapport and trust with the participant and the family as the training was carried over several weeks.

This body of research suggests that parents of young people with intellectual or developmental disabilities recognise the potential benefits of online participation. There is, however, mixed evidence regarding parents' perception of online risks. The research highlights that providing tailored training and support to young people with disabilities and their parents in building digital competencies had positive outcomes, especially if this is delivered by experts external to the immediate family.

The pandemic has raised awareness on the usefulness and importance of using digital media to connect with each other (Caton et al., 2022; Chadwick et al., 2022) and hence the need to build digital competencies in young people with disabilities. There is urgent need for developing more local and affordable solutions.

Covid-19 and the Rapid Move Online of Everyday Activities

Globally, the number of internet users grew by more than 10% in the first year of the Covid-19 crisis, which was the largest annual increase in a decade (ITU, 2021). The response to Covid-19 has potentially changed the landscape of issues around digital inclusion for people with intellectual or developmental disabilities as there has been a significant change towards embracing internet use. Research has suggested that digital competencies were needed to navigate the disruption that occurred in the lives of people with intellectual disabilities during the pandemic (Spencer et al., 2021). The necessity for support (both financial and physical) for developing digital competencies has become clear. As an example, in February 2021, the UK Government funded a £2.5 million Digital Lifeline Fund to provide devices, data and digital support to people with intellectual disabilities who could not afford to get online (Good Things Foundation, 2021).

Meanwhile, remote learning for many young people across the globe has made digital competencies more highly valued with many having to undertake rapid upskilling. However, it has also been reported by Jeste et al. (2020) that using the internet may not always be suitable for everyone, for example, the use of tele-education or telemedicine for families with children or young people with intellectual disabilities. Their recent study reported a need for an increased access to devices, as many were sharing with their families, and an increased and tailored support, and despite this not all would be able to use the digital devices and take part anyway, as the devices were not adapted to the individual needs of the person with disability (Jeste et al. 2020). Governmental and community-based projects that aim to provide access and spread digital skills to tackle digital – and indirectly – social exclusion show rather temporary achievements, arguably because they often approach the issue from the simplistic view that lack of skills and access can be distinctly targeted as main barriers to digital inclusion. The reality, as has been illustrated through this chapter, is much more complex. It has further been shown that people with intellectual and developmental disabilities who were not digitally participating before the COVID-19 have not suddenly become more digital (Chadwick et al., 2022). However, overcoming barriers to be digitally included, participate in meaningful online activities and feel socially connected through the computer screen have proven possible among young people with intellectual disabilities during the pandemic with, for example, grassroots disability organisation being able to create a digital community for its members with intellectual/developmental disabilities (Spassiani et al., 2023). This was done in offering events and activities online that members would typically participate in on-site before the pandemic, such as quiz nights and stand-up comedy events. This has even increased the number of young adult participants taking part as it was possible to do from a safe place at home (Spassiani et al., 2023).

What's Next?

The research that we have presented here shows that there are potentially important benefits for the digital participation of young people with intellectual or developmental disabilities in a wide range of areas such as for entertainment, developing a sense of self, enhancing social connections and seeking information. However, we have highlighted the multiple challenges to developing digital competencies that allow for the digital participation of people with intellectual and developmental disabilities.

Concerns about safety online as well as limited digital competencies of parents have sometimes been acting as barriers to the development of digital competencies. There is a need for a faster move towards greater regulation over privacy, regulation and protection of children that will ease the pressure put on families and supporters and allow for a more relaxed approach that embraces the benefits that online participation has to offer. Wall (2008) asserts that the majority of individuals tend to take their (good) social values with them online, and it is important that this remains at the forefront of our minds when supporting young people with intellectual and developmental disabilities in developing digital competencies to allow for digital participation.

The rapid changes in the digital environment, for example, regarding updates to software and apps and enhancements to technological devices, are one of the issues that are especially challenging for young people with intellectual disabilities to overcome in their use of the internet. This may, in part, be due to their cognitive impairment – for example, with difficulties of literacy and problem-solving – but importantly it may also be due to lack of support from others and of the digital competencies of those others (Alfredsson Ågren et al., 2020b). Co-produced research with people with intellectual and developmental disabilities and inter-professional input from occupational therapists, speech and language therapists, social workers, organisations that support people with intellectual disabilities and their families and professionals who work in the technology industry is needed to increase understanding of developing solutions for end-users with different needs.

References

Alfredsson Ågren, K., Kjellberg, A. and Hemmingsson, H. 2020a. Digital participation? Internet use among adolescents with and without intellectual disabilities: a comparative study. *New Media and Society*, 22(12), pp. 2128–2145.

Alfredsson Ågren K., Kjellberg A. and Hemmingsson H. 2020b. Access to and use of the Internet among adolescents and young adults with intellectual disabilities in everyday settings. *Journal of Intellectual and Developmental Disabilities*, 45(1), pp. 89–98.

Alfredsson Ågren, K., Kjellberg, A. and Hemmingsson, H. 2020c. Internet opportunities and risks for adolescents with intellectual disabilities: a comparative study of parents' perceptions. *Scandinavian Journal of Occupational Therapy*, 27(8), pp. 601–613.

Alper, M. and Goggin, G. 2017. Digital technology and rights in the lives of children with disabilities. *New Media and Society*, 19(5), pp. 726–740.

American Psychiatric Association. 2013. *Diagnostic and statistical manual of mental disorders*. 5th ed. DSM-5. Washington: American Psychiatric Association.

Asher, S., Hymel, S. and Renshaw, P.D. 1984. Loneliness in children. *Child Development*, 55, pp. 1456–1464.

Bannon, S., McGlynn, T., McKenzie, K. and Quayle, E. 2015. The internet and young people with Additional Support Needs (ASN): risk and safety. *Computers in Human Behavior*, 53, pp. 495–503.

Bayor, A., Bircanin, F., Sitbon, L., Ploderer, B., Koplick, S. and Brereton, M. 2018. Characterizing participation across social media sites amongst young adults with intellectual disability. In *Proceedings of ACM OzCHI'18 Conference*, Melbourne, Australia.

Blackstone, S. and Hunt Berg, M. 2012. *Social networks: a communication inventory for individuals with complex communication needs and their communication partners.* Verona, WI: Attainment Company.

Borgström, Å. 2023. Tensions between risk, coping and support: young people with intellectual disability in Sweden and internet-related support. *Disability & Society,* 38(3), pp. 460–482.

Borgström, Å., Daneback, K. and Molin, M. 2019. Young people with intellectual disabilities and social media: a literature review and thematic analysis. *Scandinavian Journal of Disability Research,* 1, pp. 129–140.

Carretero Gomez, S., Vuorikari, R. and Punie, Y. 2017. DigComp 2.1: the Digital Competence Framework for Citizens with eight proficiency levels and examples of use. Publications Office of the European Union. [online] [Accessed on 12.10.2022]. Available from: http://publications.jrc.ec.europa.eu/repository/handle/JRC106281.

Caton, S. and Chapman, M. 2016. The use of social media and people with intellectual disabilities: a systematic review and thematic analysis. *Journal of Intellectual and Developmental Disabilities,* 41(2), pp. 125–139.

Caton, S., Hatton, C., Gillooly, A., Oloidi, E., Clarke, L., Bradshaw, J., Flynn, S., Taggart, L., Mulhall, P., Jahoda, A., Maguire, R., Marriott, A., Todd, S., Abbott, D., Beyer, S., Gore, N., Heslop, P., Scior, K. and Hastings, R.P. 2022. Online social connections and internet use among people with intellectual disabilities in the UK during the Covid-19 pandemic. *New Media and Society.* https://journals.sagepub.com/doi/full/10.1177/14614448221093762

Caton, S. and Landman, R. 2022. Internet safety, online radicalisation and young people with learning disabilities. *British Journal of Learning Disabilities,* 50(1), pp. 88–97.

Committee on the Rights of the Child. 2021. General comment No. 25 (2021) on children's rights in relation to digital environment. [online] [Accessed on 12.11.22]. Available from: https://www.ohchr.org/en/documents/general-comments-and-recommendations/general-comment-no-25-2021-childrens-rights-relation

Chadwick, D. 2019. Online risk for people with intellectual disabilities. *Tizard Learning Disability Review,* 24(4) pp. 180–187.

Chadwick, D., Alfredsson Ågren, K., Caton, S., Chiner, E., Danker, Gómez-Puerta, M., Heitplatz, V., Johansson, S., Normand, C., Murphy, E., Plichta, P., Strnadová, I. and Flygare Wallén, E. 2022. Digital inclusion and participation of people with intellectual disabilities during COVID-19: a rapid review and international bricolage. *Journal of Policy and Practice in Intellectual Disabilities,* 19(3), pp. 242–256.

Good Things Foundation. 2021. *Digital Lifeline Fund: Interim Report.* [online] [Accessed on 12.11.22]. Available from: https://www.goodthingsfoundation.org/insights/dcms-digital-lifeline-fund-interim-report/

Goodman, J., Hurst, J. and Locke, C. 2008. *Occupational therapy for people with learning disabilities: a practical guide.* Edinburgh: Churchill Livingstone.

Grace, E., Raghavendra, P., Newman, L., Wood, D. and Connell, T. 2014. Learning to use the Internet and online social media: what is the effectiveness of home-based intervention for youth with complex communication needs? *Child Language Teaching and Therapy,* 30(2), pp. 141–157.

Holmes, K.M. and O'Loughlin, N. 2012. The experiences of people with learning disabilities on social networking sites. *British Journal of Learning Disabilities,* 42(1), pp. 3–7.

ITU. 2021. Measuring digital development. Facts and figures 2021. [online] [Accessed on 12.11.22]. Available from: https://www.itu.int/en/ITU-D/Statistics/Documents/facts/FactsFigures2021.pdf

Jeste, S., Hyde, C., Distefano, C., Halladay, A., Ray, S. Porath, M., Wilson, R.B. and Thurm, A. 2020. Changes in access to educational and healthcare services for individuals with intellectual and developmental disabilities during COVID-19 restrictions. *Journal of Intellectual Disability Research*, **64**(11), pp. 825–833.

Johansson, S., Gulliksen, J. and Gustavsson, C. 2020. Disability digital divide: the use of the internet, smartphones, computers and tablets among people with disabilities in Sweden. *Universal Access in the Information Society*, **20**, pp. 105–120.

Kiresuk, T. and Sherman, R. 1968. Goal attainment scaling: a general method of evaluating comprehensive community mental health programs. *Community Mental Health Journal*, **4**, pp. 443–453.

Law, M., Baptiste, S., Carswell, A., McColl, M., Opzoomer, A., Polatajko, H. and Pollock, N. 2005. *The Canadian occupational performance output measure*. 4th ed. Ottawa, ON: CAOT Publications.

Lewis, B. 2014. *Raising children in a digital age*. Oxford: Lion Books.

Literat, I., Kligler-Vilenchik, N., Brough, M. and Blum-Ross, A. 2018. Analyzing youth digital participation: aims, actors, contexts and intensities. *The Information Society*, **34**(4), pp. 261–273.

Livingstone, S. and Bober, M. 2003. UK children go online: listening to young people's experiences [online]. London: LSE Research Online. [online] [Accessed on 12.11.22]. Available from: http://eprints.lse.ac.uk/archive/0000388

Livingstone, S. and Byrne, J. 2018. Parenting in the digital age. The challenges of parental responsibility in comparative perspective. In Mascheroni, G., Ponte, C. and Jorge, A. eds. *Digital parenting. The challenges for families in the dgital age*. Göteborg: Nordicom, pp. 19–30.

Livingstone, S., Mascheroni, G. and Staksrud, E. 2018. European research on children's internet use: assessing the past and anticipating the future. *New Media & Society*, **20**(3), pp. 1103–1122.

Madell, D. and Muncer, S. 2005. A study from a 'rational actor' perspective. *Information, Communication & Society*, **8**(1), pp. 64–80.

Molin, M., Sorbring, E. and Löfgren-Mårtenson, L. 2015. Teachers' and parents' views on the Internet and social media usage by pupils with intellectual disabilities. *Journal of Intellectual Disabilities*, **19**(1), 22–33.

Molin, M., Sorbring, E. and Löfgren Mårtensson, L. 2017. New em@ncipatory landscapes? Young people with intellectual disabilities, internet use and identification processes. *Advances in Social Work*, **18**(2), 645–662.

Normand, C.L. and Sallafranque-St-Louis, F. 2016. Cybervictimization of young people with an intellectual or developmental disability: risks specific to sexual solicitation. *Journal of Applied Research in Intellectual Disabilities*, **29**(2), pp. 99–110.

Raghavendra, P., Grace, E., Newman, L., Wood, D. and Connell, T. 2013a. 'They think I'm really cool and nice': the impact of Internet support on the social networks and loneliness of young people with disabilities. *Telecommunication Journal of Australia*, **63**(2), Article 414.

Raghavendra, P., Hutchinson, C., Grace, E., Wood, D. and Newman, L. 2018. 'I like talking to people on the computer': outcomes of a home-based intervention to develop social media skills in youth with disabilities living in rural communities. *Research in Developmental Disabilities*, **76**, 110–123.

Raghavendra, P., Newman, L., Grace, E. and Wood, D. 2013b. 'I could never do that before': effectiveness of a tailored Internet support intervention to increase the social participation of youth with disabilities. *Child: Care, Health & Development*, **39**, pp. 552–561.

Raghavendra, P., Newman, L., Grace, E. and Wood, D. 2015. Enhancing social participation in young people with communication disabilities living in rural Australia: outcomes of a home-based intervention for using social media. Special issue of *Disability & Rehabilitation*, **37**(17), pp. 1576–1590.

Raghavendra, P., Olsson, C., Sampson, J., McInerney, R. and Connell, T. 2012. School participation and social networks of children with complex communication needs, physical disabilities and typically developing peers, *Augmentative and Alternative Communication*, **28**(1), pp. 33–43.

Raghavendra, P., Virgo, R., Olsson, C., Connell, T. and Lane, A. 2011. Activity participation of children with complex communication need, physical disabilities and typically developing peers. *Developmental Neurorehabilitation*, **14**(3), pp. 145–155.

Ramsten, C., Martin, L., Dag, M. and Marmatål Hammar, L. 2019. A balance of social inclusion and risks: staff perceptions of information and communication technology in the daily life of young adults with mild to moderate intellectual disability in a social care setting. *Journal of Policy and Practice in Intellectual Disabilities*, **16**(3), 171–179.

Smahel, D., Machackova, H., Mascheroni, G., Dedkova, L., Staksrud, E., Ólafsson, K., Livingstone, S. and Hasebrink, U. 2020. *EU Kids Online 2020: survey results from 19 countries*. EU Kids Online. [online] [Accessed on 12.11.22]. Available from: https://www.eukidsonline.ch/files/Eu-kids-online-2020-international-report.pdf

Small, N., Raghavan, R. and Pawson, N. 2013. An ecological approach to seeking and utilising the views of young people with intellectual disabilities in transition planning. *Journal of Intellectual Disabilities*, **17**(4), pp. 283–300.

Spassiani, N.A., Becaj, M., Miller, C., Hiddleston, A., Hume, A. and Tait, S. 2023. Now that I am connected it isn't social isolation, this is engaging with people: staying connected during the COVID-19 pandemic. *British Journal of Learning Disabilities*, **51**(1), pp. 99–110.

Spencer, P., Van Haneghan, J.P., Baxter, A., Chanto-Wetter, A. and Perry, L. 2021. 'It's ok, mom. I got it!': exploring the experiences of young adults with intellectual disabilities in a postsecondary program affected by the COVID-19 pandemic from their perspective and their families' perspective. *Journal of Intellectual Disabilities*, **25**(3), 405–414.

Valentine, G. and Holloway, S.L. 2002. Cyberkids? Exploring children's identities and social networks in on-line and off-line worlds. *Annals of the Association of American Geographers*, **92**(2), pp. 302–319.

Wall, D.S. 2008. Cybercrime, media and insecurity: the shaping of public perceptions of cybercrime. *International Review of Law, Computers & Technology*, **22**(1–2), pp. 45–63.

White, P. and Forrester-Jones, R. 2020. Valuing e-inclusion: social media and the social networks of adolescents with intellectual disability. *Journal of Intellectual Disabilities*, **24**(3), pp. 381–387.

13

AUTISTIC YOUTH AS ACTIVE AGENTS FOR SOCIETAL CHANGE

Anna Robinson and Kerrie Highcock

Introduction

In this chapter, we explore autistic youth's positioning within the current body of research and their role as active agents for societal change through their participation in research. We draw on data from a recently completed research project, 'We are the Autistic Activists' carried out in the North East of England, in the United Kingdom. Our aim in this chapter is to argue against the deficit medical model and negative narrative that dominates research carried out about autistic young people to date. We show how the neurodiversity movement is calling for a different narrative and one that positions the autistic person as an expert of their own experience. We draw from our Autistic Activist project based upon emancipatory research principles, which used creative methods to give voice to young autistic lives. We show how placing autistic young people at the centre of research enables authentic voice through both their words and art. We show how these lived experiences articulate with broader empirical research and with other lived experiences. In the final part of the chapter, we show how an emancipatory research project can empower autistic young people to become active social agents to make transformative changes in their own lives and for wider societal change.

Negative Narrative Research Agenda

Within the individual (medical) model of disability, autism spectrum disorder (ASD) is defined as a pervasive lifelong neurodevelopmental condition that affects 1%–2% of children globally (Elsabbagh et al., 2012). It is characterised by a dyad of persistent qualitative impairments in social interactions,

DOI: 10.4324/9781003102915-13

verbal and non-verbal communications, as well as restricted and repetitive thinking and behaviours (American Psychiatric Association, 2013). The difference of male to female ratio continues to indicate larger numbers of males (Zablotsky et al., 2015).

Autistic youth generally experience a lower quality of life compared to their typically developing peers (Ikeda, Hinckson, and Krägeloh, 2014). They face a range of challenges, including experiences of school bullying, extreme peer victimisation and associated difficulties in forming friendships (Rowley et al., 2012). Autistic adolescents often experience difficulties in understanding their own emotions and the emotions of others. Encounters between autistic youth and their typically developing peers (neurodivergent-neurotypical intersubjectivity) often result in emotional misattunement or misempathy. Through these repeated misempathy encounters, autistic people are vulnerable to trauma-related experiences (Robinson, 2018). Furthermore, they face poorer outcomes associated with increased mental health issues (Cooper, Smith and Russell, 2017) and high rates of self-injurious behaviours, as high as 42% compared to 8% for typically developing child and adolescent peers (Morgan et al., 2017).

These difficulties create a pathologising narrative which also dominates research emerging from parent studies that report the experiences of parenting an autistic child. The negative consequences of parenting and living with an autistic child have been well documented (Davis and Carter, 2008). Parental shock, trauma, feelings of isolation, anxiety attacks, depression and loss of employment have all been associated with going through the process of an autism childhood diagnosis (Robinson, 2016). Furthermore, parenting an autistic child results in significantly higher levels of stress than parenting a typically developing child or a child with other disabilities (Silva and Schalock, 2011).

Over the last decade, academics and members of the autistic community have voiced challenges surrounding behaviourist interventions and negative narratives of autism, arguing that these are harmful. They have called for more emphasis to be placed on positive accounts (Mottron, 2011). One study found that although parents reported parenting their autistic child as demanding, they experienced growth through learning more about themselves, becoming more empathetic, as well as experiencing moments of hope and happiness (Corman, 2009). Confirmation of this juxtaposition was found in a small group of mothers who experienced autism having a negative impact on the emotional state of the family – and they also voiced a sense of gratitude and pride in their child's achievements (Doui, 2015).

Neurodiversity: An Alternative Narrative

In parallel to this deficit portrayal, during the 1990s, connections people made via the web and autistic self-advocacy pushed the neurodiversity movement forward. A key turning point in recognising autism as difference rather than deficit came through the inspirational *Don't Mourn for Us* speech delivered in 1993 by Jim Sinclair (2010). Autistic self-advocates proposed an alternative construction in which autism is framed as a form of neurodiversity (Singer, 1999). This paradigm shift emphasised the value of neurological difference, to highlight strengths and possibilities of being autistic (van den Bosch et al., 2019). For decades, a perspective on autism as a culture has been proposed (Mesibov and Shea, 1998; Sinclair, 1993). Autistic identity forged a culture of its own with a message of positive identity with the celebration in 2005 of the first autism pride day taking place. Further interesting developments have included, in the United Kingdom, the Labour Party embracing neurodiversity (2019) with a call for acceptance of difference.

Neurodiversity intersects with the wider disability rights movement, with its central premise that variations in neurological development and functioning across humans are a natural and a valuable part of human variation (Kapp, 2020). In accordance with the social model of disability (Oliver, 1990), the most significant premise of neurodiversity is that it is not simply a deficit in the individual, but arises from the interaction between a non-standard individual (or neurotypical) and an unaccommodating environment. From this standpoint, we seek to use preferred terminology within this chapter, which in the UK is identity-first language (Kenny et al., 2016), as well as the more neutral term 'autism' rather than 'Autism Spectrum Disorder'.

The Rights of Young People: No Research about Us without Us!

The United Nations Convention on the Rights of the Child (1989) made the explicit call for adults to listen to the views and aspirations of all children, including disabled children. Obtaining the views of disabled children is a requirement of legislation and policy both national, such as the Children Act (Department for Education and Skills 2005), and international, such as the Convention on the Rights of Persons with Disabilities (2006). Additionally, the Children and Families Act (2014) called for young people's views to be centrally positioned within any decision made about the education, social and health aspects of their lives. However, the Department for Education (DFE) found only 40% of over 2000 young people had been asked if they wanted to be involved in the development of their Education, Health and Care plan (Adams et al., 2018).

Listening to the voices of children extends beyond service delivery to including them in social research, with researchers encouraged to involve children in research concerning them. Not surprisingly, research involving children and young people tends to be research *on them* and about them – the latter often involving research with proxies, such as parents or practitioners. There is limited research including young people's experiences as research participants, with much less research including them in the research process itself. The participation of autistic youth in research falls behind that of their non-autistic peers (Ellis, 2017). James and Prout (2001) claimed that children are the best informants on childhood and matters concerning them. There is increased recognition of the need to include the views of young people, including those with a disability, in research concerning their lives (Lewis, 2009). Ellis (2017) called for researchers to identify better ways to meaningfully engage with autistic youth.

Scott-Barrett, Cebula and Florian (2019) interviewed researchers who were experienced in conducting research with autistic young people. Findings identified power dynamics, building rapport, communication, meaningful processes and outputs as key issues when conducting research with autistic youth. They outlined a number of ethical imperatives to consider in how research participants experience the research process, and also how they are represented in, research outputs. Researchers have a responsibility to facilitate voices captured by those who take part in research and to represent findings in an authentic way. Furthermore, the kind of messages the research communicates about autism is important. To date, most research concerning autistic youth is mostly carried out being *done to* or *about* as opposed to *with* (Milton and Bracher, 2013). It is only by exploring their experiences we can begin to understand what they want society to know about autistic identity.

Uncovering Hidden Voices: An Emancipatory Research Approach

In research, autistic young people may be viewed as a marginalised group, but by including their voices in research can make a significant contribution to social justice and their human rights (Oliver and Barnes, 2010). Emancipatory research is transformative research, seen as emerging from the disability community. Being born out of the motto 'nothing about us, without us', it is a political action aimed to move control of the research into the hands of the community being researched (Mertens, 2015). Emancipatory inquiry employs qualitative and creative methods, allowing participants to affect the direction of the research and thus take control over their words (Shakespeare, 1996). The research participants should be positioned as experts of their own experiences, whilst being enabled to create and validate meaningful narratives (Fisher and Freshwater, 2015). These were the key drivers underpinning our research with autistic young people, as we describe below.

The 'Young Autistic Activist's' Project

The rest of this chapter draws from a research – practice collaboration (Scottish–English respectively) formed in 2019 within the North East Autistic Society in

England, placing autistic youth at the centre of the research process, with the 'Your Rights, Your Say' project. As researchers, we wanted to develop a research project that was meaningful and to explore valuable and relevant topics (Pellicano et al., 2014). We took an emancipatory standpoint, seeing the research process, as a conduit to empower autistic young people to use their lived experience to influence positive societal change. Towards the end of the research process, the participants reclaimed the project and renamed it the 'Autistic Activists' project. This in turn led them to form their own 'Autistic Activists' group.

This study included 30 autistic young people aged between 9 and 16 years of age with a gender balance of 18 males, 10 females and two people identifying as gender neutral. All those who took part in the study had a formal diagnosis of autism. The study used a mixed methods approach using semi-structured interviews, online surveys and creative art classes to garnish rich data throughout the project. This approach enabled autistic youth to engage in all or various parts of the research process. Twenty-five participants took part in a semi-structured interview lasting between 10 and 36 minutes. Five participants took part in a case study that employed creative methods through a series of art classes and a focus group to explore the significance of their art and their experiences of the creative process. This phase of the research included ten art sessions that focused on the research questions of interest: (i) what does autism mean to me? (ii) what do I want others to know about autism? Throughout the sessions, research collaborators were given the opportunity to discuss their creations both as a group and on a one-to-one basis. In the final part of the project, the five participants also took part in a semi-structured focus group where they used their artwork as a focus for an exploratory discussion.

Once the research project ideas had been discussed and to some degree co-designed, the study underwent the process of ethical approval, which was granted by the University of Strathclyde Ethics Committee. As the autistic young people were considered a vulnerable group, both their consent and parental consent were required for participation in the research project. Following the completion of the research additional consent by autistic young people, parents and the organisation was sought. Consent has been granted to use artwork, images and media photography for all societal change activities associated with the project. The data generated with the autistic young people during the project and subsequent following activities are presented below with pseudonyms except where explicit consent to use identifying names has been given (i.e. art work and demonstration photographs).

Listening to the Voices of Autistic Young People's Lived Experience

The following presents the data from the thematic analysis of 'what autism means to me?' which were organised into themes and subthemes (see Table 13.1 for Thematic Analysis). An overarching theme emerged:

TABLE 13.1 Thematic analysis of autistic young peoples' experiences of being autistic

Accept differences because we all are		
Main theme	Subtheme	Illustration
1. WHO SAYS I DON'T FEEL	1.1 Acute sensory experiences (n = 10)	'like my mouth is on fire'
	1.2 Emotion overflow (n = 14)	'and then I'll have a total meltdown'
	1.3 A state of angst (n = 19)	'I am scared, I can't really go on my own, because I am too scared all the time'
2. STUCK IN A TRAUMA LOOP	2.1 Corrosive impact of never fitting in (n = 9)	'I feel like I am not understood by anyone'
	2.2 Masking the real me (n = 7)	'I have to wear my mask at school'
3. LOGICALLY SPEAKING	3.1 All shades, measures and gradients (n = 14)	'It effects every single part of my life'
	3.2 A celebration of one's uniqueness (n = 8)	'unique and you're different from everyone... which I like'
4. LET'S TRY NEURODIVERSITY	4.1 Being more than a stereotype (n = 8)	'...it is also more than Rainman or little boys that like trains, or Sheldon Cooper...'
	4.2 Not mad, bad or dangerous to know (n = 20)	'it is not an evil condition'
	4.3 It's a human right, stop othering us	'We are not less human in anyway just because we are autistic'

Accept difference because we all are. Four themes, comprising ten subthemes, were identified. The four major identified themes are as follows:

1 *Who says I don't feel?* which recognises the extreme and pervasive impact of experiential processing reported by autistic young people.
2 *Stuck in a trauma loop* that recognises the impact autistic young people experience through a sense of feeling as if they are always on the outside looking in on the periphery of mainstream.
3 *Logically speaking* that recognises all aspects of being on the spectrum, across the continuum from the negatives to the positives of being an identified autistic youth.
4 *Let's try neurodiversity* that recognises the power that autistic young people have to assert a different place for themselves in society.

The following expands each theme with the subthemes contained within. The numbers of participants demonstrate shared significance of that subtheme.

Each is expanded upon using direct words used as illustrations from a range of autistic young people who are represented by a pseudonym.

Theme 1: Who Says I Don't Feel?

This theme encapsulates how autistic young people live with the extremes of experiential processing in different aspects of their lives. It contained three subthemes. The majority of autistic young people reported extreme and/or pervasive feelings relating to their sensory experiences, their emotional experiences and how they lived in a constant hypervigilant state most of the time.

Subtheme 1.1: Acute Sensory Experiences

A third of the autistic young people (n = 10) reported experiencing extreme sensory processing issues relating to their senses often triggering fear responses. Sensory atypicalities are commonly reported by autistic people (Robertson and Baron-Cohen, 2017). Participants described the impact of numerous sensory experiences, such as the gustatory system explained by Jenny.

> autism is not being able to eat certain foods even though you love the way they taste, but they are too mushy, or a mix of too mushy and too crunchy at the same time and its awful and you feel like your mouth is on fire.

These experiences accord with previous autistic authors who step into the role of interpretive guides, explaining atypical sensory landscapes. For example, Stephen Shore (2003) explained the impact commonly encountered stimuli had for him, such as searing pain experienced by fluorescent lights and how light touch feels link electric shocks. Similarly, the autistic young people in our research explained how they associated hypersensitivities with being autistic. Heightened sensitivities were experienced as disorientating, painful and triggered fear responses as described by Samantha 'loud noises frighten me'. Our participants spoke about the need to accommodate for hypo-hyper sensitivities of their sensory systems and the need to devise their own strategies to cope. Paul explained 'autism to me is wearing sunglasses every time I go outside because it is too bright, even if it is night time'. This is in line with other studies that stress the emotional impact of sensory experiences, and the need to develop strategies to control or avoid the sensory environment, especially when anxious (e.g. Gara et al., 2020). One young person reported the intersection of sensory processing being exacerbated by social experiences as explained by Jonny.

> the feeling of someone touching us makes me feel ill' and synesthesia in which information meant to stimulate one sense stimulates several senses, as Susie said, 'autism is certain colours being loud.

This resonates with autistic adult experiences that sensory sensitivity had negative physical, emotional and cognitive effects on their daily lives (Charlton et al., 2021).

Subtheme 1.2: Emotion Overflow

Approximately half of the participants (n = 14) spoke of overwhelming emotional experiences, including angry outbursts as described by Liam 'I have anger issues, because I can get annoyed and then I lash out'. Others expressed possessing emotions they felt no control over, as described by Niamh, 'feelings can be uncontrollable and for me I can get angry and start crying all at the same time'. Emotion regulation (ER) difficulties have been reported (Conner et al., 2021) with autistic children possessing poorer ER abilities compared to non-autistic peers (Cibralic et al., 2019) and difficulties managing strong emotions (Mazefsky and White, 2014). Our findings resonate with much that has been documented on emotion processing and understanding. Sally spoke of 'I end up freaking out' or emotional collapse illustrated by Niamh 'and then I'll have a total meltdown' to total exhaustion described by Roddie, 'I end up being burnt out'.

Subtheme 1.3: A State of Angst

Almost two-thirds of autistic young people (n = 19) made reference to some kind of anxiety, often fear-related, as Lisa stated, 'I can't really go out on my own, because I am too scared all the time'. This fear was intrusive in everyday experiences, as explained by George, 'I am always living in fear worrying about where the next noise might come from'. This finding is in line with current research which indicates that a majority of autistic young people (eight-year-olds) have at least one cooccurring psychiatric condition (Soke et al., 2018). Approximately 40% of autistic youth meeting criteria for an anxiety disorder (van Steensel, Bögels and Perrin, 2011). Higher prevalence rates of social anxiety disorder have also been found in the autistic population (Maddox and White, 2015).

Theme 2: Stuck in a Trauma Loop

This theme encapsulates how autistic young people navigate childhood with a perpetual sense of difference from those around them and how they adapt by hiding their real sense of self by putting on a fake persona to avoid exclusion.

Subtheme 2.1: Corrosive Impact of Never Fitting in

Almost a third of participants (n = 9) explained how the social rules did not make sense to them as Mark states, 'people always expect us to do the right thing, and I just don't know what this is most of the time'. This not knowing how to be coupled with a longing to be like other peers was commonly reported with similar statements to the one given here by Janie 'I just want to be normal like my friends', but this was accompanied with feelings that they could never find their place, as Colin stated, 'I feel like I am not understood by anyone'. This feeling of being like an outsider is a phenomenon reported by some of the earliest pioneering autistic authors. Temple Grandin famously describes herself as an 'anthropologist on Mars' who in everyday social situations struggled to 'figure out the natives' (Sacks 1995, p. 256). Similarly, our participants struggled to navigate typical social engagements, as Simon explained, 'just don't expect eye contact' and Paul, 'don't expect physical contact from me'.

Subtheme 2.2: Masking the Real Me

A number of autistic young people (n = 7) had shared experiences of school being a hostile place to be their real self, as Libbie states, 'I have to wear my mask at school'. Masking describes the suppression of aspects of self and identity to 'appear normal', using both conscious (i.e., mimicking facial expressions) and unconscious (i.e., unintentionally suppressing aspects of one's identity) means (Miller, Reese and Pearson, 2021).

Other participants described having to hide behaviours that help them regulate their sensory system, as explained by Laura, 'sometimes I will be spinning around, or I will echo things I have said, I am not being weird this is a coping mechanism'. This need to hide behaviours, such as stimming has been described as camouflaging. The term camouflaging, defined as strategies used to appear less autistic in social interactions (Hull et al., 2017), was a common adaptive strategy used by autistic people as a means of fitting in. Our participants spoke of shared experiences of school being a place to hide whilst home was a safe place where they could be their authentic selves, as David explained,

> as soon as I shut the door behind me and come home it's a massive sigh of relief, my dog is going crazy and it's like finally I can just be my little autistic self. I can turn the lights off and sit in the dark, and I can wear more comfortable clothes and lie on the floor.

Theme 3: Logically Speaking

This theme encapsulates how autistic young people make sense of their own profile of autism and how this impacts them on a daily basis.

Subtheme 3.1: All Shades, Measures and Gradients

Approximately half of the participants (n = 14) spoke about the impact being autistic had on them and how they could appreciate both the benefits and challenges. They spoke of pros and cons of being autistic and echoed the acceptance of identity-first language, how autism *was them* and the rejection of person-first language, not how autism was *with them* (Kenny et al., 2016). Shaun explained 'autism affects every single part of my life'. His experience today still resonates with the early statement advocated by Jim Sinclair (1993, p. 1):

> Autism isn't something a person has, or a 'shell' that a person is trapped inside. It is pervasive, it colours every experience, every sensation, perception, thought, emotion, and encounter, every aspect of existence.

This strength and challenge dichotomy was acknowledged by both Kieran, 'it's like a double-edged sword' and Amanda, 'it's a burden and a gift'. Others recognised extreme challenges, as Paul stated, 'It is good for me in some areas but in social situations its crippling'. Some of the young people held diagrammatically opposed views to being autistic, voicing the negative experience, Trudy stated, 'autism is an embarrassment' and by Adam, 'autism ruins everything'. Voicing her positive experience, Natasha stated, 'autism is the greatest thing a person can have'.

Subtheme 3.2: A Celebration of One's Uniqueness

Almost one-third (n = 8) of autistic young people spoke about viewing autism in a celebratory way from the benefits it afforded them. This related to feelings of difference, for some, like Matt they were happy, 'you're unique and you're different from everyone, which I like'. Others, like Darren explained, 'our brains are just wired differently'. Others agreed with this acceptance of difference, given here by Karen 'it doesn't really matter if you're autistic or not, everyone is different'. Others spoke about their openness about being autistic as Lorna stated, 'I tell everyone I am autistic' whilst others felt proudly autistic as Eddie said, 'autism is something to be proud of'. This accords with Swain and French's (2000) affirmation model of disability pointing to how we can promote emotional well-being by harnessing a positive celebration of being autistic. We agree that personal acceptance of autism as part of one's identity could protect against depression and anxiety, as well as having a positive view of autism being associated with a stronger sense of affiliation to the autistic community (Cooper et al., 2021).

Theme 4: Let's Try Neurodiversity

This theme encapsulates how the autistic youth reject negative narratives and advocate acceptance by society.

Subtheme 4.1: Being More Than a Stereotype

Almost one-third of participants (n = 8) complained about how autistic people are portrayed in the media, through films and on TV and how non-autistic people make assumptions about them based upon these. Portrayals of autistic characters on film and in TV series are increasing which presents both pros, such as increasing public awareness and cons, such as increasing stereotypes (Nordahl-Hansen, Øien and Fletcher-Watson, 2018). Media representations of autistic people often portray them negatively (Maras, Mulcahy and Crane, 2015). The participants took issue with how others viewed them based upon these stereotypes, as Donny stated, 'it is also more than Rainman or little boys that like trains, or Sheldon Cooper'. The way autistic people are portrayed in the media is based upon stereotypes of a narrow view of autism, as Darren explained,

> I felt the stereotypes of what autistic people were like wasn't like me. I could speak, I could walk, I could feed myself. Because when people think of autism they think of low functioning.

Other participants expressed having experienced a lack of empathy or understanding from others in a position of support or power to make a significant difference in their life, as shown here by Tommy of his experiences of pupil-teacher interactions:

> I'm very academic, so my teachers assume I can cope with last minute changes or do social activities. They sometimes find it hard to understand how I can answer complex math questions, but I would struggle to find a new seat to sit in.

Subtheme 4.2: Not Mad, Bad or Dangerous to Know

Two-thirds (n = 20) of the autistic young people experienced negative narratives and stereotyping from those around them, which they wanted to reject. This accords with autistic peoples' experiences of stigma. Sasson and colleagues (2017) found that non-autistic individuals tend to make rapid unfavourable judgements about autistic people. Autism has been associated with negative traits, such as being disruptive (White et al., 2016). Our participants reported having experienced negative attributes associated with being autistic, which they wanted to reject. Mindy said, 'we are not just naughty'; Freddie: 'we are not crazy'; Paul stated, 'we are not stupid or freaks' and a more broadly shared experience described here by Debbie, 'it doesn't make them any more or less of a person'. These experiences accord with research on stereotypes depicting autistic people as dangerous (Jones and Harwood, 2009) or emotionless (Harnum, Duffy and Ferguson, 2007). Autism as an empathy disorder was rejected, as Ronnie stated, 'some people think we have no empathy for others and this isn't true' whilst David stated, 'we are not like psychopaths'. The accuracy of autistic stereotypes has been questioned, with evidence suggesting that the vast majority of autistic people are not emotionless (Tierney et al., 2016).

Subtheme 4.3: It's a Human Right, Stop Othering Us

More than two-thirds of the participants (n = 24) expressed a feeling of being othered by society as a whole and by people they come into contact with directly, including parents, siblings, peers and teachers. Our participants had, on the basis of their experiences, concluded that autism was viewed as 'less than', as Kieran stated, countering this: 'we are not less human in any way just because we are autistic'. Others had experiences of being viewed through a deficit lens as Julie described, 'people see us as "broken", and so they pity us'. Goffman (1963) defined stigma as social process that occurs when the public responds negatively to an attribute of a person. That attribute becomes deeply discrediting and reduces the person from a whole and usual person to a tainted, discounted one. Their identity is 'spoiled'. Our findings demonstrate that at an early age young autistic people have already encountered stigma, which mirrors autistic adult experiences of a lack of autism acceptance from society contributing to their experiences of social isolation and anxiety (Griffith et al., 2012). Autistic adults view stigma as inescapable (Botha, Dibb and Frost, 2022). In order to avoid stigma, many engage in behaviours such as masking or camouflaging designed to help them to 'pass' as non-autistic in order to fit into the non-autistic world (Hull et al., 2017).

This experience of being othered, and associated rejection, was voiced by a number of autistic young people. Liam stated, 'I have human wants and ambitions' echoed by Jonny 'we deserve the same rights as everyone else and the same chances'. With this final subtheme, participants held a shared desire to advocate a strong message that they wanted society to hear, stated here by Martin, 'we don't need fixing; we don't need pitying. People need to replace that pity with a healthy respect for differences'. Some feared the implications of how this othering might manifest as described by Danny:

> I worry about them finding a way to cure us and then all autistic people going mad, and that wouldn't be good because I know probably about one billion people on the planet are autistic.

This section presented the thematic analysis of autistic young people's lived experiences of being autistic. These demonstrate not only the strong negative messages that surround their childhoods but also their capacity as active agents for future change. Their voiced experiences help us see how such negative narratives are already pervasive at such a young age. These come from many sources including parents, peers, teachers, the media portrayal of sensationalist narratives, the characters portrayed in films and TV and the ever increasing presence of social media.

Using Creative Methods to Elicit Voice: Our Pictures Are as Good as Our Words!

Staying close to the young people's words and meanings was an important process within data analysis of the Autistic Activist project. Harrington et al. (2014) proposed that researchers need to plan creatively and flexibly for the interactive dynamic that is unique to each autistic individual to enable them to provide rich and meaningful insights into their own lives. This is supported through the use of creative methods and the use of art pieces within focus groups as real active agents within research.

Whilst the spoken word can give us an in-depth understanding from such narrative accounts, the use of art includes more emotional connection (Eales and Peters, 2016), thus making research more appealing to youth and accessible to those who may encounter barriers. This research project used art not only as a means of giving voice to experience but also as a vehicle for self-agency. Our aim was to provide a sense of empowerment by facilitating individual and collective messages to a society that often oppresses. Through this creative research process, the pieces of art had a themed message that tended to flip the narrative that largely surrounds autism to date. The messages expressed through the artwork affirm that autistic young people have already experienced life through a deficit lens. Their artwork rejected the negative narrative but was indicative that they had already experienced ableist encounters. Many drawings flipped the deficit narrative by insisting on acceptance of difference and challenging those aspects of what is commonly portrayed as an intrinsic part of the dyad of 'impairments'.

All those who took part in the creative art classes, interviews and focus groups were asked to select one piece of artwork that they felt gave the most important message to society and one piece was chosen (see Figure 13.1) by all those who made a selection. It was felt collectively that 'not looking, still listening' represented their lived experience the most. It was one thing that was expressed in differing ways by many, and the one thing they really wanted non-autistic people to get, encapsulated in Annie's statement, 'This message is very true, I have experienced people thinking I am not listening because I am not looking at them. Looking at people when communicating is embarrassing and really uncomfortable. I wish people would know this'.

FIGURE 13.1 'Not Looking: Still Listening' by Lucie Kendall, age 13

When asked to talk about the art piece and its significance, Lucie said,

> I have focused on using eyes in this picture as it really annoys me when people think I am not listening to them because I am not looking. This is not the case at all, I do it because it is easier for me.

This view was echoed by other participants when asked to select the piece of art they felt best represented the message they wanted other people to hear and what they wanted society to know about autism. Amanda said she chose this artwork because 'you don't need eye contact, to be able to hear. In fact, it can be much easier to hear without eye contact' and Lee 'people not understanding eye contact is difficult for me, is something I face at school, and at home and represents my life on a daily basis'.

The artwork brought the subthemes to life and their creativity enabled the autistic young people to have a stronger voice than was afforded through words alone. Understanding and acceptance of difference is shown in one piece of artwork that *celebrates autism uniqueness* (see Figure 13.2). When discussing his artwork in the focus group, Ed said, 'Every autistic person is unique and many of us have lots of strengths that non autistic people do not have'.

FIGURE 13.2 'Every Autism is Unique' by Edward Armstrong, age 12

Another piece of art that also counters the negative narrative encapsulated in the theme *not mad, bad, or dangerous to know* (see Figure 13.3). When sharing what his artwork represented, James said, 'It's clear, you need to listen, we are not stupid or freaks and yes, of course I can still learn'. The message represented in the art is clear and comes from a place that rejects the ableist attitudes and the stigma that surrounds them. This chimes with the view that the most disabling factors are the structures of society, the oppression of stereotypes and the power of the majority (Haraldsdóttir, 2013). The participants gave voice to a strong message for educators calling for change. Furthermore, they call for a need to teach autistic young people in the way that they learn, to break down barriers set up through ableist views and to incorporate a strength-based approach to teaching, that draws upon autistic strengths of creativity, in love of nature, in humour. After all, as James states, laughing wryly with the others, 'What's not to love about a rhinoceros wearing shades?'

From Research to Action!

The previous section demonstrates how the artwork contained messages that the young people wanted to voice and for society to hear which resulted in an art exhibition (see Figure 13.4) displaying all artwork. This aligns with

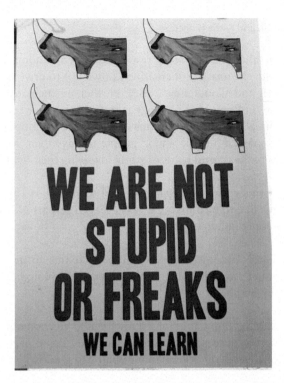

FIGURE 13.3 'We are not Stupid or Freaks' by James Parker, aged 13

FIGURE 13.4 Artwork displayed at the Autistic Activists Art Exhibition at the 'Thought Foundation', Birtley, England

recommendations that emancipatory researchers need to adopt a transformative paradigm with the mission of creating knowledge to drive positive change in society (Danieli and Woodhams, 2005). Further, emancipatory researchers' key objective and underpinning ideology is to foster positive social change for those living with disabilities. Taking this emancipatory standpoint during the research project enabled autistic young people to have their voices heard; essentially, they were the central focus of study involving their lives. As Ed states,

> Being part of this exhibition made me feel so proud as I want people to know what it's like to be autistic. It was great to be part of something that might help people understand more.

During the research process, some of the participants formed the 'Autism Activists' becoming empowered as active agents of change. This impact is best explained by Stephen,

> Being part of this group has changed my life and view on autism. I used to think that there was something wrong with me. Being part of this group empowers me to educate others about what being autistic means.

Following on the research came a shared sense of social justice, to fight for the rights of all autistic youth, which culminated in a march against Special Educational Needs and Disabilities (SEND) cuts (see Figure 13.5). Some of the Autism Activists transformed art into placards and their hard-hitting messages were carried to Westminster calling on the government to end SEND funding cuts. They joined thousands of other families protesting over funding cuts that left many pupils without appropriate support and unable to attend school. After delivering a 13,000-name petition to Downing Street, James stated, 'I was excited to hand over the petition so what happened to me doesn't happen again'.

These often hidden voices are keen to educate others so they can be understood, as Jonny states,

> it's not just the message that's important ('not looking, still listening'), but what is behind the message. It shows that we are very different to neurotypicals, yet they still insist we behave like them. Why would you expect one thing to act like another, it makes no sense!

Autistic young people want to contribute to positive societal change through indirect and direct action. Those who took part in the Autistic Activist project demonstrate how they take their place as social actors who actively shape and respond to their social world (James, Jenks and Prout, 1998). When

FIGURE 13.5 March Against SEND Cuts (from left to right James Parker, Albie Rose, Quinn Rose and Alex Parker)

spaces are created they can suggest changes to service provision, such as possible impacts within education as Lexi stated, 'we need to have neurodiversity in curriculum like LGBT issues'.

Overall, the project was a positive experience for those involved and findings resonate with the conclusion advocated by Pellicano (2018) that the only real way to best support young people is to ask them what they need. Autistic young people have much to say and are empowered when spaces are created where they can be heard. Lucie stated, 'I feel like a weight has been lifted off my shoulders by talking'. Our study found that autistic young people want the opportunity to have their experiences heard and acknowledged. We found a lack of engagement of autistic young people in research about their lives, as Ronnie stated, 'people study us like lab rats instead of just asking us', but most significantly how they felt empowered through engagement with the research questions and activities, as Jenny stated, 'I'd never been asked questions about autism before'. A shared sense of activism and empowerment emerged during the research process facilitated a range of research outputs as autistic youth became actors of societal change.

Conclusion

By involving autistic young people in research about their lives, we have shown how they can articulate autistic childhoods from this insider perspective. In this chapter, we give voice to their experience. We show how ableist attitudes surround most aspects of their lives, and how experiences of stigma manifest by autistic young people engaging in camouflaging behaviours in an attempt to hide their authentic self in an attempt to pass as being non-autistic. This in turn impacts their mental health, increasing cooccurring conditions such as anxiety and depression, which ultimately erodes their sense of self. We argue that we need to listen to the insights afforded to us in order to prevent future spoiled identities (Goffman, 1963). Through creative methods, autistic young people become empowered to become active agents for societal change. We argue that the gains of involving autistic young people in emancipatory research about their lives are two-fold. Not only is it a life-affirming experience enabling them to become self-advocates, but it also creates a space for shared empathy. As we see their empathic response is to prevent other autistic young people from experiencing the pain they have experienced. We call for autistic young people to be involved in shaping all aspects of their lives.

References

Adams, L., Tindle, A., Basran, S., Dobie, S., Thomson, D., Robinson, D. and Codina, G. 2018. *Education, health and care plans: a qualitative investigation into service user experiences of the planning process*. London: DfE.

American Psychiatric Association. 2013. *Diagnostic and statistical manual of mental disorders*. 5th ed. Washington, DC: American Psychiatric Association.

Botha, M., Dibb, B. and Frost, D.M. 2022. 'Autism is me': an investigation of how autistic individuals make sense of autism and stigma. *Disability & Society*. 37(3), pp. 427–453.

Charlton, R.A., Entecott, T., Belova, E. and Nwaordu, G. 2021. 'It feels like holding back something you need to say': Autistic and Non-Autistic Adults accounts of sensory experiences and stimming. *Research in Autism Spectrum Disorders*. 89, pp. 101864.

Cibralic, S., Kohlhoff, J., Wallace, N., McMahon, C. and Eapen, V. 2019. A systematic review of emotion regulation in children with autism spectrum disorder. *Research in Autism Spectrum Disorders*. 68, pp. 1–21.

Conner, C.M., Golt, J., Shaffer, R.C., Righi, G., Siegel, M. and Mazefsky, C.A. 2021. Emotion dysregulation is substantially elevated in autism compared to the general population: impact on psychiatric services. *Autism Research*. 14(1), pp. 169–181.

Convention on the Rights of the Child. 1989. [online] [Accessed on 10.10.2022]. Available from: https://treaties.un.org/doc/Treaties/1990/09/19900902%2003-14%20AM/Ch_IV_11p.pdf

Cooper, D.K., Smith, L. and Russell, A. 2017. Social identity, self-esteem, and mental health in autism. *European Journal of Social Psychology*. 47, pp. 844–854.

Cooper, R., Cooper, K., Russell, A.J. and Smith, L.G.E. 2021. 'I'm proud to be a little bit different': the effects of autistic individuals' perceptions of autism and autism social identity on their collective self-esteem. *Journal of Autism and Developmental Disorders*. **51**, pp. 704–714.

Corman, M.K. 2009. The positives of caregiving: mothers' experiences caregiving for a child with autism. *Families in Society: The Journal of Contemporary Social Services*. **90**(4), pp. 439–445.

Danieli, A. and Woodhams, C. 2005. Emancipatory research methodology and disability: a critique. *International Journal of Social Research Methodology*. **8**(4), pp. 281–296.

Davis, N.O. and Carter, A.S. 2008. Parenting stress in mothers and fathers of toddlers with autism spectrum disorders: associations with child characteristics. *Journal of Autism and Developmental Research*. **38**, pp. 1278–1291.

Department for Education and Skills. 2005. *Departmental Report*. [online] [Accessed on 1.11.2022]. Available from: https://assets.publishing.service.gov.uk/government/uploads/system/uploads/attachment_data/file/272106/6522.pdf

Doui, I. 2015. The experiences of parents for emotional interaction with children with autism: a systemic approach. *Journal of Psychiatry*. **18**(5), pp. 310–319.

Eales, L. and Peters, D. 2016. Moving adapted physical activity: the possibilities of arts-based research. *Quest*. **68**(1), pp. 55–68.

Ellis, J. 2017. Researching the social worlds of autistic children: an exploration of how an understanding of autistic children's social worlds is best achieved. *Children and Society*. **31**(1), pp. 23–36.

Elsabbagh, M., Divan, G., Koh, Y.J., Kim, Y.S., Kauchali, S., Marcín, C. ... Yasamy, M.T. 2012. Global prevalence of autism and other pervasive developmental disorders. *Autism Research*. **5**, pp. 160–179.

Fisher, P. and Freshwater, D. 2015. An emancipatory approach to practice and qualitative inquiry in mental health: finding 'voice' in Charles Taylor's ethics of identity. *Ethics and Social Welfare*. **9**(1), pp. 2–17.

Gara, S.K., Chhetri, A.G., Alrjoob, M., Abbasi, S.A.A. and Rutkofsky, I.H. 2020. The sensory abnormalities and neuropsychopathology of autism and anxiety. *Cureus*. **12**(5), p. 8071.

Goffman, E. 1963. *Stigma*. Englewood Cliffs, NJ: Prentice-Hall.

Griffith, G.M., Totsika, V., Nash, S. and Hastings, R.P. 2012. 'I just don't fit anywhere': support experiences and future support needs of individuals with Asperger syndrome in middle adulthood. *Autism*. **16**(5), pp. 532–546.

Haraldsdóttir, F. 2013. Simply children. In Curran, T. and Runswick-Cole, K. eds. *Disabled children's childhood studies: critical approaches in a global context*. Basingstoke, UK: Palgrave Macmillan, pp. 13–21.

Harnum, M., Duffy, J. and Ferguson, D.A. 2007. Adults' versus children's perceptions of a child with autism or attention deficit hyperactivity disorder. *Journal of Autism and Developmental Disorders*. **37**(7), pp. 1337–1343.

Harrington, C., Foster, M., Rodger, S. and J. Ashburner. 2014. Engaging young people with autism spectrum disorder in research interviews. *British Journal of Learning Disabilities*, **42**(2), pp. 153–161.

Hull, L., Petrides, K.V., Allison, C., Smith, P., Baron-Cohen, S., Lai, M. and Mandy, W. 2017. 'Putting on my best normal': social camouflaging in adults with autism spectrum conditions. *Journal of Autism and Developmental Disorders*. **47**(8), pp. 2519–2534.

Ikeda, E., Hinckson, E. and Krägeloh, C. 2014. Assessment of quality of life in children and youth with autism spectrum disorder: a critical review. *Quality of Life Research*. **23**, pp. 1069–1085.

James, A., Jenks, C. and Prout, A. 1998. *Theorizing childhood*. Cambridge: Polity Press.

James, A. and Prout, J. 2001. *Constructing and reconstructing childhood*. London: Routledge.

Jones, S.C. and Harwood, V. 2009. Representations of Autism in Australian print media. *Disability & Society*. **24**(1), pp. 5–18.

Kapp, S.K. 2020. *Autistic community and the neurodiversity movement*. Singapore: Palgrave Macmillan.

Kenny, L., Hattersley, C., Molins, B., Buckley, C., Povey, C. and Pellicano, E. 2016. Which terms should be used to describe autism? Perspectives from the UK autism community. *Autism*. **20**, pp. 442–462.

Lewis, A. 2009. Methodological issues in exploring the ideas of children with autism concerning self and spirituality. *Journal of Religion Disability & Health*. **13**, pp. 64–76.

Maddox, B.B. and White, S.W. 2015. Comorbid social anxiety disorder in adults with autism spectrum disorder. *Journal of Autism and Developmental Disorders*. **45**, pp. 3949–3960.

Maras, K., Mulcahy, S. and Crane, L. 2015. Is autism linked to criminality? *Autism*. **19**(5), pp. 515–516.

Mazefsky, C.A. and White, S.W. 2014. Emotion regulation. *Child and Adolescent Psychiatric Clinics of North America*. **23**(1), pp. 15–24.

Mertens, D.M. 2015. *Research and evaluation in education and psychology*. Thousand Oaks: Sage.

Mesibov, G. and Shea, V. 1998. *The culture of autism: from theoretical understanding to educational practice*. Plenum: New York.

Miller, D., Rees, J. and Pearson, A. 2021. 'Masking is life': experiences of masking in autistic and nonautistic adults. *Autism in Adulthood*. **3**(4), 330–338.

Milton, D.E. and Bracher, M. 2013. Autistics speak but are they heard? *Medical Sociology Online*. **7**(2), pp. 61–69.

Morgan, C., Wedd, RT., Carr, M.J., Kontopantelis, E., Green, J., Chew-Graham, C.A., Kapur, N. and Ashcroft, D.M. 2017. Incidence, clinical management, and mortality risk following self-harm among children and adolescents: cohort study in primary care. *British Medical Journal*. **359**, j4351.

Mottron, L. 2011. Changing perceptions: the power of autism. *Nature*. **479**(7371), pp. 33–35.

Nordahl-Hansen, A., Øien, R.A. and Fletcher-Watson, S. 2018. Pros and cons of character portrayals of autism on TV and film. *Journal of Autism and Developmental Disorders*. **48**, pp. 635–636.

Oliver, M. 1990. *The politics of disablement*. London: Palgrave.

Oliver, M. and Barnes, C. 2010. Disability studies, disabled people and the struggle for inclusion. *British Journal of Sociology of Education*. **31**(5), pp. 547–560.

Pellicano, E. 2018. Engaging 'seldom heard' individuals in participatory autism research. In: Milton, D. and Martin, N. eds. *Autism and learning disability annual*. London: Pavilion Publishing, pp. 29–34.

Pellicano, E., Dinsmore, A. and T. Charman. 2014. What should autism research focus upon? Community views and priorities from the United Kingdom. *Autism*. 18(7), pp. 756–770.

Robertson, C.E. and Baron-Cohen, S. 2017. Sensory perception in autism. *Nature Reviews Neuroscience*. 18(11), pp. 671–684.

Robinson, A. 2016. An evaluation report of the Right Click Parent Training Programme. *Scottish Autism*. [online] [Accessed on 18.02.2022]. Available from: https://www.scottishautism.org/sites/default/files/right_click_report_by_anna_robinson.pdf

Robinson, A. 2018. Emotion-focused therapy for autism spectrum disorder: a case conceptualization model for trauma-related experiences. *Journal of Contemporary Psychotherapy*. 48(3), pp. 133–143.

Rowley, E., Chandler, S., Baird, G., Simonoff, E., Pickles, A., Loucas, T. and Charman, T. 2012. The experience of friendship, victimization and bullying in children with an autism spectrum disorder: associations with child characteristics and school placement. *Research in Autism Spectrum Disorders*. 6, pp. 1126–1134.

Sacks, O. 1995. *An anthropologist on Mars*. London: Picador.

Sasson, N.J., Faso, D.J., Nugent, J., Lovell, S., Kennedy, D.P. and Grossman, R.B. 2017. Neurotypical peers are less willing to interact with those with autism based on thin slice judgments. *Scientific Reports*. 7, p. 40700.

Scott-Barrett, J., Cebula, K. and Florian, L. 2019. Listening to young people with autism: learning from researcher experiences. *International Journal of Research and Method in Education*. 42(2), pp. 163–184.

Shakespeare, T. 1996. Rules of engagement: doing disability research. *Disability & Society*. 11(1), pp. 115–119.

Shore, S. 2003. *Beyond the wall: personal experiences with autism and Asperger syndrome*. 2nd ed. Kansas: Autism Asperger Pub.

Silva, L.M.T. and Schalock, M. 2011. Autism parenting stress index: initial psychometric evidence. *Journal of Autism Developmental Disorder*. 42, pp. 566–574.

Sinclair, J. 1993. Don't mourn for us. Our Voice, 1(3). [online] [Accessed on 15.12.2022]. Available from: https://philosophy.ucsc.edu/SinclairDontMournForUs.pdf

Sinclair, J. 2010. Cultural commentary: being autistic together. *Disability Studies Quarterly*. 30(1), pp. 1–4.

Singer J. 1999. "Why can't you be normal for once in your life?" From a "problem with no name" to the emergence of a new category of difference. In: Corker, M. and French, S. eds. *Disability discourse*. Buckingham: Open University Press, pp. 59–67.

Soke, G.N., Maenner, M.J., Christensen, D., Kurzius- Spencer, M. and Schieve, L.A. 2018. Prevalence of co-occurring medical and behavioral conditions/symptoms among 4-and 8- year-old children with autism spectrum disorder in selected areas of the United States in 2010. *Journal of Autism and Developmental Disorders*. 48, pp. 2663–2676.

Swain, J. and French, S. 2000. Towards an affirmation model of disability. *Disability & Society*. 15(4), pp. 569–582.

Tierney, S., Burns, J. and Kilbey, E. 2016. Looking behind the mask: social coping strategies of girls on the autistic spectrum. *Research in Autism Spectrum Disorders*. 23, pp. 73–83.

UN General Assembly, Convention on the Rights of Persons with Disabilities: resolution/adopted by the General Assembly, 24 January 2007, A/RES/61/106. Available from: https://www.refworld.org/docid/45f973632.html

van den Bosch, K.E., Krzeminska, A., Song, E.Y., van Hal, L.B.E., Waltz, M.M., Ebben, H. and Schippers, A.P. 2019. Nothing about us, without us: a case study of a consumer-run organization by and for people on the autism spectrum in the Netherlands. *Journal of Management and Organization*. **25**, pp. 464–480.

van Steensel, F.J., Bögels, S.M. and Perrin, S. 2011. Anxiety disorders in children and adolescents with autistic spectrum disorders: a meta-analysis. *Clinical Child and Family Psychology Review*. **14**, pp. 302–317.

White, D., Hillier, A., Frye, A. and Makrez, E. 2016. College students' knowledge and attitudes towards students on the autism spectrum. *Journal of Autism and Developmental Disorders*. **49**, pp. 2699–2705.

Zablotsky, B., Black, L.I., Maenner, M.J., Schieve, L.A. and Blumberg, S.J. 2015. Estimated prevalence of autism and other developmental disabilities following questionnaire changes in the 2014 National Health Interview Survey. *National Health Statistics Reports*. **87**, pp. 1–20.

14

'NORMAL, DIFFERENT, OR SOMETHING IN BETWEEN'

Young People with Autism and Down Syndrome and Psycho-Emotional Disablism

Alice Scavarda

Introduction

> *Having a defect means that each of us is incomplete*
> *And this defect may be remedied*
> *Only by someone you care about*
> *And who loves you.*
> Camillo, 28-year-old man with Down syndrome

The idea of the incompleteness of every human being, which can only be compensated through interdependence (Goodley and Runswick-Cole 2016; Mladenov 2016), inspires the research presented in this chapter. The chapter, thus, opens with the words of a poem by a young man with Down syndrome: 'Your own defect' to give voice to young people with cognitive disabilities and to reflect upon the possession of defects as inherent in humanity, beyond the category of cognitive disabilities. The term 'cognitive disability' refers to a group of people who face barriers in a society that requires proficiency in certain cognitive abilities (Kittay and Carlson 2010). Among others, it includes people with intellectual/developmental disabilities, autistic people, and people with Alzheimer's. The focus of this chapter is on the experiences of adolescents with autism or Down syndrome, because they are considered as different in terms of visibility of the condition and timing of the diagnosis.

People with cognitive disabilities have been long marginalised both within disability studies (Goodley and Van Hove 2005) and within qualitative research (Stalker 2019). On the one hand, as far as early disability studies are concerned, cognitive disabilities did not fit into the original definition of

DOI: 10.4324/9781003102915-14

disability advanced by the first generation of disability studies scholars. The original UPIAS (Union of the Physically Impaired Against Segregation) social interpretation of disability focused on the group of 'physically impaired people' (UPIAS 1976, p. 4). On the other hand, as far as qualitative research is concerned, people with cognitive disabilities present specific sensorial and communication skills, and certain ways of interacting with and perceiving the outside world, which may be challenging for traditional qualitative methodologies (Gilbert 2004). However, a number of methods have been developed that enable persons with cognitive disabilities to participate in research (see, for instance, Walmsley 2010; Milner and Frawley 2019). These methods have been largely based on the social model of disability. Although widely experienced by people with cognitive disabilities, psycho-emotional disablism has been underexplored in relation to this group (Stalker 2019). The study presented herein investigated the psycho-emotional dimensions of disablism and their impact on the social identities of young people with autism and Down syndrome, by using arts-based research methods (Kara 2015; Leavy 2017).

The Concept of Psycho-Emotional Disablism

Carol Thomas (1999), in her renowned book *Female forms*, contributed to the theoretical development of the social model of disability by considering not only the unequal access to social opportunities of disabled people but also the personal experience of disability and the daily effects of impairment. To Thomas, disability is 'a form of social oppression involving the social imposition of restrictions of activity on people with impairments and the socially engendered undermining of their psycho-emotional wellbeing' (Thomas 1999, p. 60).

Disability, therefore, is a form of oppression at both the structural and the personal level, affecting what people can do as well as who they can be. Thomas (1999) draws a distinction between 'barriers to doing', namely the restrictions of activity due to social structure design (transports, inaccessible buildings) and 'barriers to being', caused by psycho-emotional disablism. The latter refers to the hurtful or hostile behaviour of others – for example, being stared at, laughed at, and made to feel unattractive or inferior – which diminishes a person's sense of self-worth. The agents of this disablism can be family members or individuals with whom disabled people have direct contact such as professionals, in addition to disablism experienced within society at large. Both the experiences of structural and of psycho-emotional disablism can prevent disabled people from being socially included. According to Donna Reeve (2004), psycho-emotional dimensions of disablism assume three different forms: responses to experiences of structural disablism, namely the emotional costs of being excluded; social interactions with others, for example being stared at with the consequent feeling of shame and vulnerability; and internalised oppression (Mason 1990), the acceptance and internalisation of prejudices widespread in society which make disabled people feel devalued and disempowered.

Numerous international studies have shown that people with cognitive disabilities are often patronised, pitied, bullied, and the victims of hate crime (see, for instance, Björnsdóttir and Traustadóttir 2010 for the Icelandic context; Levin 2012 for the US context; Lewis 2002; Macdonald 2015 for the British context; Ralli et al. 2011 for the Greek context). There is therefore much potential in applying the concept of psycho-emotional disablism to this group in the field of disability studies. However, these issues have been indirectly addressed by the self-advocacy movement led by people with cognitive disabilities.

Psycho-Emotional Disablism and Cognitive Disabilities: A Missing Link?

People with cognitive disabilities were largely ignored by the first generations of disability studies scholars (Stalker 2019). They were 'left out in the cold', as the title of Chappell's (1997) article states. Aspis (2000) argues that the social model of disability, in its first version, failed to address their barriers to social inclusion. These were often 'barriers to being', as well as access to information (Stalker and Lerpiniere 2009) invisible and hard to detect, rather than 'barriers to doing', the material barriers experienced by people with physical and sensory disabilities. This omission, among others, reinforced disempowerment of people with cognitive disabilities (Docherty et al. 2010).

The 'barriers to being' faced by people with cognitive disabilities have been put into light by self-advocacy movements, like People First (Goodley 2001; Stalker 2019) and social groups based upon the neurodiversity approach (Scavarda and Cascio 2022). People First, as well as the multifaceted neurodiversity movement, shed light on stigmatised and labelling conceptions of cognitively disabled people, based on biomedical knowledge. Both types of organisations criticise the biomedical perspective of cognitive disabilities because it implies a normative way of thinking, learning, and behaving and, consequently, it frames deviations from the norm as deficits. Activists maintain that people with cognitive disabilities are systematically discriminated against and have access to fewer life chances because of their presumed inability to adapt to the social environment. This inability, in the biomedical view, is due to genetic dysfunctions and disorders, brought forth by diagnostic labels which are constitutive of people's identity (Gillman, Heyman and Swain 2000). The international People First movement provides a self-definition, alternative to other terms used outside the UK, like intellectual disability. Activists put forward the expression 'learning difficulties', a specific expression used in the UK, which implies people's willingness to learn and a distributed notion of ability (Goodley 2001), like interdependence, alluded to by the poem at the beginning of the chapter. These more dignified conceptions, alongside the change in the US from 'mental retardation' to 'intellectual disability' (Goodley and Rapley 2001) challenge genetically oriented definitions of personhood, according to which inability is grounded in organic and immutable impairments. Likewise, the term 'neurodiversity', firstly developed within autistic advocacy movements and then extended to other conditions, like Attention Deficit Hyperactivity Disorder (ADHD), schizophrenia, and mood disorders, promotes a de-medicalised perspective of neurological differences as part of human variation (Armstrong 2010).

While many disabled activists advance a positive concept of disability, as a form of pride, self-advocacy movements of people with cognitive disabilities tended to reject being labelled as disabled and reclaimed their humanity. As a matter of fact, the slogan of People First movement, as Stalker pointed out (2019) is 'Label jars, not people'. Although the author reported examples of people with cognitive disabilities who celebrated their impairments, she concluded that the most common strategy for this group is to refuse the stigmatised traits related to their condition and to differentiate themselves from people with more profound impairments.

Nonetheless, self-advocacy groups (such as People First) and neurodiversity groups can be a collective means of representation of persons with cognitive disabilities to combat psycho-emotional disablism, speak up for themselves, and articulate their experiences from their perspectives. One crucial way to allow people with cognitive disabilities express their points of view – in line with the motto 'Nothing about us, without us' – is to involve them within the research process.

Research 'With' and Not 'On' Cognitively Disabled People

Until relatively recently, academia seemed to be unable to take cognitively disabled researchers seriously (Bjornsdottir and Svensdóttir 2008). There were several reasons for this. Firstly, what is often termed the 'strong' version of the social model of disability arguably neglected personal experience of oppression as a relevant site of knowledge and power. Conversely, many people with cognitive disabilities focused on their own stories by using life history methods (Atkinson 2004). Secondly, for a long time people with sensory or physical disabilities distanced themselves from people with cognitive disabilities, by creating a sort of a hierarchy of impairments within disability studies (Docherty et al. 2010). Thirdly, emancipatory research was the methodological approach applied by social model proponents because disabled people control the research process, unlike participatory research, where the researcher leads the research activities (Watson 2019). As Atkinson (1997) highlighted, some people with cognitive disabilities have little or no access to written and spoken words and find research activities extremely challenging. To be involved in a research process, people with cognitive disabilities must often develop alliances with people without cognitive disabilities, but with resulting questionable power relationships (Walmsley 2010). Thus, emancipatory research, whilst not impossible, is more challenging to achieve for people with cognitive disabilities.

Whilst the debate continues within disability studies regarding the possibility of people with cognitive disabilities to conducting research and developing theoretical concepts without the help of academics or non-disabled supporters (Stalker 2019), moves have been made to enable their participation in this regard. Over the past couple of decades, a number of scholars have maintained that researchers should develop ways to engage people with cognitive disabilities in both theorising and researching (Goodley and Lawthom 2005; Walmsley 2001). Various attempts have been made to involve cognitively disabled people (for example: Bigby, Frawley and Ramcharan 2014; Milner and Frawley 2019; Genova, Scavarda, and Świątkiewicz-Mośny 2023; Scavarda et al. 2021) and particularly children and young people (Liddiard et al. 2022) within research, thus producing a considerable body of knowledge on the topic. They used not only narrative methods, like life history (see, for example, Atkinson 2004) or (auto)biographical accounts (Booth 2018; Milner and Frawley 2019) but also action research (Burke et al. 2003) or quality of life research (Rapley 2003).

Inclusive Research with Cognitively Disabled (Young) People

While research with cognitively disabled people developed, it simultaneously gave rise to a controversy about the use of participatory or emancipatory techniques (see, for instance, Danieli and Woodhams 2005). Both the techniques imply the involvement of the subject, but while participatory techniques are usually implied to answer the research questions, emancipatory techniques are mainly aimed at empowering people, thus implementing civil rights (ibidem). Walmsley's (2001) concept of 'inclusive research' aims to overcome this dispute, by denoting research involving people with cognitive disabilities as more than just subjects or respondents but also as co-researchers. This definition involves research approaches that have been termed 'participatory', 'action', and 'emancipatory', implying that the distinction between participatory and emancipatory research is not clear cut. Participatory research seems to be a key methodological approach in the research with cognitively disabled people (Watson 2019) and its distinctive feature lies in the attitudes of researchers and in how they design and conduct research. What is at stake is either the ability to consider participants' requests in the formulation of research aims and objectives, or to actively involve them in the process of data collection, by challenging the researcher's own assumptions, within a co-productive framework (Liddiard et al. 2019). Co-production has been also extended to research with cognitively disabled children and young people (Kellet 2005) as people who have legitimate expertise, also in relation to disabling conditions. If the aim is to put into light the psycho-social dimensions of disablism, participatory research needs to make the expression of resistant identities possible (Goodley and Lawthom 2005).

Using Arts-based Methods with Persons with Cognitive Disabilities

Conducting research with cognitively disabled people can be challenging in many respects. From a methodological point of view, in-depth interviews or focus groups present some common issues like acquiescence, the tendency to choose the last option and to answer 'yes' (Stalker 1998). Moreover, verbal communication may not be the preferred way of expression of many people with cognitive disabilities (Scavarda et al. 2021). From an ethical point of view, mainstream qualitative methods may prevent cognitively disabled people to freely express their points of view and thus foster perceptions of personal inadequacy (Booth 2018). However, Atkinson (2004) and Booth (2018) showed that involvement within research may be empowering for participants, if the techniques employ creativity, such as storytelling. While previous studies, such as the one by Liddiard et al. (2019), show the potentialities of digital methods, the use of arts-based methods (Kara 2015; Leavy 2017) – drawing on forms of creative writing and on the visual arts, like painting, drawing, collage, or photography – with cognitively disabled young people has not been assessed in any depth, to date.

Arts-based methods may be particularly useful to adapt to the specific abilities of the interviewees and to allow them to depict their experiences, because they 'assist people in expressing feelings and thoughts that are difficult to articulate in words' (Blodgett et al. 2013, p. 313). Furthermore, arts-based research is considered beneficial in social justice and identity work not only to challenge dominant ideas but also to include marginalised voices and to induce people to think differently (Leavy 2017). Arts-based practices evoke multiple meanings and thus they may relativise the researcher's knowledge and democratise meaning-making processes. Moreover, arts-based methods are widely applied in research on children's experiences (see, for example, Freeman and Mathison 2009) based on the use of prompts to elicit verbal responses. Generally, the elicitation prompts (objects or role-playing scenarios) are effective in both evoking interviewees' memories and feelings, and for exploring their lived experiences (Freeman and Mathison 2009).

A Case Study on the Use of Arts-based Methods with Cognitively Disabled Young People

The rest of the chapter discusses the results of a research study carried out in the North-West of Italy as an example on how arts-based methods can be used to investigate the impact of psycho-emotional disablism on autistic children and adolescents ('autistic people' is the preferred term in Italy, promoted also by self-advocacy movements) and young people with Down syndrome. The qualitative research study involved in-depth interviews with parents, children, young people, and young adults with autism with low levels of support and Down syndrome, as well as healthcare professionals. Moreover, it included shadowing sessions, namely a long-standing non-participant observation (Czarniawska 2007), with two families: one with a ten-year-old autistic child and one with a fifteen-year-old boy with Down syndrome.

For this chapter, I focus upon the results of 21 in-depth interviews with 15 children and young people with autism and six with Down syndrome. I also refer to interviews with parents and other young adults where relevant, applying a distributed methodology that blends the perspectives of the child/young person, with that of significant others in their lives, carefully and ethically. The sample was composed primarily of young people aged 13–21 years but also included some younger children aged 8–10 years. Interviewees were predominantly male, because of the unbalanced gender ratio of autism (Loomes et al. 2017). Finally, participants were from both families with middle-low and middle-high socioeconomic status. Participants were recruited from neuropsychiatric and paediatric units, as well as from local parents' associations (see Table 14.1), to have a heterogeneous sample in terms of attitudes towards

TABLE 14.1 Sociodemographic characteristics of the sample

Type of condition	
Autism	15
Down Syndrome	6
Age	
3–10	2
13–21	19
Gender	
Male	16
Female	5
Socioeconomic status (SES)	
Middle-low	10
Middle-high	11
Types of recruitment sites	
Neuropsychiatric units	9
Paediatric units	2
Parents' associations	10
Total	21

cognitive disabilities. This is because in Piedmont, where the study took place, local parents' associations are inspired by both a medical approach, neuro-biologically oriented (particularly in the case of autism, Scavarda and Cascio 2022), and by a Catholic view of disability (Scavarda 2020b). These associations, therefore, promote a perspective that mixes up the medical one and the Catholic one approaches. Therefore, recruiting respondents only from parents' associations would have resulted in a homogeneous sample in terms of parents' narratives, because they share similar cultural backgrounds.

Interviews were conducted by the author and lasted on average 40 minutes. They were all recorded and fully transcribed. The interview guide was created with the help of parents and people with autism and Down syndrome themselves, based on the principles of flexibility, openness, and ethical symmetry (Cardano 2020). Moreover, I also took into consideration Booth and Booth's (1996) advice to use different approaches within the same interview situation. I applied firstly Photovoice (Wang and Burris 1994), a participatory research strategy which involves the active production of images by participants. This method enabled the elicitation of interviewees' representations of their living contexts and main interests. It fitted particularly well with the visual abilities of some autistic respondents, and it offered an alternative outlet of expression to interviewees with Down syndrome. Moreover, it also contributed to balance the power relationship between me and the participants. As a matter of fact, the latter had greater control over both the research interaction and findings, and they affirmed to feel empowered by this activity. Secondly, I used the spidergram, a visual method, to help participants portray their social networks (Draper, Hewitt and Rifkin 2010). Thirdly, I asked participants to draw themselves and to comment on the picture. The use of these visual techniques was intended to encourage participants' self-definitions and representations of impairment and disability, because drawing usually gives time to reflect on the issues depicted (Gauntlett 2007). I also made a collage with participants to depict their daily activities on weekdays and on weekends. They finally played with a magic wand, which I created, and with a hat containing some sentences to be completed. These activities were aimed at making interviewees think what they would change about themselves and about their lives. Some of the visuals produced are presented below.

All the participants were aware of what was going on during the interview and I asked for an oral consent to do the activities together. They were also told they could interrupt the interview at any time. Interview transcripts and fieldnotes were fully anonymised and analysed with thematic template analysis (Cardano 2020), which combines the use of codes derived from the literature and from the analysis. A template was applied to the interview transcripts made up of these codes: impairment, disability, psycho-emotional disablism, self-representation, autism, and Down syndrome. In what follows, pseudonyms are used for the participants.

'Special or Normal with an Extra Chromosome'

Both children and adolescents with Down syndrome expressed representations of their condition largely derived from parents and healthcare professionals. In general, they interiorised their parents' narratives, related both to their special talents, sometimes overstated, without a clear communication about Down syndrome, and to the normalisation of the condition, when it was acknowledged. What is largely missing is a thematisation of Down syndrome as a form of difference, which implies both particular strengths and weaknesses.

The first situation is represented by Monica, a 15-year-old girl, and by Alina, a 21-year-old woman. Monica's mother has never used the word 'Down syndrome', but she always told her daughter that she is a 'special one'. She suggested the idea of her 'slowness' through the metaphor of the turtle, which can go wherever it wants, at its own pace. Moreover, she stated that Monica is lucky because her family members love her and she will always have their support. In what follows, we can see how Monica partially reproduced her mother's arguments, without using the metaphor of the turtle:

> I am special because I have a beautiful mum, a beautiful dad, and a beautiful brother too. I am special because my parents love me, and I am brilliant in all the disciplines.
>
> *(Monica)*

During the interview, Alina, a young woman with Down syndrome, also gave a positive self-description, and she highlighted her talents in specific fields, like singing, drawing, and acting, but when she manifested difficulties in writing the word 'mamma' (mum) – she wrote 'ammma' – in her drawing (see Figure 14.1), she expressed anxiety and anger. While completing it, she shouted, with an annoyed voice: 'I am not incompetent as those people with Down syndrome!'.

Her mother expressed a type of overprotective and symbiotic attitude, reported also by Alina's drawing, since she was the only interviewee to portray herself with her mother. The mother also asked to read the interview guide beforehand, because she wanted to be sure that no references to Down

FIGURE 14.1 Alina's original drawing. The name has been changed for privacy issues.

syndrome were present. She had never told Alina about her difference be-cause she wanted to raise her in a 'pure world', avoiding any sources of pain or anxiety. She added that Alina felt both compassion and irritation towards 'people with Down syndrome' (Cardanoet al. 2020). She protected a schoolmate with the condition who was bullied, but at the same time she refused to watch television shows where people with Down syndrome are protagonists. Alina stated that the audience applauds out of pity. In fact, the pitiful attitude often reported by parents (Scavarda 2020a) – which portrays the presence of a member with Down syndrome as a negative occurrence and a family tragedy (Scavarda 2020b) – was somehow interiorised by most of the interviewees. It resulted in a refusal of belonging to the condition, either by denying it or by stressing normalcy, both of which Alina did. The latter strategy is applied by Matteo, a 15-year-old young boy whom I shadowed for a week. In the following extract, Matteo while commenting on his drawing (Figure 14.2) represented himself as a normal person, with an extra chromosome:

FIGURE 14.2   Matteo's original drawing. Matteo, his sister and his cousin's names have been deleted for privacy issues.

Interviewer:	How other people are different from you?
Matteo:	They aren't.
Interviewer:	Are you different from other people?
Matteo:	No, I am not.
Interviewer:	Are there things difficult for you?
Matteo:	I struggle in Maths.
Interviewer:	What did your parents tell you?
Matteo:	That I have got Down syndrome, I have got an extra chromosome and I am normal.

In line with Stalker's claims (2019), most of the interviewees who were aware of their condition refused the association with Down syndrome, widely conceived as a stigmatised trait, associated with powerlessness, and dependence. This strategy of 'identification through denial' was also widespread among young adults, as an indication that these stereotypes are carried on into adulthood. This means that the main identity strategy of people with Down syndrome consists in distancing themselves from their peers and in refusing their gap from normalcy. Disability, related to Down syndrome, is therefore a master status (Aull Davies and Jenkins 1997) a negative category that conceals individual characteristics, to be widely refused. This strategy is suggested by parents who, in their bid to ensure acceptance of their sons and daughters with Down syndrome, are reinforcing the stigma attached to the condition rather than seeking to remove it.

'Am I Shy, Crazy or Stupid?'

In line with the results of the interviews with persons with Down syndrome, children and young people with autism (with low level of support needs) reported descriptions of impairment and disability largely drawn from their parents' accounts. They were often unaware of their condition and manifested confusion about their identity. During the interviews, their parents referred to autism as a neurobiological disorder (Scavarda 2020a; Scavarda and Cascio 2022) – which implied specific deficits in social communication and interaction – Child and adolescent interviewees consequently assumed the idea of their radical otherness, without being able to properly name it. They described themselves as either 'crazy' or 'stupid'.

Michael, a ten-year-old autistic child, drew himself with his twin sister, Claire, but he affirmed that he was different from her, because sometimes he became crazy at home. He pretended to be in a science fiction movie (Figure 14.3).

When I asked him how he knew that he was crazy when he behaved in such a manner, he replied by referring to a temporary concept of madness:

> Maybe dad told me that I am crazy, like people who drank too much wine, the face turns red. I feel embarrassed because I become too crazy, and I can't come back to reality. (Michael)

Samuele, a 14-year-old autistic young boy, during the Photovoice session commented on one of his pictures (Figure 14.4) of the swimming class, by stressing his swimming abilities, compared to his learning difficulties: 'I am good at swimming, although I am stupid'.

Samuele was highly stressed during the research session, particularly while discussing his pictures, because it was a flexible activity, without a clear structure and timing. For this reason, I explored the topic further by changing the activity to reduce his stress. He felt immediately relieved during the magic wand activity. For this activity, I gave him a magic wand I had created with a twig, and I asked him what he would change of himself. He replied that he would rather be normal, without being stupid, because of his language

FIGURE 14.3   Michael's original drawing. Michael and her sister's names have been changed for privacy issues.

problems. Moreover, he mentioned that his parents told him that he could improve his communication abilities.

Interviewer:	Let's imagine that the magic wand is real, what will you change about yourself?
Samuele:	I wish I were normal, without being stupid.
Interviewer:	Are you stupid?
Samuele:	I have always been stupid … because I always get my Italian homework wrong. But my parents told me that I can get better.

The urge to be normal is therefore proposed by Samuele's parents, who forced him to attend social skills training classes and to meet other young people, both neurodivergent and neurotypical ones. Samuele, during the interview, clearly stated that he did not like these activities, and he expressed his desire to be on his own: 'The educators told me what to do and these are all boring activities. They make me stay with other people, while I prefer to be alone'.

FIGURE 14.4 Samuele during his swimming class. Picture taken by his mother.

Mattia, a 14-year-old young boy diagnosed with Asperger's Syndrome, similarly affirmed that he would 'get rid of' going to the daily centre, because he does not like group activities. While expressing their disapproval of cognitive behavioural programmes, most of the interviewees acknowledged their relational difficulties, to be overcome through specialised interventions. Consequently, they interiorised the therapeutical orientation embraced by their parents (Scavarda and Cascio 2022), and they attributed their problems to internal and not to contextual issues, without acknowledging the presence of invisible barriers like discrimination and exclusion, including bullying experiences. They did not notice these forms of psycho-emotional disablism and did not question the negative attitudes and the lack of empathy from other people. They often blamed themselves for being unable to interact with peers properly, maybe to unconsciously comply with parents' requests. This is how Massimo, 13 years old, put it:

Massimo: I am shy, and I struggle to be with other people. My parents told me that it is true, but I must try. By my character I was not wanted by my schoolmates, they weren't coming for me. Sometimes I am obnoxious, and I happen to get angry. I am

    sorry if I scare them, and I get nervous if I can't play games.
    I need to change this aspect.

Interviewer: Why?

Massimo: To not be alone all the time, that's why I must improve.

In parallel with the interviewees with Down syndrome, autistic adolescents who were aware of their condition distanced themselves from it (Stalker 2019) and therefore these attitudes persist until adulthood. Adult interviewees either stressed their normalcy or applied décalage strategies, in line with a previous study on psychiatric patients (Cardano 2007), meaning they mitigated the severity of the traits associated to their condition, by choosing the Asperger's Syndrome label.

  Finally, only one autistic young girl, Luna, 16 years old, explicitly referred to the neurodiversity paradigm. Luna's spidergram (Figure 14.5) revealed the presence of a social network made up of both neurodivergent young people (Elisabetta, Ezio, and Nana, members of a local association; and Machali, a young autistic boy met within an Aspie pride forum) and neurotypical ones (Luca, her boyfriend; and Eleonora, her schoolmate) as well as her family members ('mamma' – mum – 'papa' – dad – and 'madrina' – godmother).

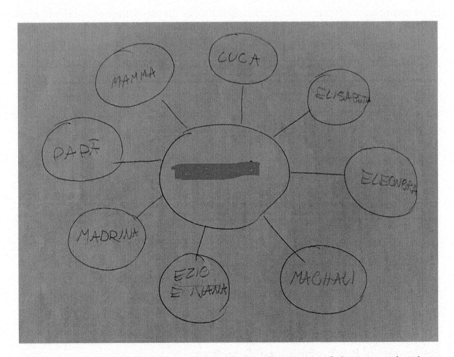

FIGURE 14.5 Luna's spidergram. Her name, at the centre of the image, has been deleted for privacy issues.

Luna asserted that she was 'neither normal nor different, but something in between'; she later explained that she had both abilities and difficulties, not wholly traceable to Asperger's Syndrome. Therefore, disability in this case is not turned into a master status (Aull Davies and Jenkins 1997) because it does not overshadow individual characteristics. When Luna described her condition, she affirmed that in the past she experienced psycho-emotional disablism (Reeve 2004, 2019; Thomas 1999), in terms of conflicts and misunderstandings with schoolmates and teachers. They did not understand her sensory specificities, as well as her troubles in processing idioms and metaphors, which were widely considered as signs of either 'madness' or 'laziness', with negative consequences on her self-esteem. However, she discovered the neurodiversity approach by connecting with some online communities and she was able to turn the stigma into a form of charisma (Cardano 2010) and to develop a positive interpretation of her characteristics:

> When I was in elementary and middle school, I had conflicts with teachers and classmates, so I had low self-esteem, I felt like a nobody. Now, however, I have more self-esteem, I have made myself stronger, I have realized that I have specialties and I am proud of them, I am proud of being smart.

Luna expressed a form of Asperger's pride like the disability pride developed by disability studies scholars and activists (Tregaskis 2002). Coming out as an autistic/Asperger's person, therefore, became a strategy of resistance to psycho-emotional disablism, to rebuff the stigma related to be part of a discredited group. In the end, Luna was able to acknowledge the need to raise other people's awareness of neurodiversity and she asked to be accepted with her peculiar characteristics. At the same time, she proposed a form of mutual respect between neurodivergent and neurotypical people during the magic wand game:

> If I had a magic wand, I would change myself but also the other people. I'd like to keep my peculiarity, some specific characteristics. Being neurodiverse, that's fine with me, but I also wish the others could accept me, as I accept them.

The neurodiversity movement often challenges parent and professional perspectives on autism, especially those aiming to cure autistic people or change them into non-autistic people and these discourses are also influential for young people alongside autism acceptance (Fein 2020; Milton 2020).

The Impact of Psycho-Emotional Disablism

The results of the inclusive study presented herein show how children and young people with cognitive disabilities are still consistently subject to psycho-emotional disablism (Reeve 2004, 2019; Thomas 1999). This form of disablism adds to structural disablism to make people with cognitive disabilities feel worthless and socially incompetent. In the interviewees' accounts, the psycho-emotional dimensions of disablism assume two main forms (Reeve 2004): social interactions with others, during which participants' behaviours may be misunderstood and judged also by close friends or schoolmates; and internalised oppression, the acceptance and incorporation of negative representations of both autism and Down syndrome widespread in society which make cognitively disabled people feel devalued and disempowered. In line with Stalker (2019), people with cognitive disabilities were patronised and pitied for their 'tragic condition' or were bullied by schoolmates who did not accept and understand their specific way of functioning. The consequent feelings of shame and vulnerability were often expressed by the interviewees, while they commented on their drawings, their pictures or they were involved in the magic wand activity.

As previous studies have shown (see, for example,; Walmsley 2010), autism and Down Syndrome are widely considered as stigmatised traits, related to deficits and dysfunctions in cognitive, as well as social abilities, to be fixed with specialised interventions. This medical approach to disability results in specific attitudes and behaviours assumed by people in direct contact with cognitively disabled ones: not only healthcare professionals, teachers, and friends but also parents, who may be the agents of these forms of disablism. Interviewees' internalisation of these negative images of autism and Down syndrome fosters and reproduces the instances of psycho-emotional disablism to which they are subject.

Parents represent the interviewees' main source of information about their condition, but they are stigmatised and subject to the same instances of psycho-emotional disablism of their children (Scavarda 2020b). The strategies of resistance to stigma that parents put in place – labelled elsewhere as normalisation and medicalisation (Scavarda 2020a) – are therefore interiorised by their children, resulting in both therapeutical and ableist orientations. Interviewees tended to attribute their negative experiences to their impairments or to stress the affiliation to normalcy, by distancing themselves from people with their own condition. Therefore, the results from this research highlight the absence of a process of peer socialisation amongst cognitively disabled people, even for those who attend local associations. This would be distinctive of disability that, unlike other social statuses such as ethnicity, is not shared by other family members (Reeve 2014, see also chapter by Zirnsak in this volume). As a consequence, 'barriers to being' and psycho-emotional disablism are specifically challenging, because children, young people, and young adults with cognitive disabilities lack positive role models. They are often torn between the desire to deny the belonging to a discredited category and the need to overcome the stereotypes attributed to them during social interactions. This is outlined by the concept of 'identification through denial', which refers to the interviewees' strategies of refusal of their condition, portrayed as an undesirable one, and to the practices of resistance to their presumed abnormality (either related to madness or stupidity), promoted by the neurodiversity approach. While the two rhetorical strategies used by parents – medicalisation and normalisation – imply both suppressing disability, by curing it, or assimilating it into the norm, this study suggests that neurodiversity may offer a specific language to value cognitive disability (Scavarda and Cascio 2022). The acknowledgement of cognitively disabled people's own talents, alongside their difficulties, can foster their self-esteem and favour their empowerment, triggered by the active involvement in the research process.

Conclusion

The research presented here shows the importance of listening to the voices of disabled children and adolescents and gather their views about their own lives, by using suitable research methods. In this context, arts-based methods are effective in eliciting participants' emotions (Leavy 2017) and points of view, particularly in relation to sensitive topics like disablism and self-awareness. They offer an innovative contribution to inclusive research (Bigby et al. 2014; Milner and Frawley 2019; Scavarda et al. 2021; Walmsley 2001) because they entail different forms of expression and resistance to binary thinking (Kara 2015). The potential of arts-based methods in challenging conceptual categories is useful to make participants reflect about their self-ideas and to overcome the researcher's own assumptions, related to interviewees' disempowerment. This may allow interviewees to challenge the negative images related to their conditions and to express resistant identities. However, the tailoring of methods to the range of the individuals involved is crucial both to collect participants' narratives – avoiding acquiescence and researcher's patronisation – and to strengthen these scant attempts of resistance to disablism, up to develop a new form of cognitive disability pride.

References

Armstrong, T. 2010. *The power of neurodiversity: unleashing the advantages of your differently wired brain*. Boston: Da Capo Lifelong Books.

Aspis, S. 2000. Researching our history. Who is in charge? In: Brigham, L., Atkinson, D., Jackson, M., Rolph, S. and Walmsley, J. eds. *Crossing boundaries: change and continuity in the history of disability*. Kidderminster: British Institute for Learning Disability, pp. 1–5.

Atkinson, D. 1997. *An auto/biographical approach to learning disability research*. Ashgate: Aldershot.

Atkinson, D. 2004. Research and empowerment: involving people with learning difficulties in oral and life history research. *Disability & Society*, **19**(7), pp. 691–702.

Aull Davies, C. and Jenkins, R. 1997. 'She has different fits to me': how people with learning difficulties see themselves. *Disability & Society*, 12(1), pp. 95–110.

Bigby, C., Frawley, P. and Ramcharan, P. 2014. Conceptualizing inclusive research with people with intellectual disability. *Journal of Applied Research in Intellectual Disabilities*, 27(1), pp. 54–64.

Bjornsdottir, K. and Svensdóttir, A.S. 2008. Gambling for capital: learning disability, inclusive research and collaborative life histories. *British Journal of Learning Disabilities*, 36(4), pp. 263–270.

Björnsdóttir, K. and Traustadóttir, R. 2010. Stuck in the land of disability? The intersection of learning difficulties, class, gender and religion. *Disability & Society*, 25(1), pp. 49–62.

Blodgett, A.T., Coholic, D.A., Schinke, R.J., McGannon, K.R., Peltier, D. and Pheasant, C. 2013. Moving beyond words: exploring the use of an arts-based method in Aboriginal community sport research. *Qualitative Research in Sport, Exercise and Health*, 5(3), pp. 312–331.

Booth, T. 2018. Sounds of still voices: issues in the use of narrative methods with people who have learning difficulties. In Barton, L. eds. *Disability and society. Emerging issues and insights*. London: Routledge, pp. 237–255.

Booth, T. and Booth, W. 1996. Sounds of silence: narrative research with inarticulate subjects. *Disability and Society*, 11(1), pp. 55–69.

Burke, A., McMillan, J., Cummins, L., Thompson, A., Forsyth, W., McLellan, J., Snow, L., Fraser, A., Fraser, M., Fulton, C., McCrindle, E., Gillies, L., LeFort, S., Miller, G., Whitehall, J., Wilson, J., Smith, J. and Wright, D. 2003. Setting up participatory research: a discussion of the initial stages. *British Journal of Learning Disabilities*, 31, pp. 65–69.

Cardano, M. 2007. 'E poi cominciai a sentire le voci...'. Narrazioni del male mentale ['And then I started hearing the voices …'. A narration of mental illness]. *Rassegna Italiana di Sociologia*, 48(1), pp. 9–56.

Cardano, M. 2010. Mental distress: strategies of sense-making. *Health*, 14(3), pp. 253–271.

Cardano, M. 2020. *Defending qualitative research: design, analysis, and textualization*. London: Routledge.

Cardano, M., Cioffi, M. and Scavarda, A. 2020. Sofferenza psichica, follia e disabilità [Mental suffering, madness and disability]. In: Cardano, M., Giarelli, G. and Vicarelli, G. eds. *Sociologia della Salute e della medicina* [Sociology of Health and Medicine]. Bologna: Il Mulino.

Chappell, A.M. 1997. From normalisation to where? In Barton, L. and Oliver, M. eds. *Disability studies: past, present and future*. Leeds: Disability Press, pp. 45–61.

Czarniawska, B. 2007. *Shadowing: and other techniques for doing fieldwork in modern societies*. Copenhaghen: Copenhagen Business School Press DK.

Danieli, A. and Woodhams, C. 2005. Emancipatory research methodology and disability: a critique. *International Journal of Social Research Methodology*, 8(4), pp. 281–296.

Docherty, D., Hughes, R., Phillips, P., Corbett, D., Regan, B., Barber, A., Adams, M., Boxall, K., Kaplan, I. and Izzidien, S. 2010. This is what we think. In: Davis, L. eds. *The disability studies reader*. London: Routledge, pp. 432–440.

Draper, A.K., Hewitt, G. and Rifkin, S. 2010. Chasing the dragon: developing indicators for the assessment of community participation in health programmes. *Social Science & Medicine*, 71(6), pp. 1102–1109.

Fein, E. 2020. *Living on the spectrum: autism and youth in community*. New York: NYU Press.

Freeman, M. and Mathison, S. 2009. *Researching children's experiences*. New York: Guilford Press.

Gauntlett, D. 2007. *Creative explorations: new approaches to identities and audiences*. London, Routledge.

Genova, A., Scavarda, A. and Świątkiewicz-Mośny, M. eds. 2023. *Disability welfare policy in Europe: cognitive disability and the impact of the Covid-19 pandemic*. London: Emerald Group Publishing.

Gilbert, T. 2004. Involving people with learning disabilities in research: issues and possibilities. *Health & Social Care in the Community*, **12**(4), pp. 298–308.

Gillman, M., Heyman, B. and Swain, J. 2000. What's in a name? The implications of diagnosis for people with learning difficulties and their family carers. *Disability & Society*, **15**(3), pp. 389–409.

Goodley, D. 2001. 'Learning difficulties', the social model of disability and impairment: challenging epistemologies. *Disability & Society*, **16**(2), pp. 207–231.

Goodley, D. and Lawthom, R. 2005. Epistemological journeys in participatory action research: alliances between community psychology and disability studies. *Disability & Society*, **20**(2), pp. 135–151.

Goodley, D. and Rapley, M. 2001. How do you understand 'learning difficulties'? Towards a social theory of impairment. *Mental Retardation*, **39**(3), pp. 229–232.

Goodley, D. and Runswick-Cole, K. 2016. Becoming dishuman: thinking about the human through dis/ability. *Discourse: Studies in the Cultural Politics of Education*, **37**(1), pp. 1–15.

Goodley, D. and Van Hove, G. 2005. Disability studies, people with learning difficulties and inclusion. In: Goodley, D. and Van Hove, G. eds. *Another disability studies reader. People with learning difficulties and a disabling world*, Antwerpen/Apeldoorn: Garant, pp. 15–25.

Kara, H. 2015. *Creative research methods in the social sciences: a practical guide*. Bristol: Policy Press.

Kellett, M. 2005. *How to develop children as researchers: a step-by-step guide to teaching the research process*. London: Paul Chapman/Sage.

Kittay, E.F. and Carlson, L. eds. 2010. *Cognitive disability and its challenge to moral philosophy*. Chichester: John Wiley & Sons.

Leavy, P. ed. 2017. *Handbook of arts-based research*. New York: Guilford Publications.

Levin, J. 2012. Disablist violence in the US: unacknowledged hate crime. In: Roulstone, A. and Mason-Bish, H. eds. *Disability, hate crime and violence*. London and New York: Routledge, pp. 95–105.

Lewis, A. 2002. *Children's understanding of disability*. London and New York: Routledge.

Liddiard, K., Runswick-Cole, K., Goodley, D., Whitney, S., Vogelmann, E. and Watts MBE, L. 2019. 'I was excited by the idea of a project that focuses on those unasked questions' co-producing disability research with disabled young people. *Children & Society*, **33**(2), 154–167.

Liddiard, K., Whitney-Mitchell, S., Evans, K., Watts, L., Spurr, R., Vogelmann, E., Runswick-Cole, K. and Goodley, D. 2022. *Living life to the fullest: disability, youth and voice*. Bingley: Emerald Publishing Limited.

Loomes, R., Hull, L. and Mandy, W.P.L. 2017. What is the male-to-female ratio in autism spectrum disorder? A systematic review and meta-analysis. *Journal of the American Academy of Child & Adolescent Psychiatry*, **56**(6), pp. 466–474.

Macdonald, S.J. 2015. 'Community fear and harassment': learning difficulties and hate crime incidents in the north-east of England. *Disability & Society*, **30**(3), pp. 353–367.

Mason, M. 1990. Internalized oppression. In Reiser, R. and Mason, M. eds. *Disability equality in education*. London: ILEA, pp. 27–28.

Milner, P. and Frawley, P. 2019. From 'on' to 'with' to 'by': people with a learning disability creating a space for the third wave of inclusive research. *Qualitative Research*, **19**(4), pp. 382–398.

Milton, D. 2020. Neurodiversity past and present - an introduction to the neurodiversity reader. In: Milton, D., Murray, D., Ridout, S., Martin, N. and Mills, R. eds. *The neurodiversity reader*. Hove, UK: Pavilion, pp. 3–6.

Mladenov, T. 2016. Disability and social justice. *Disability & Society*, **31**(9), pp. 1226–1241.

Ralli, A.M., Margeti, M., Doudoni, E., Pantelemidou, V., Rozou, T. and Evaggelopoulou, E. 2011. Typically developing children's understanding of and attitudes towards diversity and peers with learning difficulties in the Greek setting. *European Journal of Special Needs Education*, **26**(2), pp. 233–249.

Rapley, M. 2003. *Quality of life research: a critical introduction*. Sage: London.

Reeve, D. 2004. Psycho-emotional dimensions of disability and the social model. In: Barnes, C. and Mercer, G. eds. *Implementing the Social model of disability: theory and research*. Leeds: The Disability Press, pp. 83–100.

Reeve, D. 2014. Psycho-emotional disablism and internalised oppression. In: Swain, J., Thomas, C., Barnes, C. and French, S. eds. *Disabling barriers–enabling environments*. London: Sage, pp. 92–98.

Reeve, D. 2019. Psycho-emotional disablism: the missing link? In: Watson, N., Roulstone, A. and Thomas, A. eds. *Routledge handbook of disability studies*. London: Routledge, pp. 78–92.

Scavarda, A. 2020a. 'Come pinguini nel deserto'. Strategie di resistenza allo stigma di famiglie con figli autistici e con Trisomia 21 ['Like penguins in the desert'. Strategies of resistance to stigma of families with children with autism and with Trisomy 21]. *Rassegna Italiana di Sociologia*, **61**(3), pp. 537–561.

Scavarda, A. 2020b. *Pinguini nel deserto. Strategie di resistenza allo stigma da autismo e trisomia 21* [Penguins in the desert. Strategies of resistance to stigma of families with children with autism and with Trisomy 21]. Bologna: Il Mulino.

Scavarda, A. and Cascio, M.A. 2022. Embracing and rejecting the medicalization of autism in Italy. *Social Science & Medicine*, **294**, p. 114728.

Scavarda, A., Cascio, M.A. and Quaglia, V. 2021. Fare ricerca qualitativa con persone disabili: possibili sfide e benefici. Fare ricerca qualitativa con persone disabili: possibili sfide e benefici. *Welfare ed Ergonomia*, **1**, pp. 117–127.

Stalker, K. 1998. Some ethical and methodological issues in research with people with learning difficulties. *Disability and Society*, **13**(1), pp. 5–19.

Stalker, K. 2019. Theorising the position of people with learning difficulties within disability studies: progress and pitfalls. In: Watson, N., Roulstone, A. and Thomas, A. eds. *Routledge handbook of disability studies*. London: Routledge, pp. 158–171.

Stalker, K. and Lerpiniere, J. 2009. 'It's against our law, never mind anyone else's': the Disability Discrimination Act 1995 and adults with learning disabilities. *Disability & Society*, 24(7), pp. 829–843.

Thomas, C. 1999. *Female forms: experiencing and understanding disability*. New York: McGraw-Hill Education.

Tregaskis, C. 2002. Social model theory: the story so far. *Disability & Society*, 17(4), pp. 457–470.

UPIAS. 1976. Fundamental principles of disability. London: Union of the Physically Impaired Against Segregation. [online] [Accessed on 06.05.2023]. Available from: https://disability-studies.leeds.ac.uk/wp-content/uploads/sites/40/library/UPIAS-fundamental-principles.pdf

Walmsley, J. 2001. Normalisation, emancipatory research and inclusive research in learning disability. *Disability & Society*, 16(2), pp. 187–205.

Walmsley, J. 2010. Research and emancipation: prospects and problems. In: Grant, G., Ramcharan, P., Flynn, M. and Richardson, M. eds. *Learning disability: a life cycle approach*. 2nd ed. Maidenhead: McGraw Hill: Open University Press, pp. 489–502.

Wang, C. and Burris, M.A. 1994. Empowerment through photo novella: portraits of participation. *Health Education Quarterly*, 21(2), pp. 171–186.

Watson, N. 2019. Agency, structure and emancipatory research. In: Watson, N., Roulstone, A. and Thomas, A. eds. *Routledge handbook of disability studies*. London: Routledge, pp. 127–141.

15

WE ARE SEXUAL TOO

Sexuality in the Lives of Disabled Adolescents

Claire Azzopardi Lane and Alan Santinele Martino

Introduction

Sexual expression and exploration are a part of development from childhood to adolescent and adulthood. Studies have consistently shown that most disabled youth are interested in having intimate relationships and maintaining a sexual life (Alexander and Taylor Gomez, 2017). Yet, disabled sexualities are commonly regulated, restricted, and surveilled (Bahner, 2019). The beginning of intimate relationships and sexual experiences is often a marker of the transition between childhood and adulthood. During adolescent and early adulthood years, youth usually start experimenting with their sexuality, building relationships, and learning about their gender and sexual identities. A recent survey conducted by the Centers for Disease Control and Prevention found, for example, that around 55% of teenagers in the United States had sex by age 18 (Abma and Martinez, 2017).

Youth as defined by the United Nations (UN) is the fluid period of transition from childhood to adulthood. For statistical purposes, the UN defines youth as persons between the ages of 15 and 24 years. Although it is understood that the definition of youth might be prone to situational variations including socio-cultural settings, this definition is seen as adequately supporting the assessment of needs and the provision of guidelines related to youth development (UNDESA, no date).

Ironically, disabled youth are either infantilised and de-sexualised, on the one hand, or seen as having uncontrollable sexualities that pose a danger to others in the community on the other hand (Bahner, 2021). As a disabled person once noted to one of the authors in the context of a research project focused on disability and sexuality, 'no matter where you end up in those

DOI: 10.4324/9781003102915-15

[extremes], you are screwed either way'. In this chapter, we look at some of the barriers that keep disabled youth from engaging in forms of sexual expression and developing their own sense of gender and sexual identities. This chapter draws on relevant research literature to illustrate the experiences of sexual exploration and expression of disabled youth conducted by us in Canada and Malta in particular. We begin by examining the long history of surveillance and social control that continues to shape the intimate lives of disabled youth.

A 'Bad' Sexuality: Surveillance and Social Control

It is important to acknowledge the longstanding history of social control over the sexualities of disabled people. Historically, the sexualities of disabled people have been constructed as 'problematic', as a 'bad sexuality' (McRuer, 2011; Rubin, 1984), that deviate from normative, valued, and privileged forms of sexuality. Being constructed as having a 'bad sexuality' (Rubin, 1984) as a social group can impact the sexualities, specifically the sexual self-confidence of marginalised groups, including disabled people. This is illustrated by the most common portrayal of disabled people in the media; either as child-like and naive and/or deviant and unattractive as intimate partners (Alexander and Gomez, 2017; Renwick, Fudge Schormans and Shore, 2013). As Shakespeare (2000, p. 161) notes, 'being sexual demands self-esteem'. Disabled people, who continue to be 'systematically devalued and excluded by modern western societies', are 'often not in the right place to begin that task of self-love and self-worth' (Shakespeare, 2000, p. 161).

The sexuality of marginalised groups in particular is seen as potentially dangerous and disruptive (McRuer, 2011). Scholars in disability studies have long been calling out these 'new regimes of sexual control and domination' (McConnell and Phelan, 2022, p. 3) and the prevailing narrative of oppression that surrounds them.

Sexual oppression is often an amplified experience throughout the lifespan of disabled women and girls, extending from the first signs of puberty to menopause (McCarthy, 2002). Disabled women and girls are known to be at the centre of the infringements of reproductive justice and bodily autonomy. Loss of bodily autonomy is explored in Kittay's (2011) work on the gendered aspects of de-sexualisation, performed upon a six-year-old child with intellectual disability, known as Ashley X, through the surgical removal of her reproductive organs. Kittay's work highlights how the disabled body is problematised, infantilised, and invaded in the name of protection against sexual exploitation. Kittay draws from her personal experience with her daughter Sesha and gives a very different perspective on her daughter's physical maturation. In her article 'Forever Small', that addresses the growth attenuation treatment received by Ashley X, Kittay says:

> As the childishness in her face fades, Sesha's body has taken the form of a woman. I don't know if Sesha can rejoice in her breasts, if she notices them at all, if she would miss them, or if she compares herself to other girls [...] I can say that I, as her mother, delight in her womanliness. It is very much a part of Sesha, as she is now.
>
> *(p. 621)*

While in the case of Ashley X, the growth attenuation treatment she undergoes obstructs her natural physical development and keeps her in a suspended childhood, Sesha's transition to womanhood is celebrated as a milestone in the life of any woman would be. Kittay's ability to see beyond her daughter's intellectual impairment and through her identity as a woman is uncommon. However, this notion of disablement is specifically experienced by girls and women with disability who are not perceived as sexual beings, as potential lovers, partners, and mothers.

For many disabled women and girls, decisions over contraceptive care are dictated by others or negotiated as a condition in exchange of what is considered the privilege of socialisation and intimacy (Malacrida, 2020). McCarthy (2009) conducted semi-structured in-depth interviews with 23 women with intellectual disabilities living in the UK to explore if these women have any agency over their bodies. She investigated whether her participants could exercise choice and control when it came to their use of contraception. Her findings revealed a lack of bodily autonomy, where decisions were mostly taken by others and, when some of those women did make their own choices, these were often heavily influenced. Social control exerted on women's reproductive capacities is being challenged all over the world; however, disabled women's reproductive rights are never at the forefront of this fight. A residue of eugenic beliefs still contributes to the sexual repression of disabled persons, especially those with intellectual disability and culminates in discourse on the reproductive capacity of women with intellectual disability (Kallianes and Rubenfeld, 1997; McCarthy, 2009). Because of the concern that disabled women will produce a child with similar conditions (Othelia Lee and Oh, 2005), at times, irreversible contraceptive methods and invasive surgical procedures such as sterilisation have been performed without their consent, with the aim of protecting them against unwanted pregnancy (Kittay, 2011, McCarthy, 2009). Research shows that sexual and reproductive rights of disabled women and girls are still not a par with those of their non-disabled counterparts. In practise, this translates to limited access to quality sexual healthcare, questionable retention of fertility, and no choice over contraception use and which method of contraception is preferred (Azzopardi and Azzopardi Lane, 2021; Retznik et al, 2022a, b; Schuengel et al., 2022).

A study by O'Shea and Frawley (2020) has also shown how many disabled people, especially people with intellectual disabilities, are often pushed into stereotypical gendered performances. For example, women with intellectual disabilities are sometimes led to perform an 'emphasized femininity' that is a form of femininity that relies on traditional gendered expectations (Björnsdóttir et al., 2017, p. 296). Young girls with disabilities tend not to be encouraged to go to work, to go out, or to date. This limited understanding about gender identity and performance has the potential to reproduce gender inequality.

The Conversation Around Vulnerability

Disabled people's sexuality is predominantly framed around discourses of vulnerability, risk, and danger leaving little room for conversations about more holistic and positive aspects of sexuality (Shildrick, 2007). Disabled children and youth are commonly perceived to require additional protection, especially when conversations involve sexuality (Retznik et al., 2021). More importantly, being labelled 'vulnerable' can at times be used to justify restrictions on the sexual expression and rights of disabled youth and lead to their overprotection in a way that can trump the decision-making power by disabled youth themselves and curtail opportunities for sexual exploration (Fish, 2016). Ableist assumptions tend to fuel the narrative of vulnerability, privileging non-disabled standpoints whilst endorsing the discrimination perpetrated towards disabled persons. Chouinard et al. (1997, p. 379) defined ableism as 'ideas, practises, institutions and social relations that presume able-bodiedness, and by so doing, construct persons with disabilities as marginalised [...] and largely invisible "others"'. Being considered vulnerable automatically assumes incompetence, most significantly sexual incompetence. These ableist beliefs translate into dogmas, such as that disabled persons cannot control their sexuality and associating them further with gendered assumptions of promiscuity and sexual offending and predatorship. Not to allow these sexual behaviours to evolve and flourish, control, coercion, and suppression of sexual exploration and expression are typically perpetrated on disabled persons by non-disabled others in positions of power.

Studies have consistently shown that disabled people have a higher risk of experiencing forms of abuse in their lives compared to non-disabled people (Collins and Murphy, 2022; Murphy, 2003; Roswell, Claire and Murphy, 2013). Collins and Murphy (2022) conducted a systematic review of a total of 48 articles when collecting evidence related to how abuse is detected and prevented within services was reviewed. Twenty-one of these employed a qualitative design, 15 used a quantitative design, and 13 used a mixed methodology. The studies were conducted in the UK, Australia, Sweden, Norway, the Netherlands, and the USA. Key methods of data collection varied but included interviews, questionnaires, focus groups, and participant observation amongst other methods. Participants with intellectual disabilities and other developmental disabilities were recruited in 14 of the 48 studies. They identified a series of risk factors, including individual characteristics, perpetrator characteristics, and organisational factors, that explain the disproportional experiences of abuse among people with disabilities. These factors have remained consistent in the last three decades. It is estimated that people with intellectual disabilities, for example, are approximately four times more likely to experience sexual abuse at some point in their lives compared to non-disabled people (Gil-Llario et al., 2019; Liasidou and Gregoriou, 2021; Majeed-Ariss, Rodriguez and White, 2020).

Research by Hollomotz (2013) and Liasidou and Gregoriou (2021) suggest that giving disabled people evidence-based sexuality-related information is an effective way of reducing the risk of sexual abuse. However, because people with intellectual disabilities generally lack access to sexuality education, they do not have the knowledge to help them identify unsafe sexual encounters and abusive intimate relationships (Gil-Llario et al., 2019). As Schaafsma et al. (2017) also note, the lack of involvement of persons with intellectual disability in the development of sex education programmes and their limited effectiveness as a result may further contribute to this vulnerability. In addition to this barrier to accessing sexuality-related information, there is the combination of various social factors, including for example, socio-economic status, availability of support, and dedicated services (Fisher et al., 2016; Langdon et al., 2011). Thus, as noted by Hollomotz (2011), it is essential to move discussions about vulnerability away from an individualising approach. Instead, it is crucial to understand how disabled people are made vulnerable, for example, through institutional and structural barriers, such as lack of sex education (Azzopardi Lane, 2022; McDaniels and Fleming, 2016).

While information about abuse prevention is crucial, there is also a need for more sex-positive sex education, with more attention paid to more positive aspects of sexuality, including romance, love, and sexual pleasure. This is illustrated by Frawley and O'Shea (2020) who, in their research, present an alternative sex education programme focused on sexual rights, developed in collaboration with people with intellectual disabilities, which uses the lived experiences of people with an intellectual disability and employs them as peer educators.

A Limited Menu of Options

In many contexts, often due to the social-cultural climate, during both formal and informal sex education, disabled youth are exposed only to information about heterosexual penetrative sexual activities that lead to procreation and the perils of engaging in such activities, such as unwanted pregnancies, sexual abuse, and sexually transmitted infections (Campbell, Löfgren-Mårtenson and Martino, 2020). Socio-cultural aspects further curtail their sexual exploration and expression, especially in those contexts that have strong religious influences (Azzopardi Lane and Callus, 2015, Nelson, Odberg Pettersson and Emmelin, 2020). In their work with young people with intellectual disability, Azzopardi Lane and Callus quote a participant saying, 'we follow God not the devil' (p. 5) when a discussion about sexual intimacy was taking place as part of their research. The context of the latter can be said to be one where traditional Christian morality leaves few possibilities for persons with intellectual disability to engage with their sexuality (Liégeois, 2022). This morality places sexual behaviour within a relationship between a man and a woman, therefore encapsulating sexual activity, especially intercourse, within the sacrament of heterosexual marriage and for the purpose of procreation. The same moral beliefs tend to reject all forms of sexual expression emerging from diverse sexualities, thus from people who identify as Two-Spirit, lesbian, gay, bisexual, transgender, and queer (2SLGBTQ+). Masturbation is also likely to be seen as a disordered sexual pleasure and a sin against the dignity of marriage within the framework of this moral stance (Liégeois, 2022), leaving disabled persons with very narrow possibilities to discover and experience their sexuality. In his revision of sexual ethics in the context of Church morality, Liégeois (2022) argues the importance to 'fully recognise sexuality as a valuable and essential dimension of human life' (p. 7). His reflections endorse a sexuality that can be experienced both through one's own body and with another person. This is crucial since not all disabled persons, especially those with intellectual disability, have the opportunity to develop intimate and sexual relationships with others and many express their sexuality through masturbation (Cicero, 2019; Gill, 2012, Morales et al., 2016).

Many disabled youths grow up with a very limited 'menu of options' (Santinele Martino, 2022) in their opportunities for sexual exploration and expression. Due to social isolation and exclusion from spaces where non-disabled children and youth participate, disabled youth may lack the platform to develop social relations and potential intimate relationships. For instance, there is the notion that disabled people cannot deal with diversity, or that conversations around disability and queerness, for example, means 'going too far' (Stoffelen et al., 2013, p. 265). Even sex education, more generally, tends to be heteronormative and cisnormative (Hobaica and Kwon, 2017; Tordoff et al., 2021). The everyday experiences of LGBT+ people with disability are reported by Leonard and Mann (2018, p. 6) who claim that stigma and prejudice against LGBT+ people with disability are also felt through the exclusion of sexual and gender diversity in 'sex and relationships education and resources', thus augmenting risky sexual behaviour that could lead to issues with sexual health and wellbeing, reducing the capacity to develop respectful, intimate relationships.

Sexual exploration and expression outside the gender binary and heterosexual norms have been and are still to date major challenges for disabled youth (Abbott and Howarth, 2007; Rodríguez-Roldán, 2020; Smith et al., 2022). Parental reactions to coming out of 2SLGBTQ+ disabled youth have been described as unpredictable and diverse but overall negative (Abbott and Burns, 2007; Vassallo and Azzopardi Lane, 2022). As a consequence, 2SLGBTQ+ disabled youth tend to remain in the closet for longer, because of the fear of being rejected or losing support. Feelings of loneliness and isolation are intertwined with experiences of homophobia and transphobia that increase the likelihood of developing mental health issues (Dinwoodie, Greenhill and Cookson, 2020). 2SLGBTQ+ disabled persons report feeling equally excluded from both LGBT+ and disabled persons' communities, leading to increased social exclusion (Dispenza, Harper and Harrigan, 2016; Santinele Martino, 2017; Vassallo and Azzopardi Lane, 2022). A participant in Vassallo and Azzopardi's (2022) research carried out with persons who had intersecting identities claimed that it was difficult to be part of the disabled community as a person who identifies as LGBT+ and the other way around:

It was difficult on the other hand since the local community is mostly about parties and bars. You know? It's quite stereotypical. I don't like people touching me and the noise, so I don't really find where to go, so I stay alone a lot (p. 46).

Research carried out in Australia by Leonard and Mann (2018) similarly reported disabled persons experiencing health disparities were discriminated from within both the LGBT+ and disability communities. This, the authors report, compounds their 'sense of social marginality and isolation and contributing to their increased risk of mental health problems' (Leonard and Mann, 2018, p. 6).

Still a Taboo Topic: The Lack of Conversations and Supports about Sexuality

Disabled youth experience barriers in terms of accessing services and supports related to sexuality (Heller et al., 2016; Toft, Franklin and Langley, 2020). A study by McDaniels and Fleming (2016) suggests that disabled adolescents tend to have lower levels of knowledge about sexuality as well as fewer opportunities to learn about sexuality in comparison with non-disabled youth. Sex education tends to be inaccessible for disabled youth.

Some students with disabilities are even removed from sex education classes under the assumption that they do not need such information, that they might not understand, or that they should not receive such information. Disabled people commonly report their experiences of sex education to be limited and unhelpful (Gougeon, 2009; Swango-Wilson, 2011). When information is provided, it is primarily, if not solely, focused on biology, risk and rules continues to perpetrate shame, fear, and negativity (Frawley and Wilson, 2016). Furthermore, disabled youth are rarely given an opportunity to discuss sexual pleasure. Sexuality education for disabled youth tends to only address abuse and risk while ignoring other more positive aspects of sexuality, including sexual pleasure (Frawley and Bigby, 2014; Tepper, 2000). In their research with self-advocates, Hole, Schnellert, and Cantle (2021, p. 6) quote a person with intellectual disability who suggested that those delivering sex education should work with couples, stating:

> Yes, work with couples, see if their relationships are doing well. . . It's like do you take birth control pills? Or do you have something special in your tummy so you don't get pregnant?

Retznik et al. (2022b) interviewed 42 parents and caregivers of young people with intellectual disability (aged 14–25), asking them for their perspectives on experiences of intimate relationships. The participants were reported to minimise the importance of the young people's relationships although they wished for a future stable partnership. Yet again they recognised how their children had limited social opportunities, partner selection possibilities, and time spent with their partner was not of the desired quality.

There is often great reluctance from family members, caregivers, and support staff to talk about sex and sexuality with disabled youth (Correa, Castro and Barrada, 2021; Lewis et al., 2020). Service providers often report feeling unprepared to provide supports related to sexuality and sexual expression (Secor-Turner, McMorris and Scal, 2017). Caregivers may sometimes feel uncomfortable initiating conversations about sexuality and may choose to avoid having such discussion altogether (East and Orchard, 2014). Some service providers may also be hesitant to approach the topic with clients due to concerns that family members and caregivers may have different values and create conflicts. Pariseau-Legault et al. (2019) explored support workers' ethical implications when addressing relationships of service users. Participants in a Canadian context reported a lack of policies that acknowledge and guide staff in addressing the sexual needs of their clients, leaving it up to 'the sensitivity of individual support workers' (Pariseau-Legault et al., 2019, p. 5). Yet, while understanding the need for sexual expression, supporting such expression was described as 'transgressing professional and organisational boundaries' (Pariseau-Legault et al., 2019, p. 5) thus making it an informal part of their role rather than an essential one.

According to some studies, disabled people want access to sex education that is factual, comprehensive, and ongoing (Brown and McCann, 2018; Vassallo and Azzopardi Lane, 2022). Frawley and Wilson (2016) led focus groups with young men and women with intellectual disability in Australia. Their participants knew facts and rules related to sexual behaviour but not 'the "how to" of relationships' (Frawley and Wilson, 2016, p. 469). They also wanted to learn more and to have more opportunities to explore their sexuality more. More problematically, even though a lot of learning about intimate relationships and sex happens through trial and error, just like in the rest of the general population, the room for mistakes that is afforded to disabled people tends to be a lot smaller compared to non-disabled people (Santinele Martino, 2019). In Malta, the last National Sexual Health Survey (Department of Health, 2012) revealed that the average age for first sexual intercourse of participants between the ages of 16 and 18 was 15 years old. While the average age for the first sexual intercourse of the entire participant population was 18 years old, the survey also showed how the average age of first intercourse decreases with the respondents' age and was reported to be 19 in those 30–40 years old and 17 years old amongst those participants aged 19–29. Yet, when it comes to disabled youth, the topic of disability and sexuality tends to be seen as 'too sensitive' and taboo to be discussed and addressed and most disabled youths do not have access to the same sexual experiences as non-disabled youth (Azzopardi Lane and Callus, 2015).

Spaces for Relationships and Sexual Exploration

Disabled youth often lack access to social networks, opportunities, and spaces typically granted to non-disabled youth to explore their sexuality and form intimate relationships. Disabled people face obstacles to accessing 'spaces and processes that teach and prepare young people for sex/uality and intimacy' (Liddiard and Slater, 2018, p. 326). For instance, children and youth with intellectual disabilities are commonly denied access to the formal sex education curriculum but also to the hidden curriculum of sexuality that takes place through interactions outside of the classroom (Gougeon, 2009). In research with people with intellectual disabilities in Canada, Santinele Martino (2021) found that, due to social isolation and access to a limited range of spaces, participants' pool of potential partners was commonly restricted to other disabled people. Participants were often restricted to 'intellectual disability sexual fields', meaning spaces that primarily occupied by people with intellectual disabilities, such as group homes and day programmes (Santinele Martino, 2021, p. 1233). Though not intended to be used as a sexual space, disabled people were using those spaces to find love and partnership with other disabled people. The challenge though is that these spaces contain rules in place that disallow forms of sexual expression, such as kissing, touching, and holding hands (Frawley and Wilson, 2016; Santinele Martino, 2021). Even spaces that should supposedly provide disabled people with some level of privacy for sexual expression, such as one's own bedroom, can be highly controlled and monitored my family members and support workers (Retznik et al., 2022a). Sometimes, people are not allowed to sexually explore their bodies, masturbate, have partners over, or watch pornography in their own bedroom (Azzopardi Lane and Callus, 2015; Björnsdóttir and Stefánsdóttir, 2020; Wilson et al., 2011). Unfortunately, this lack of privacy, rather than protect, can push some disabled people into potentially risky situations. For example, the lack of privacy can lead some to find other, perhaps less appropriate spaces, to engage in sexual expression, such as public parks (Hollomotz and Speakup Committee, 2009; Santinele Martino, 2021).

Some disabled youth also live in certain housing arrangements that are simply not conducive or that do not allow for sexual expression. This can be seen in the case of disabled youth living in nursing homes and long-term facilities. Because it is commonly assumed that only older adults live in these types of facilities, young disabled people receive little attention in terms of their unique needs. However, in the province of Nova Scotia in Canada, for instance, 87 people between ages 30–40 lived-in long-term care facilities, and at least another 21 were under the age of 30 (Gillmore, 2021). Canada has ratified the United Nations Convention on the Rights of Persons with Disabilities (2006), which states in Article 19 that disabled people have the right to 'live in the community with choices equal to others'. This includes having access to different residential options and the opportunity to choose where and with whom to live with. Furthermore, Article 22 refers to the right to privacy 'regardless of place of residence or living arrangements' and Article 23 refers to the right to explore and express one's sexuality, engage and maintain relationships, and have children on equal basis with non-disabled persons. Yet, this social phenomenon of disabled youth in long-term care facilities is seen in other Canadian provinces and countries as well. As one can imagine, living in a nursing home can curtail the community participation and opportunities for disabled youth to have romantic relationships and sexual experiences. This is similarly reported by Callus, Bonello and Micallef (2022, p. 3) who claim, following Bezzina's (2018) systematic review of studies carried out in a Maltese context, that many persons with intellectual disability 'do not enjoy the right to choose where to live, with who and with which arrangements even if this right is in the UNCRPD Act (2021)'. However, disabled youth can be resilient and transgress socio-sexual norms ascribed to them. Mark, a participant in research carried out by Azzopardi Lane and Callus (2015, p. 5), for example, has claimed that 'physical intimacy is important, otherwise what do you stay doing, watching TV?'.

Disabled people are seeking and finding alternative spaces to be sexual. This includes digital sexual spaces. There is evidence that digital spaces, such as dating websites and mobile applications, are being used by disabled people to meet potential intimate partners and pursue relationships (Santinele Martino and Kinitz, 2022). In addition, social media platforms are changing people's opportunities to meet others and date and share their experiences with love, romance, and intimacy. One could say that, by posting photos online with their partners and sharing their experiences as a couple, people are challenging de-sexualising ideas and making other people seeing that – shifts of mentality and progress (Santinele Martino and Campbell, 2019). For instance, with over a million followers on their YouTube channel (Squirmy and Grubs), Shane (disabled) and Hannah (non-disabled) document the role of disability in their relationship, including the ways in which disability brings the two closer together. Disabled youth are entitled to intimate citizenship, meaning our 'rights to choose what we do with our bodies, our feelings, our identities, our relationships, our genders, our eroticisms and our representations' (Plummer, 1995, p. 17). Although disabled youth may at times require additional support and protection to have a satisfying and safe intimate life, they should still have the opportunity to learn about sexuality, form intimate relationships, and make mistakes and learn from them.

Learning from Disabled Youth

The mantra from disabled activists, 'nothing about us without us', emphasises the inclusion of disabled people in the process of knowledge production (Charlton, 1998). This is in response to how disabled people have historically not been recognised as knowers nor been at the front line of knowledge production (Santinele Martino and Fudge Schormans, 2018). This commitment to challenging hierarchies of knowledge can start by working with disabled youth as co-researchers, as meaningful partners in research and change making. It can sometimes be challenging to obtain ethical approval for research projects involving disabled adults, especially intellectual disabilities (Santinele Martino and Fudge Schormans, 2018). It can be even more challenging to gain such approval when research involves disabled children and youth, especially in research related to gender and sexuality, due to notions of vulnerability and protectionism (Azzopardi Lane, 2022; Earle and Blackburn, 2020; Santinele Martino, 2022). Both of us have witnessed instances when graduate students and early career scholars have been actively discouraged by ethics review boards and faculty members from doing research with disabled youth, due to concerns that participants are just 'too vulnerable', or that ethics application processes may take too long and delay students' progress, or that it would just 'be wiser' to rely on the knowledge and perspectives of other social actors, such as the family members and support workers or other professionals working with disabled youth. Regardless of the reason, the problem is that disabled youth may be left out from research due to gate-keeping by people in their lives and processes that silence and disempower a social group that is so often silenced in research.

As Santinele Martino (2020, p. 23) has noted, 'disability studies has been largely adult-focused, driven by adults' agenda and perspectives' and, at the same time, the 'experiences explored in childhood studies is often that of the non-disabled, "normal" child with less space for disabled children and youth' (see also Curran and Runswick-Cole, 2014; Goodley and Runswick-Cole, 2012). Activism in the area of sexuality contributes to disability activism by highlighting the multifaceted experiences of disabled persons and highlighting their intersectional identities and the relationship of these aspects to the social model of disability rather than focusing on the impairment. Disabled youth should have the opportunity and space to help set the agenda for disability activism and scholarship. Meanwhile, disabled youth can also count on an impressive network of disabled activists who are using creative platforms, including YouTube videos, blogs, podcasts, and comic books, to question the silences around discussions related to disability and sexuality (Santinele Martino, 2020; Santinele Martino and Campbell, 2019). In Canada, for example, Andrew Gurza (2023) – a queer disabled man – is behind the podcast, Disability After Dark, which explores different aspects of disability and sexuality.

Rather than simply reproducing normative understandings of sexuality, disabled youth are sometimes engaging in the act of 'cripping' sex and sexuality. By challenging and transforming, non-disabled understandings of sexuality, they are calling into question 'what and who is sexy' and 'what counts as sex' (McRuer and Mollow, 2012, p. 32). They are 'cripping' sexuality by, for example, questioning the idea that sex needs to follow a specific order and script that sex cannot involve the support of a third party, or what counts as a meaningful intimate relationship (Santinele Martino and Fudge Schormans, 2021). At the end of the day, everyone – disabled and non-disabled – can benefit from a more expansive understanding of sexuality and a menu of possibilities. Normative understandings of what counts as sexual, for example, limit our attention to only exploring certain parts of the body (i.e., reproductive organs) while denying the possibility for other erogenous and pleasure zones, such as ear lobes and the scalp. By cripping sexuality, disabled people are expanding the overall repertoire of sexual possibilities for all sexual actors in our social world.

Conclusion

This chapter places a spotlight on the experiences of sexual exploration and expression that disabled youth are likely to embark upon, including those youth going through the adolescent years, where their sexuality is steadily developing. The social factors affecting disabled youth's sexuality are highlighted against a backdrop of cultural restraints, ranging from infantilisation to prohibition. A bold gendered element can also be clearly identified as an inhibitor to sexual emancipation. This form of disempowerment is common amongst other minorities including persons with intellectual disability and persons from sexual and gender diverse origins. Sex education plays an important role in this area, its availability and accessibility serving as the catalyst to informed decision making, self-determination, and sexual advocacy. The sexual citizenship of disabled youth cannot be shelved till their adult years are due and needs to be seen as a holistic aspect of the person's life on an equal basis with non-disabled youth. Their sexuality needs to be given social, education, and political platforms where to evolve and flourish and their voices need to be given the opportunity to not just be heard but to lead the conversation.

References

Abbott, D. and Burns, J. 2007. What's love got to do with it?: Experiences of lesbian, gay, and bisexual people with intellectual disabilities in the United Kingdom and views of the staff who support them. *Sexuality Research & Social Policy*, 4(1), pp. 27–39.

Abbott, D. and Howarth, J. 2007. Still off-limits? Staff views on supporting gay, lesbian and bisexual people with intellectual disabilities to develop sexual and intimate relationships? *Journal of Applied Research in Intellectual Disabilities*, 20(2), pp. 116–126.

Abma, J.C. and Martinez, G.M. 2017. Sexual activity and contraceptive use among teenagers in the United States, 2011–2015. *National health statistics reports*; no 104. Hyattsville, MD: National Center for Health Statistics.

Alexander, N. and Taylor Gomez, M. 2017. Pleasure, sex, prohibition, intellectual disability, and dangerous ideas. *Reproductive Health Matters*, 25(50), pp. 114–120.

Azzopardi, A. and Azzopardi Lane, C. 2021. Positive Parenting Project. [online] [Accessed on 8 April 2022]. Available from: https://www.um.edu.mt/library/oar/handle/123456789/95822

Azzopardi Lane, C. 2022. Disability and sexuality; rewriting the narratives of vulnerability. In: Grassi, P. and Zammit, R. eds. *La bioetica e il paradoso delle apparenze: Fragilità, dipendenza, disabilità nelle varie fasi della vita*. Rome, Italy: Armando Editori

Azzopardi Lane, C. and Callus, A.M. 2015. Constructing sexual identities: people with intellectual disability talking about sexuality. *British Journal of Learning Disabilities*, 43(1), pp. 32–37.

Bahner, J. 2019. Mapping the terrain of disability and sexuality: from policy to practice. *Ars Vivendi Journal*, 11, pp. 27–47.

Bahner, J. 2021. Access to sexuality: disabled people's experiences of multiple barriers. In: Egard, H., Hansson, K. and Wasterfors, D. eds. *Accessibility denied: understanding inaccessibility and everyday resistance to inclusion for persons with disabilities*. London: Routledge, pp. 123–139.

Bezzina, L. 2018. Systematic review [Masters' and L.L.D. Dissertations on Disability in Malta]. https://www.um.edu.mt/__data/assets/pdf_file/0011/373781/MADissertationsSystematicReviewNovember2018.pdf

Björnsdóttir, K. and Stefánsdóttir, G.V. 2020. Double sexual standards: sexuality and people with intellectual disabilities who require intensive support. *Sexuality and Disability*, 38(3), pp. 421–438.

Björnsdóttir, K., Stefánsdóttir, A. and Stefánsdóttir, G.V. 2017. People with intellectual disabilities negotiate autonomy, gender and sexuality. *Sexuality & Disability*, 35(3), pp. 295–311.

Brown, M. and McCann, E. 2018. Sexuality issues and the voices of adults with intellectual disabilities: a systematic review of the literature. *Research in Developmental Disabilities*, 74, pp. 124–138.

Callus, A.M., Bonello, I. and Micallef, B. 2022. Advocacy and self-advocacy in Malta: reflections on the lives of Maltese people with intellectual disability from the 1950s to the present day. *British Journal of Learning Disabilities*, 50(2), pp. 156–165.

Campbell, M., Löfgren-Mårtenson, C. and Martino, A.S. 2020. Cripping sex education. *Sex Education*, 20(4), pp. 361–365.

Charlton, J.I. 1998. *Nothing about Us without Us: Disability Oppression and Empowerment*. Berkeley, CA: University of California Press.

Chouinard, V., Cormode, L., Golledge, G., Butler, R., Bowlby, S. and Parr, H. 1997. Geographies of disability. *Environment and Planning. D. Society & Space*, 15(4), pp. 379–480.

Cicero, F.R. 2019. Shaping effective masturbation in persons with developmental disabilities: a review of the literature. *Sexuality and Disability*, 37(1), pp. 91–108.

Collins, J. and Murphy, G.H. 2022. Detection and prevention of abuse of adults with intellectual and other developmental disabilities in care services: a systematic review. *Journal of Applied Research in Intellectual Disabilities*, 35(2), pp. 338–373.

Convention on the Rights of Persons with Disabilities and Optional Protocol. 2006. [online] [Accessed on 10 October 2021]. Available from: www.un.org/disabilities/documents/convention/convoptprot-e.pdf.

Correa, A.B., Castro, Á. and Barrada, J.R. 2021. Attitudes towards the sexuality of adults with intellectual disabilities: a systematic review. *Sexuality and Disability*, 40(2), pp. 261–287.

Curran, T. and Runswick-Cole, K. 2014. Disabled children's childhood studies: a distinct approach? *Disability & Society*, 29(10), pp. 1617–1630.

Department of Health. 2012. National Sexual Health Survey. [25 January 2023]. Available from: https://deputyprimeminister.gov.mt/en/dhir/Pages/Surveys/sexualhealthsurvey2012.aspx

Dinwoodie, R., Greenhill, B. and Cookson, A. 2020. 'Them two things are what collide together': understanding the sexual identity experiences of lesbian, gay, bisexual and trans people labelled with intellectual disability. *Journal of Applied Research in Intellectual Disabilities*, 33(1), pp. 3–16.

Dispenza, F., Harper, L.S. and Harrigan, M.A. 2016. Subjective health among LGBT persons living with disabilities: a qualitative content analysis. *Rehabilitation Psychology*, 61(3), pp. 251–259.

Earle, S. and Blackburn, M. 2020. Involving young people with life-limiting conditions in research on sex: the intersections of taboo and vulnerability. *International Journal of Social Research Methodology*, 24(5), pp. 545–551.

East, L.J. and Orchard, T.R. 2014. Somebody else's job: experiences of sex education among health professionals, parents and adolescents with physical disabilities in southwestern Ontario. *Sexuality and Disability*, 32(3), pp. 335–350.

Fish, R. 2016. "They've said I'm vulnerable with men": doing sexuality on locked wards. *Sexualities*, 19(5–6), pp. 641–658.

Fisher, M.H., Baird, J.V., Currey, A.D. and Hodapp, R.M. 2016. Victimisation and social vulnerability of adults with intellectual disability: a review of research extending beyond Wilson and Brewer. *Australian Psychologist*, 51(2), pp. 114–127.

Frawley, P. and Bigby, C. 2014. "I'm in their shoes": experiences of peer educators in sexuality and relationship education. *Journal of Intellectual and Developmental Disability*, 39(2), pp. 167–176.

Frawley, P. and O'Shea, A. 2020. 'Nothing about us without us': sex education by and for people with intellectual disability in Australia. *Sex Education*, 20(4), pp. 413–424.

Frawley, P. and Wilson, N.J. 2016. Young people with intellectual disability talking about sexuality education and information. *Sexuality and Disability*, 34(4), pp. 469–484.

Gil-Llario, M.D., Morell-Mengual, V., Díaz-Rodríguez, I. and Ballester-Arnal, R. 2019. Prevalence and sequelae of self-reported and other-reported sexual abuse in adults with intellectual disability. *Journal of Intellectual Disability Research*, 63(2), pp. 138–148.

Gill, M. 2012. Sex can wait, masturbate: the politics of masturbation training. *Sexualities*, 15(3–4), pp. 472–493.

Gillmore, M. 2021. Stuck in long-term care. [Online]. [Accessed on 10 February 2023]. Available from: https://www.abilities.ca/abilities-magazine/stuck-in-long-term-care-2/

Goodley, D. and Runswick-Cole, K. 2012. Decolonizing methodology: disabled children as research managers and participant ethnographers. In: Azzopardi, A. and Grech, S. eds. *Inclusive communities* (Volume 16). Rotterdam; Boston: Sense Publishers, pp. 215–232.

Gougeon, N.A. 2009. Sexual education for students with intellectual disabilities, a critical pedagogical approach: outing the ignored curriculum. *Sex Education*, 9(3), pp. 277–291.

Gurza, A. 2023. Episode 323: My Gimpy Life w/ Teal Sherer. Disability After Dark. [Podcast]. [Accessed on 14 February 2023]. Available from: https://podcasts.apple.com/ca/podcast/episode-323-my-gimpy-life-w-teal-sherer/id1151890990?i=1000598058891.

Heller, M.K., Gambino, S., Church, P., Lindsay, S., Kaufman, M. and McPherson, A.C. 2016. Sexuality and relationships in young people with Spina Bifida and their partners. *Journal of Adolescent Health*, 59(2), pp. 182–188.

Hobaica, S. and Kwon, P. 2017. "This Is How You Hetero:" sexual minorities in heteronormative sex education. *American Journal of Sexuality Education*, 12(4), pp. 423–450.

Hole, R., Schnellert, L. and Cantle, G. 2021. Sex: what is the big deal? Exploring individuals' with intellectual disabilities experiences with sex education. *Qualitative Health Research*, 32(3), pp. 453–464.

Hollomotz, A. 2011. *Learning difficulties and sexual vulnerability: a social approach*. London: Jessica Kingsley Publishers.

Hollomotz, A. 2013. Disability, oppression and violence: towards a sociological explanation. *Sociology*, 47(3), pp. 477–493.

Hollomotz, A. and Speakup Committee. 2009. 'May we please have sex tonight?'–people with learning difficulties pursuing privacy in residential group settings. *British Journal of Learning Disabilities*, 37(2), pp. 91–97.

Kallianes, V. and Rubenfeld, P. 1997. Disabled women and reproductive rights. *Disability & Society*, 12(2), pp. 203–222.

Kittay, E.F. 2011. Forever small: the strange case of Ashley X. *Hypatia*, 26(3), pp. 610–631.

Langdon, P.E., Murphy, G.H., Clare, I.C.H., Steverson, T. and Palmer, E.J. 2011. Relationships among moral reasoning, empathy, and distorted cognitions in men with intellectual disabilities and a history of criminal offending. *American Journal on Intellectual and Developmental Disabilities*, 116(6), pp. 438–456.

Leonard, W. and Mann, R. 2018. *The everyday experiences of lesbian, gay, bisexual, transgender and intersex (LGBTI) people living with disability*. [Online]. [Accessed on 2 April 2023]. Available from: https://apo.org.au/node/193361

Lewis, B., Richards, S., Rice, S. and Collis, A. 2020. A response to Bates, C et al. 2020. "Always trying to walk a bit of a tightrope": the role of social care staff in supporting adults with intellectual and developmental disabilities to develop and maintain loving relationships. *British Journal of Learning Disabilities*, 48(4), pp. 269–271.

Liasidou, A. and Gregoriou, A. 2021. A longitudinal analysis of disability-related interpersonal violence and some implications for violence prevention work. *Journal of Interpersonal Violence*, 36(15–16), pp. NP8687–NP8705.

Liddiard, K. and Slater, J. 2018. 'Like, pissing yourself is not a particularly attractive quality, let's be honest': learning to contain through youth, adulthood, disability and sexuality. *Sexualities*, 21(3), pp. 319–333.

Liégeois, A. 2022. Sexuality in persons with intellectual disabilities: a challenge to Church morality. *International Journal for the Study of the Christian Church*, 22(1), pp. 35–46.

Majeed-Ariss, R., Rodriguez, P.M. and White, C. 2020. The disproportionately high prevalence of learning disabilities amongst adults attending Saint Marys Sexual Assault Referral Centre. *Journal of Applied Research in Intellectual Disabilities*, 33(3), pp. 595–603.

Malacrida, C. 2020. Mothering and disability: from eugenics to newgenics. In: Watson, N., Roulstone, A. and Thomas, C. eds. *Routledge handbook of disability studies*. 2nd ed. London: Routledge, pp. 467–478.

McCarthy, M. 2002. Going through the menopause: perceptions and experiences of women with intellectual disability. *Journal of Intellectual and Developmental Disability*, 27(4), pp. 281–295.

McCarthy, M. 2009. 'I have the jab so I can't be blamed for getting pregnant': contraception and women with learning disabilities. *Women's Studies International Forum*, 32(3), pp. 198–208.

McConnell, D. and Phelan, S. 2022. The devolution of eugenic practices: sexual and reproductive health and oppression of people with intellectual disability. *Social Science & Medicine*, 298, p. 114877.

McDaniels, B. and Fleming, A. 2016. Sexuality education and intellectual disability: time to address the challenge. *Sexuality and Disability*, 34(2), pp. 215–225.

McRuer, R. 2011. Disabling sex: notes for a crip theory of sexuality. *GLQ*, **17**(1), pp. 107–117.

McRuer, R. and Mollow, A. 2012. *Sex and disability*. Durham: Duke University Press.

Morales, E., Gauthier, V., Edwards, G. and Courtois, F. 2016. Women with disabilities' perceptions of sexuality, sexual abuse and masturbation. *Sexuality and Disability*, **34**(3), pp. 303–314.

Murphy, G.H. 2003. Capacity to consent to sexual relationships in adults with learning disabilities. *BMJ Sexual and Reproductive Health*, **29**(3), pp. 148–149.

Nelson, B., Odberg Pettersson, K. and Emmelin, M. 2020. Experiences of teaching sexual and reproductive health to students with intellectual disabilities. *Sex Education*, **20**(4), pp. 398–412.

O'Shea, A. and Frawley, P. 2020. Gender, sexuality and relationships for young australian women with intellectual disability. *Disability and Society*, **35**(4), pp. 654–675.

Othelia Lee, E.K. and Oh, H. 2005. A wise wife and good mother: reproductive health and maternity among women with disability in South Korea. *Sexuality and Disability*, **23**(3), pp. 121–144.

Pariseau-Legault, P., Holmes, D., Ouellet, G. and Vallée-Ouimet, S. 2019. An ethical inquiry of support workers' experiences related to sexuality in the context of intellectual disabilities in Quebec, Canada. *British Journal of Learning Disabilities*, **47**(2), pp. 116–125.

Plummer, K. 1995. *Telling sexual stories: power, change, and social worlds*. London: Routledge.

Renwick, R., Schormans, A.F. and Shore, D. 2014. Hollywood takes on intellectual/developmental disability: cinematic representations of occupational participation. *OTJR: Occupation, Participation and Health*, **34**(1), pp. 20–31.

Retznik, L., Wienholz, S., Höltermann, A., Conrad, I. and Riedel-Heller, S.G. 2021. "Everyone would like their child to have a boyfriend or a girlfriend." Young people with intellectual disability and their experiences with intimate relationships: a follow-up analysis of parents' and caregivers' perspectives. *Sexuality and Disability*, **40**, pp. 299–314.

Retznik, L., Wienholz, S., Höltermann, A., Conrad, I. and Riedel-Heller, S.G. 2022a. Young people with intellectual disability and their experiences with intimate relationships: a follow-up analysis of parents' and caregivers' perspectives. *Sexuality and Disability*, **40**(2), pp. 299–314.

Retznik, L., Wienholz, S., Höltermann, A., Conrad, I. and Riedel-Heller, S.G. 2022b. 'It Gives Me, as her Caregiver, a Sense of Security.' Young people with intellectual disability and their experiences with sexuality, menstruation, gynecological treatment and contraception: a follow-up analysis of parents' and caregivers' perspectives. *Sexuality and Disability*, **41**(1), pp. 97–116.

Rodríguez-Roldán, V. 2020. The intersection between disability and LGBT discrimination and marginalization. *American University Journal of Gender, Social Policy & the Law*, **28**(3), pp. 429–440.

Rowsell, A.C., Clare, I.C. and Murphy, G.H. 2013. The psychological impact of abuse on men and women with severe intellectual disabilities. *Journal of Applied Research in Intellectual Disabilities*, **26**(4), pp. 257–270.

Rubin, G. 1984. Thinking sex: notes for a radical theory of the politics of sexuality. In: Vance, C.S. ed. *Pleasure and danger: exploring female sexuality*. Boston: Routledge, pp. 267–319.

Santinele Martino, A. 2017. Cripping sexualities: an analytic review of theoretical and empirical writing on the intersection of disabilities and sexualities. *Sociology Compass*, **11**(5), e12471–n/a.

Santinele Martino, A. 2019. "It is totally a power struggle": struggles over the sexuality of individuals with intellectual disabilities in Southern Alberta. In: Malinene, K. ed. *Dis/consent: perspectives on sexual violence and consensuality*. Nova Scotia: Fernwood Press, pp. 98–107.

Santinele Martino, A. 2020. Also here, also queer: the work of queer disabled activists/scholars in "cripping" sexualities. In: Toft, A., Frankline A. and Langley, E. eds. *Young, disabled and LGBT+: voices, identities and intersections*. New York: Routledge, pp. 13–28.

Santinele Martino, A. 2021. 'I don't want to get in trouble': a study of how adults with intellectual disabilities convert and navigate intellectual disability sexual fields. *Culture, Health & Sexuality*, **24**(9), pp. 1230–1243.

Santinele Martino, A. 2022. The intersection of sexuality and intellectual disabilities: shattering the taboo. In: Fischer, N.L., Westbrook, L. and Seidman, S. eds. *Introducing the new sexuality studies: original essays*. 4th ed. New York: Routledge, pp. 460–469.

Santinele Martino, A. and Campbell, S.M. 2019. Exercising intimate citizenship rights and (re)constructing sexualities: the new place of sexuality in disability activism. In: Berghs, M., Chataika, T., El-Lahib Y. and Dube, K. eds. *The new disability activism: current trends, shifting priorities and (uncertain) future directions*. New York: Routledge, pp. 97–109.

Santinele Martino, A. and Fudge Schormans, A. 2018. When good intentions backfire: university research ethics review and the intimate lives of people labelled with intellectual disabilities. *Forum: Qualitative Social Research*, **19**(3), n/p.

Santinele Martino, A. and Fudge Schormans, A. 2021. Theoretical developments: queer theory meets crip theory. In: Shuttleworth, R. and Mona, L. eds. *Routledge handbook of disability and sexuality*. London: Routledge, pp. 53–67.

Santinele Martino, A. and Kinitz, D.J. 2022. "It's just more complicated!": experiences of adults with intellectual disabilities when navigating digital sexual fields. *Cyberpsychology: Journal of Psychosocial Research on Cyberspace*, **16**(2), Article 6.

Schaafsma, D., Kok, G., Stoffelen, J.M.T. and Curfs, L.M.G. 2017. People with intellectual disabilities talk about sexuality: implications for the development of sex education. *Sexuality and Disability*, **35**(1), pp. 21–38.

Schuengel, C., Cuypers, M., Bakkum, L. and Leusink, G.L. 2022. Reproductive health of women with intellectual disability: antenatal care, pregnancies and outcomes in the Dutch population. *Journal of Intellectual Disability Research*. https://doi.org/10.1111/jir.12982.

Secor-Turner, M., McMorris, B.J. and Scal, P. 2017. Improving the sexual health of young people with mobility impairments: challenges and recommendations. *Journal of Pediatric Health Care*, **31**(5), pp. 578–587.

Shakespeare, T. 2000. Disabled sexuality: toward rights and recognition. *Sexuality & Disability*, **18**(3), pp. 159–166.

Shildrick, M. 2007. Contested pleasures: the sociopolitical economy of disability and sexuality. *Sexuality Research & Social Policy*, **4**(1), pp. 53–66.

Smith, E., Zirnsak, T.M., Power, J., Lyons, A. and Bigby, C. 2022. Social inclusion of LGBTQ and gender diverse adults with intellectual disability in disability services:

a systematic review of the literature. *Journal of Applied Research in Intellectual Disabilities*, **35**(1), pp. 46–59.

Squirmy and Grubs. [Video]. Squirmy and Grubs. [Online]. [Accessed on March 2023] https://www.youtube.com/c/squirmyandgrubs.

Stoffelen, J., Kok, G., Hospers, H. and Curfs, L.M.G. 2013. Homosexuality among people with a mild intellectual disability: an explorative study on the lived experiences of homosexual people in the Netherlands with a mild intellectual disability. *Journal of Intellectual Disability Research*, **57**(3), pp. 257–267.

Swango-Wilson, A. 2011. Meaningful sex education programs for individuals with intellectual/developmental disabilities. *Sexuality & Disability*, **29**(2), pp. 113–118.

Tepper, M.S. 2000. Sexuality and disability: the missing discourse of pleasure. *Sexuality and Disability*, **18**(4), pp. 283–290.

Toft, A., Franklin, A. and Langley, E. 2020. 'You're not sure that you are gay yet': the perpetuation of the 'phase' in the lives of young disabled LGBT + people. *Sexualities*, **23**(4), pp. 516–529.

Tordoff, D.M., Haley, S.G., Shook, A., Kantor, A., Crouch, J.M. and Ahrens, K. 2021. "Talk about Bodies": recommendations for using transgender-inclusive language in sex education curricula. *Sex Roles: A Journal of Research*, **84**(3), pp. 152–165.

UNDESA [no date]. *Definition of Youth. United Nations Department of Economic and Social Affairs*. [Online]. [Accessed on 3 January 2023]. Available from: https://www.un.org/esa/socdev/documents/youth/fact-sheets/youth-definition.pdf

Vassallo, M. and Azzopardi Lane, C. 2022. *Intersectionality and People with Disability*. [Online]. [Accessed on 3 January 2023]. Available from: https://www.crpd.org.mt/resources/research/

Wilson, N.J., Parmenter, T.R., Stancliffe, R.J. and Shuttleworth, R.P. 2011. Conditionally sexual: men and teenage boys with moderate to profound intellectual disability. *Sexuality and Disability*, **29**(3), pp. 275–289.

16

ACCESS TO HIGHER EDUCATION AND PREPARATION FOR ADULTHOOD OF YOUNG PERSONS WITH INTELLECTUAL DISABILITY IN MEXICO

Challenges of the *Somos Uno Más* [*We Are One of the Same*] Programme

Jesica Paola Gomez Muñoz, Maria Edith Reyes Lastiri and Tomas Puentes Leon

Introduction

The increase in inclusive programmes and initiatives to widen access to higher education have also expanded the opportunities for persons with intellectual disability, with positive benefits and transformational aspects that enrich the life of students with regard to their autonomy, friendship, relationships and qualification-levels (Corby et al., 2020). These experiences have highlighted the importance of building skills for future employment (Grigal et al., 2021) and promoting wider opportunities for the life-course trajectories of persons with disabilities that will impact on their adult life (Uditsky and Hughson, 2012). Access to higher education for persons with disabilities has been also recognised for enhancing the educational experience for stakeholders, staff and peers by valuing diversity and inclusion (Corby et al., 2022; Tucker et al., 2020). However, the practice of inclusion tends to differ between initiatives designed as spaces for socialising and those offering a more involved academic experience, with a clearer impact on a 'normative' pathway for future adulthood (Uditsky and Hughson, 2012).

The transition to adulthood is considered a complex and meaningful step in the life-course (De Los Santos and Tinoco, 2013). It is often related to personal changes such as acquiring responsibilities and obligations and developing new aspects of social identity (Miller and Arvizu, 2016). In the case of persons with disabilities, this transition can be truncated, with misconceptions and barriers that lead to infantilisation along their life-course trajectories (Morris, 2002; Priestley, 2003). Thinking anew about how to develop

DOI: 10.4324/9781003102915-16

a more flexible and wider support-system might help challenge the current barriers, allowing young people to develop autonomy and independent skills for future adulthood. This rethinking may, in turn, increase opportunities for accessing employment, developing identities, exploring sexuality or leaving the family home to live in one's own place, among other life-course events often associated with adulthood (Ferrer Cerdà, 2001; Pallisera et al., 2014; Valls Fernández and Martínez Vicente, 2005). However, supports are often unavailable and participation is often restricted from key aspects of adulthood. Education is a key example. Additionally, the lack of support can even position these young people in a vulnerable position, facing situations of abandonment, institutionalisation, poverty or abusive conditions (Comisión Nacional de los Derechos Humanos, 2018).

The Mexican Legislative and Social Context

Mexico has ratified the Convention on the Rights of the Child (CRC) and the Convention on the Rights of Persons with Disabilities (CRPD), although some barriers can still be seen in education, where lower literacy (Male and Wodon, 2017) and lesser educational attainment (Unesco Institute for Statistics [UIS], 2018) are seen in persons with disabilities, when compared to persons without disabilities. Most recent data have shown that 31.7% of persons with disabilities between 6 and 17 years of age are illiterate (Secretaría de la Educación Pública, 2020). In addition, there is currently a schooling gap between persons with and without disability, which is exacerbated in the case of persons with intellectual disabilities, where only 28.3% have at least completed basic education (Leite, 2020). This data helps in evidencing that education is still far from being guaranteed as a right, leading to a situation that often detracts from experiencing full equality in society (Committee on The Rights of Persons with Disabilities, 2022).

This lack of access to education shows the disadvantaged position and successive structural difficulties experienced by persons with disabilities in Mexico (Leite, 2020). In 2017, the National Survey of Discrimination in Mexico reported that discrimination persists, with persons with disabilities facing multiple barriers for their full development, and stereotypes and prejudice around disability persisting nationally (Consejo Nacional para Prevenir la Discriminación, 2019). Education, as a key facilitator of the participation of persons with disabilities in mainstream activities (Pallisera et al., 2014), also contributes to fighting discrimination across different life domains (Padilla Muñoz, 2011).

In the case of persons with intellectual disability, access to higher education has gained some attention during recent years. However, it remains an emerging topic, with initiatives occurring predominantly in European countries (Björnsdóttir, 2017), the USA (Grigal et al., 2012) and Canada (Uditsky and

Hughson, 2012), where concepts of integration and inclusion are often mixed and different levels of inclusion can be recognised (Hart et al., 2004). Inclusion has been understood as involving the creation of the conditions for all people to be welcomed; unlike *integration*, which is a strategy specifically aimed at the inclusion of people with disability into the existing context (Cobeñas and Santuccione, 2022). In Latin America, inclusion of persons with disabilities in higher education has been a recent concern (Moreno, 2006), with strategies focusing on persons with intellectual disability still being in an emerging phase.

This chapter discusses issues in accessing to higher education and its role in preparing young persons with intellectual disabilities for adulthood in the Mexican context. It explores how the *Somos Uno Más* Programme [*We are one of the same*] has been implemented by Universidad Iberoamericana [Iberoamerican University] in Mexico City and analyses the support provided to their students with intellectual disability in their transition to adulthood.

Disability and Education in Mexico

Historical Milestones

In 1995, the *National Programme for Wellbeing and the Incorporation to Development of Persons with Disabilities* was created (CONVIVE), coordinated by the Integral Development for the Family System (DIF) and based on the United Nations Standard Rules on the Equalisation of Opportunities for Persons with Disabilities (General Assembly of United Nations, 1993). This change led to a transition in the country from a paternalistic to a social model of disability approach, with a focus on rights and dignity of persons with disabilities. In 2000, the creation of the Representation Office for the Promotion and Social Integration of Persons with Disabilities (ORPIS) and the National Council for the Integration of Persons with Disabilities (CONADIS) facilitated an institutional response to disability matters (CONADIS, 2017). During this time, the Public Education Secretary managed to articulate with different institutions and organisations for persons with disabilities forming part of CONADIS, which promoted intersectoral work together with health, work and social security secretaries.

Although previous decades were characterised by the promotion of programmes and institutions for persons with disabilities (Gobierno de México, 2014), access to higher education was still postponed, which led in 2002 to the publication of the *Manual for the Integration of Persons with Disabilities in Higher Education Institutions* by the National Association of Universities and Higher Education Institutions (ANUIES). This manual was designed to define guidelines for including persons with disabilities in higher education in Mexico (Asociación Nacional de Universidades e Instituciones de Educación Superior, 2002).

Moreover, in 2008, during the second Mexico-Spain binational meeting for the rights of persons with disabilities, held between universities in Mérida and Yucatán, the *Declaration of Yucatán on the Rights of Persons with Disabilities* was adopted and published. This Declaration recognised the need for guaranteeing persons with disabilities the right to study at universities without discrimination and promoting respect for diversity and the human condition, promoting a human rights approach and a gender perspective.

These efforts were helpful in making visible the problems faced by many persons with disabilities. However, despite the potential of these two initiatives, critiques have pointed towards its lack of actual implementation and reduced transformational power, with only minor changes being the result (Guajardo and Góngora, 2018). As noted by Cruz Vadillo (2016), higher education for persons with disabilities has been characterised by omissions and exclusions.

Current Situation

Article 3 of the *Political Constitution of the United Mexican States* (México, 1917, Art. 3) establishes the right to education for every person, where the State must guarantee education in all of its levels, including mandatory primary and secondary education. Since 2021, the *Higher Education General Law* understands higher education as a right that contributes to the well-being and development of persons (Ley General de Educación Superior, 2021). The law establishes that higher education must include a human rights perspective based on equality and inclusion. In addition, it also acknowledges the need to account for gender, interculturality, disability and youth. The law recognises the importance of multidisciplinary teams who work with persons with disabilities to identify their needs and the barriers that they face for studying and participating in mainstream activities.

The *Sectoral Education Programme 2020–2024* of the Public Education Secretary in Mexico proposed to achieve a higher level of inclusion and equality in education through a strategy focused on creating accessible conditions for students with disabilities in all types and levels of regular education services. Despite the effort, this policy has raised questions regarding its positive evaluation of special education, defining it as:

[An] educational service destined to persons with disabilities, transitory or definitive, but also to those with outstanding aptitudes, seeking that students be treated in an adequate way to their conditions, with an inclusive social equity and gender perspective.

(Secretaría de la Educación Pública, 2020, p. 21)

Therefore, exclusion and segregation are a constant present in the educational trajectory of students with disability, with a dual system of regular and specialised education that reinforces exclusion as a legitimated strategy (Pérez-Castro, 2019).

As noted before, most persons with disabilities experience a restricted educational pathway, where 46.9% of persons with disabilities present 'school gaps' compared to 14.5% of persons without disabilities (Leite, 2020). This difference has also been seen in terms of higher numbers of school dropouts (Acle Tomasini et al., 2007). The *UN Committee Concluding Observations on the Mexican State* also reported a high level of school dropouts in children with disabilities over 15 years of age, with women being more excluded from the first stages of education and secondary school by reasons of gender and disability, lack of accessibility and reasonable accommodation, among other issues (Committee on the Rights of Persons with Disabilities, 2022).

Additionally, only 22.1% of all persons with disabilities are included in secondary education level or higher settings, with a starker scenario in the case of persons with intellectual disabilities, where 40.9% have not received a formal education. In 2018, there were 1,100,000 persons with disabilities aged from 3 to 22 years, of whom 28,000 had access to higher education (Committee on the Rights of Persons with Disabilities, 2018), highlighting a situation where access to higher education is limited to the few.

As noted, it is during the young lives of people with disabilities when dropouts tend to occur, coinciding with the situation in the wider Latin America and Caribbean region (UNESCO, 2020). The barrier to accessing quality education after secondary school can be seen as even more problematic when considering that this is the period when persons with disabilities are involved in their transitions to adulthood and starting to negotiate decisions, develop autonomy, transition to the labour market and explore their sexuality and identities. Acknowledging the importance of these milestones in the life-course helps us to comprehend how this process needs to be supported and to consider the role that higher education is taking for persons with disabilities, with specific focus on persons with intellectual disabilities, in Mexico.

Transition to Adulthood in the Mexican Context

Generally, the transition to adulthood is analysed from the presence or absence of certain events, such as leaving school, the beginning of work, becoming independent from the family, developing new family-units and changing from an economic dependence to independence (Echarri Cánovas and Pérez Amador, 2007). These events tend to be presented as individual processes, rather than as part of an interrelated/interdependent experience. Additionally, it could be considered that the idealised approach taken is that most often achieved by a particular group within society: mainly a white, upper class, heterosexual and non-disabled male. Many of these life-course achievements are not entirely or easily available, or are more complex to achieve for women, members of minoritised ethnic and indigenous groups, persons with non-normative sexual orientations and gender identities, persons without disabilities and other marginalised groups in a situation of poverty (UNESCO, 2020). Although social inequalities based on class, gender, ethnicity, education, geography and disability are present in various parts of the world, it has been observed that in Latin America they are intertwined, generating cycles of exclusion, vulnerability and poverty (ECLAC, 2016).

In the case of disability and adulthood in Mexico, Skivington (2011) conducted an ethnography with the community of Cuernavaca, a city in South Central Mexico, the capital of the state of Morelos. This area has 18 schools for children with disabilities. Skivington (2011) found that most persons with disabilities have seen their ideas of adulthood limited by roles assigned to them, fostered by prejudice. They were often depicted as eternal children, holy innocents and objects of pity. In this sense, as noted by Brogna (2013), the community plays a significant role in shaping opportunities for transitioning from childhood to adulthood, conveying the idea that adulthood is constructed in a relational manner.

Brogna (2013), who studied the transition of persons with intellectual disability in Mexico, identified four components of adulthood: (i) self-care, (ii) self-determined physical distance, (iii) work and (iv) reproductivity and sexuality. This classification provided a flexible understanding of an adult life experience, where skills are developed within a varied spectrum that are dependent on interactions with wider relationships, instead of specific life-course markers. In that way, access to education and work enhance the opportunities for interactions that could help develop these different components. Subsequently, Brogna (2014) adds a second feature, explaining that there is an ongoing differentiation between 'them' and 'us', which positions persons with intellectual disability in the former and persons without disabilities in the latter. This represents a cultural barrier confronted by persons with intellectual disability, where there is a constant need to prove wrong the assumed idea of what is expected by 'them' and to challenge spaces that are assumed to be only for the non-disabled 'us'. Education, and higher education more specifically, is a space where young persons with intellectual disability can challenge expected adulthood pathways and can expand their future lives, not only concerned with being employed but also in terms of how they relate to their own communities.

Higher Education as a Space for Transitions

Higher Education in Mexico

Higher education in Mexico is characterised by its heterogeneity and complexity, with 13 subsystems, divided by their government dependence and accountability, source of funding, size, enrolment, field of studies, location and mission focus (OECD, 2019). Eleven are funded from either federal government or a mixed state and federal funding. Only two of all the subsystems are private institutions, independent from the government (Cruz López and Cruz López, 2008). The public institutions can be differentiated by their autonomy: the first group includes federal and state universities, and is dependent on government funding, but has autonomy with regard to their decisions; a second group is administered by decentralised government agencies and follows guidelines from the Secretariat of Public Education a third group is managed by other government agencies from different ministries.

In terms of enrolment, the majority – one-third – of students are in private universities, followed by public state and public federal universities. In recent years, there has been an increase from smaller direct provision subsystems, which considers technological universities, decentralised institutes of technology and intercultural universities (OECD, 2019). These have the objective to support the national production of industries by generating intensive programmes of two to three years, often reflecting the needs of the entrepreneur sector and based on a strong university-enterprise relationship (Aguirre García, 2022). Technological and polytechnic universities focus on providing education in engineering and technology areas, in line with productive and service sector priorities.

Experiences in Higher Education for Persons with Disabilities in Mexico

According to research on Spanish-speaking countries, there has been an increase in the number of universities offering programmes for persons with disabilities to access higher education (Paz-Maldonado, 2020). In the Latin American region, Cortés (2015) reviewed websites from 12 Latin American countries, identifying 48 universities with programmes aimed at supporting students with disabilities. In the case of Mexico, Cruz Vadillo and Casillas Alvarado (2017) researched the local scenario, finding that only 12 Mexican universities had activities, policies or programmes for inclusion of persons with disabilities. Only five of these 12 institutions had a specific programme as part of their institutional policy supporting students with disabilities from the beginning of their programme, during their studies and after they graduate. The remaining universities implemented inclusive practices with specific arrangements such as support for deaf or hearing-impaired students, web accessibility initiatives and disability anti-discrimination strategies. However, there was no mention of ideas supporting transition to adulthood in these inclusive initiatives (Cruz Vadillo and Casillas Alvarado, 2017).

A year later, Guajardo and Góngora (2018) found that approximately 15 autonomous universities had students with disabilities. These authors inquired beyond the university institutions and found that the technological subsystem of higher education had also begun to receive students with disabilities, although, at that time, only two technological institutions had ventured into the inclusive education model. Reyes Lastiri (2021) reviewed programmes designed for the access of students with intellectual disability, finding that the majority of such students are not enrolled in programmes where the aim is to achieve an official bachelor's degree. Rather, such programmes focus on providing students with disabilities the experience of an institutional academic context.

The educational formation and support of young persons with intellectual disabilities has occurred as a consequence of civil society organisations working collaboratively with higher education institutions (Saad Dayán et al., 2019). A clear example in Mexico has been the 'Construyendo Puentes' (Building Bridges) Programme, born in 2006 as a civil society initiative by the Centre for Personal and Social Autonomy (CAPYS). The objective was to provide training for young persons with intellectual disabilities, to support their transition to an independent adulthood. It sought to enable persons to gain more control over their lives and was developed by the Iberoamerican University, a private institution (Saad Dayán et al., 2017). It was replicated later by another five private and public universities.

Despite new approaches to inclusion in higher education institutions, recent research has identified structural barriers within universities: slow progress on making the environment accessible or lack of policy measures helping to counteract attitudinal barriers (Pérez-Castro, 2019). This echos previous studies which found that within inclusive initiatives from higher education institutions, those who have not incorporated these measures at an institutional policy level tend to provide actions for specific groups, rather than inculcating change within the wider learning community (Cruz Vadillo and Casillas Alvarado, 2017).

As a result of the barriers impeding access to education of persons with disabilities and the lack of disaggregated data existing on these experiences, the experience of the *Somos Uno Más* [*we are one of the same*] Programme from the Iberoamerican University of Mexico City is of particular interest, allowing us to understand some of the features involved in access to higher education of persons with intellectual disability in Mexico.

Somos Uno Más Programme [We Are One of the Same]

The *Somos Uno Más* [*we are one of the same*] Programme started in autumn in 2014, aiming to develop competences in young persons with intellectual disabilities to gain autonomy in a higher education context (Reyes Lastiri, 2021). It has been presented as an inclusive practice of the Iberoamerican University in the city of Mexico, a private institution based on a Jesuit educational model (Reyes Lastiri, 2021). The Programme provides the possibility for young persons with intellectual disability to participate in academic spaces in higher education. The inclusion of young persons with disabilities has been considered as a learning experience, not only for students of the programme but also for the entire university community.

In order to gain a better understanding of the context in which the Programme originated, it is necessary to acknowledge that from the beginning of the University, in March 1943, this institution has intended to promote a humanist and philosophical perspective in higher education, based on Christian faith values and on principles of the Society of Jesus, promoting a welcoming environment that values diversity (Patiño Domínguez, 2018). Despite valuing diversity, there is no institutional policy for persons with disabilities or other policy that includes references to the access of this group to the different degrees offered. However, there is an equity and equality policy that aims to define guidelines for a culture of justice, tolerance, inclusive equity and gender equality that must be implemented at all institutional levels (Universidad Iberoamericana Ciudad de México, 2016 [no page]).

Although there is currently no institutional policy on disability, some initiatives have been developed, such as actions to enhance accessibility on campus for persons with physical disabilities by the Rehabilitation Technology and Engineering Centre, which has been focused on developing technology for persons with physical disabilities; and the *Somos Uno Más* Programme. The latter obtained the Inter-American Award of Innovative Educational Models (MEIN) coordinated by the Inter American University Organisation in 2018. This award serves to promote knowledge, to learn from different experiences and to share good educational practices that are perceived to be an example of innovation (Fundación Organización Universitaria Interamericana, 2019).

Objectives of the Programme

The *Somos Uno Más* Programme is currently under the administration of the University Medium of the General Directorate, with four objectives:

i   to promote adaptive behaviours and necessary competencies for inclusion at work;
ii to develop aspects of self-determination and autonomy in students, by strengthening their identity as active participants in society;
iii to favour a spiritual development and social responsibility for an integral development of the student and
iv to strengthen adaptive behaviour in a specific context for the development of independence competencies.

It is composed of three phases, the first focuses upon adaptation to an academic life, and is based upon an initial evaluation of the interests and abilities of each student, an entry-level profile and an Individualised Education Plan (PEI); the second phase implements the PEI and focuses upon academic, cultural and sport inclusion; the final stage involves students working in an apprenticeship, which takes place in the university. This PEI approach seeks to identify individualised practices that are helpful for the person with disability, based on their own capacity, providing an education that is adapted to their situation and to their level of ability (Valls Fernández and Martínez Vicente, 2005).

Structure of the Programme

The Programme is structured into five areas.

i Basic academic formation that promotes competence development which favours the incorporation of students in the university context. Then, in the second phase, the work focuses upon strengthening and increasing student achievement levels. The goal is for students to be able to follow indications correctly, to comprehend readings of different types of text, along with preparing summaries or short pieces of writing on specific topics, and to focus on a context that prepares them for adulthood. The objective is to help students to develop their language, communication, cognitive, arithmetic and digital abilities.

ii University life formation, which encourages inclusion and educational possibilities that relying on a support system, favours the contact and socialisation of students with intellectual disabilities in the university community. The general objective here is to strengthen adaptive behaviour and to develop competencies in the context of specific subjects, with tutorial activities. This work centres on inclusion through academic, cultural and sport activities.

In this area, there is an opportunity for students with intellectual disabilities to integrate into academic modules of undergraduate degrees and to participate in university spaces that allow for interaction with the community, such as conferences, workshops and seminars. Students have access to the same digital platforms designed for learning processes that are used by other students, and online services where students can interact with their peers, upload their submissions and find resources for the lectures, all of which help increase interactions between students and lecturers.

One key support service is the involvement of students from other programme degrees, who, as part of their own Social Services module, can volunteer to participate as 'pedagogical peers', guiding and supporting students from different levels in this Programme. The goal is to foster a buddy figure that supports the student with intellectual disabilities in different spaces and contexts – at the gym, in lectures, laboratories and auditoriums.

iii Preformation Labour develops responsibilities and notions that facilitate future access to the labour market. These tasks are part of the contribution that employment provides to the quality of life of persons with intellectual disability, along with support for autonomy in areas such as family, social and self-esteem, economic self-determination and leisure management.

iv Social and Personal Formation focuses on the psychological well-being of the students through emotional support and personal guidance on daily and university activities, assistance in shaping family dynamics and guidance on personal situations affecting and acting as barriers to social inclusion or at an interpersonal relationship level. This scheme serves the purpose to support and promote the inner reflection and development of adaptive abilities that will help students to increase their autonomy and be included within society.

In addition, from August to September of 2021, this programme implemented a workshop on sexuality topics, where students had the opportunity to meet and reflect on their identities, working through questions about who they were, how they lived and how they expressed their sexualities. These sessions were complemented with practical lectures focused on the use of contraceptive methods, relationships, body health and care and other related topics.

v Integral Formation is inspired by person-centred learning and seeks to generate a space of openness, freedom and esteem for diversity. It promotes the integration of the Iberoamerican University values, working with students in spiritual actions and inner development, which encourage volunteering and care for others.

This Programme can be classified under the three types of models proposed by Hart et al. (2004), who provide an evaluation of models of accessing higher education by students with disabilities, known as (i) substantially separated, which considers differentiated activities between persons with and without disabilities, with a strong focus on developing life skills in students with disabilities and bringing them closer to a work experience; (ii) hybrid or mixed, promoting activities without major interactions with the rest of the students and participating in specific lectures and shared spaces in the educational institution; and (iii) inclusive activities, in which personalised support and services are implemented so that students with disabilities are part of the modules, apprenticeship and degrees, with a certification involved. From this categorisation, the *Somos Uno Más* could be considered within the mixed or hybrid category, where it seeks to enhance participation of the students in most of the areas of the university, with a curriculum designed for them specifically, and seeking to strengthen their social participation, autonomy and independence for a future working life.

Reflections on the Implementation of Somos Uno Más

The Programme constitutes an initiative that seeks to enhance the participation of persons with intellectual disabilities in higher education in a context of ongoing advances in Mexico. It was designed to enable opportunities for accessing the university and to promote independent and autonomy skills for future adult life. However, even though it has promoted the value of diversity in the university and its community, it has experienced challenges in its implementation that has prompted reflections on a practical and conceptual level. The practical issues relate to context and family involvement, and the conceptual issues relate to inclusion and ways to prepare for adulthood under a constant presence of exclusionary aspects.

Conceptual Challenges

There have been different initiatives with the objective of improving access to persons with disabilities in the post-secondary or higher education level. In relation to persons with intellectual disability, efforts to promote their access to this level of education have tended to maintain tensions between educational understandings that maintain special education and, at the same time, seek to develop inclusive programmes. The central tension in this programme can be identified in the way that it has been designed with the purpose of providing inclusion, while only being able to seek to achieve that inclusion *incrementally*. Being a new initiative within the Mexican context means that it definitely endeavours to bring about change, in line with similar experiences within Latin America (Calderón Albornoz and Rodríguez Herrero, 2021). However, its design requires a review of how students are actually getting involved in career development and further professionalisation along with obtaining a career diploma.

Throughout this chapter, the Mexican context has been described as an emerging state aiming for access to higher education for persons with disabilities. Therefore, these efforts are situated on a national stage where opportunities are recently being provided and have been positively valued as a contribution in developing competences and self-esteem in students with intellectual disability (Alqazlan et al., 2019). For instance, when students were asked for their motivation to be part of this type of programmes, they valued the fact that it might increase their opportunities to be employed, but also that these programmes improved their social relations with persons without disabilities (Alqazlan et al., 2019). These motivations are in line with certain achieved objectives seen from students with intellectual disabilities who participated in higher education, where they saw an improvement in their preparation for work. Even more, however, it has contributed to enhanced relations with persons without disabilities and increased participation in learning processes oriented towards developing autonomy (Corby et al., 2020).

The *Somos Uno Más* Programme encourages another reflection – it prompts us to consider whether the adult life – the transition to which students are being prepared – could itself be framed according to ableist thinking. Ableism is understood as a set of beliefs where certain abilities are preferred and valued, and against which people are judged (Wolbring, 2008). The ideal adult life seems to be focused primarily on the capacity to be productive, because in our society, productive labour has been conceived as a key element involved in access to independence and to citizenship (Guzmán and Platero, 2012). This point of discussion finds its relevance when applied to the *Somos Uno Más*, which seeks an integral development of the students that not only enhances their suitability to be included in the labour market but also provides a curriculum focused on self-exploration. The recent modifications of the curriculum that added modules on sexuality and identity are ways to defy the impoverished ideal of adult life as merely 'productive'. The core of the programme still aims to develop essential skills for transitioning to the labour market. However, through promoting discussions on sexuality it provides a wider understanding of adulthood and contributes to inclusion within communities, which tend to play a crucial role as seen in research on transitions to adulthood in Mexican contexts (Brogna, 2013; Skivington, 2011).

The discussion on the Programme also invites reflection on the objective of higher education, which sometimes may have its aim restricted to merely improving the employment skills of students. In this sense, a wider understanding of the role of higher education role might account for the integral development of the person through experiencing multiple aspects of the university. Moreover, modules that are not directly related to labour skills, such as those treating topics like sexuality, could be influential in conversations around identity and how adulthood is perceived. Curricular developments in areas such as sexuality may be of particular significance given that the identity of persons with intellectual disabilities tends to be stigmatised and defined solely by their impairment (Wilkinson et al., 2015). These innovations are helping to produce alternative identities and identifications and challenge the assumed classifications according to which people with intellectual disabilities are often framed (Midjo and Aune, 2018).

Practical Challenges

The *Somos Uno Más* has also experienced challenges at a practical level. Barriers have been observed during its implementation, deriving from administrative or logistical issues. These have impacted upon the student experience.

Access to higher education for persons with disabilities is not isolated from socioeconomic barriers that affect young persons who come from disadvantaged backgrounds. In terms of *Somos Uno Más*, it can be noted that even though students do not pay for a registration process, the cost of 12 months of payments is equivalent to 642 US dollars, which tends to limit the access to those with capacity to afford it. Understanding that poverty and lower socioeconomic status tend to be more present in the population with disability (Pinilla-Roncancio, 2018), this type of barrier impacts negatively, undermining efforts to ameliorate the disparities in equal opportunities.

A key aspect in the implementation of this programme has been the role of families. Their importance has been considered in the programme design by including them in the evaluation process for students, first in the welcome interview, where the programme is described and, in a later stage, when the results of the evaluation are confirmed. However, their involvement has been noticed to be more present than required in some cases, with some parents taking decisions regarding which modules their children study. The complex role of families is well-recognised within research. Studies have evidenced both positive and less positive aspects of family involvement: some parents can push for more opportunities (positive) whilst other parents do not perceive the relevance of higher education for their children (negative) (Alqazlan et al., 2019). Their involvement will likely influence how young adults with intellectual disabilities see themselves and how they are supported during their education (Corby et al., 2020). Therefore, it is important for family involvement to provide support, while not interfering with the development of autonomy and independence of the students.

Finally, the COVID-19 pandemic has impacted the whole world and its subsequent economic problems are still present in Latin America, intensifying inequality and vulnerability in marginalised groups, such as persons with disabilities who, as noted previously, already experienced difficulties in accessing higher education pre-pandemic (CEPAL, 2021; Meresman and Ullmann, 2020). Covid-19 negatively affected participation in inclusive spaces (Dickinson et al., 2021) that had previously promoted interactions amongst the university community. These non-lecture spaces were when most of the interactions among students, staff and lecturers were occuring (CEPAL, 2021). As a result of the pandemic and its impacts on the pre-labour sessions, the programme was extended by an additional year.

Additionally, the COVID-19 pandemic exposed the fragility of these types of programmes (Smith, 2021). Most of the companies that usually offered work experience placements for the students, cancelled their previous contributions. There was an increased burden on families as teachers had to depend on them for implementing the online modules. From the perspective of students, the impossibility of leaving their homes meant that not going to the university meant that they lost that important, much needed distance from their families that had contributed to them developing autonomy and independence. Therefore, families were in position of being key actors for on-line learning, but at the same time overprotection was more difficult to avoid.

Conclusion

Access to higher education is recognised not only as an unfulfilled right but also as a key aspect that contributes to developing conditions for an adulthood pathway. During the last decades, Mexico has progressed in legal and policy mechanisms to regulate discrimination and promote participation in university and higher education institutions. The *Somos Uno Más* Programme should be acknowledged for its objective of providing independence and autonomy skills, preparing young people not only for their entrance to the labour market, but also providing a space that helps to include students with intellectual disability in higher education in a more meaningful manner.

With regard to the implementation of the Programme, some reflections have been shared on conceptual and practical levels. As noted, the programme's main purpose is to work towards inclusion. However, it is acknowledged that it is important to advance in terms of providing degree certifications and curriculum changes that enable students to participate under equal terms and conditions, alongside peers who do not have disabilities. A positive move has been promoting changes in the curriculum that have helped students to explore issues around sexuality, expanding the notion of adulthood underpinning the programme. On a practical level, as a result of the pandemic, the role of families was recognised as crucial, as they worked together with educators to ensure their young people were able to continue their studies; but it also highlighted the ongoing problem of families overprotecting students or being to determining of their studies. Finally, the COVID-19 pandemic presented administrative and logistical challenges and made evident the fragility of this programme condition as an emerging inclusive initiative.

References

Acle Tomasini, G., Roque Hernández, M. del P., Zacatelco Ramírez, F., Lozada García, R. and Martínez Basurto, L.M. 2007. Discapacidad y rezago escolar: riesgos actuales [Disability and educational lagging: current risks]. *Acta Colombiana de Cuidado Intensivo*, 10(2), pp. 19–30.

Aguirre García, J.A. 2022. *La educación superior en México, 1980–2018: una reflexión crítica* [Higher education in Mexico: a critical reflection]. Master thesis. Faculty of Economy. Universidad Nacional Autónoma de México.

Alqazlan, S., Alallawi, B. and Totsika, V. 2019. Post-secondary education for young people with intellectual disabilities: a systematic review of stakeholders' experiences. *Educational Research Review*, 28, p. 100295.

Asociación Nacional de Universidades e Instituciones de Educación Superior. 2002. *Manual para la integración de personas con discapacidad en las instituciones de educación superior* [Maual for the integration of persons with disavility in higher education institutions]. [Online]. [Accessed on 23 January 2023]. Available from: https://www.conapred.org.mx/documentos_cedoc/Manual_integracion_educacion_superior_UNUIES.pdf

Björnsdóttir, K. 2017. Belonging to higher education: inclusive education for students with eintellectual disabilities. *European Journal of Special Needs Education*, 32(1), pp. 125–136.

Brogna, P.C. 2013. *Condición de adulto con discapacidad intelectual. Posición social y simbólica de 'otro'* [Adult with intellectual disability condition. Social and symbolic position of the 'other']. Tesis de Doctorado [Doctorate thesis]. Universidad Nacional Autónoma de México.

Brogna, P.C. 2014. *Adultez, trabajo y discapacidad: el trabajo de crecer* [Adulthood, work and disability: the process of growing]. Benito Juárez, México: Editorial Trillas.

Calderón Albornoz, M.P. and Rodríguez Herrero, P. 2021. Social representations of intellectual impairments in universities: the educational implications of a case study in Chile. *Disability & Society*. ahead-of-print(ahead-of-print), pp. 1–18.

CEPAL. 2021. *Personas con discapacidad y sus derechos frente a la pandemia de COVID-19: que nadie se quede atrás* [Persons with disabilities and their rights in the COVID-19 pandemic: leaving no one behind]. Santiago: CEPAL. [Accessed on 20 June 2022]. Available from: https://repositorio.cepal.org/handle/11362/46600.

Cobeñas, P. and Santuccione, G. 2022. *La influencia de la producción de Ainscow en una experiencia de incidencia en Argentina* [Influence from the production of Ainscow on an implemented experience in Argentina]. In: Peña, C., Contu, M. and Huaiquián, C. eds. *Aportes a la inclusión educativa. Trayectorias y perspectivas. Homenaje a la obra de Mel Ainscow* [Contributions on education inclusion. Perspectives and trajectories. An homage to the work of Mel Ainscow]. Chile: Editorial Cuadernos de Sofía, Santiago, Chile/Fondazione Giovannino Pinna, Cerdeña, Italia / Centro de Apoyo Psicopedagógico de Aragón, México.

Comisión Nacional de los Derechos Humanos. 2018. Análisis cuantitativo y cualitativo de las violaciones a los derechos humanos de grupos vulnerables [Qualitative and quantiative analysis of violations to human rights of vulnerable groups]. [Online]. [Accessed on 6 April 2022]. Available from: https://www.cndh.org.mx/sites/default/files/documentos/2019-11/Analisis-Cuantitativo-Cualitativo-Violaciones-DH-Grupos-Vulnerables.pdf.

Committee on the Rights of Persons with Disabilities. 2018. Combined second and third periodic reports submitted by Mexico under article 35 of the Convention, due in 2018. CRPD/C/MEX/2-3 [Online]. [Accessed on 13 April 2022]. Available from: https://tbinternet.ohchr.org/_layouts/15/treatybodyexternal/Download.aspx?symbolno=CRPD%2FC%2FMEX%2F2-3&Lang=en.

Committee on the Rights of Persons with Disabilities 2022. Concluding observations on the combined second and third periodic reports of Mexico. CRPD/C/MEX/CO/2–3 [Online]. [Accessed on 13 April 2022]. Available from: https://tbinternet.ohchr.org/_layouts/15/treatybodyexternal/Download.aspx?symbolno=CRPD%2FC%2FMEX%2FCO%2F2-3&Lang=en&fbclid=IwAR3LL-bMRkk4uuGkeozjugYZpQ_0Oqqg6iboV7XogIyRVpn9-yw3MN5j3w.

CONADIS. 2017. *CONADIS, seis años trabajando por un México Incluyente, Consejo Nacional para el Desarrollo y la Inclusión de las Personas con Discapacidad*

[CONADIS, six years working for an inclusive Mexico, National council for inclusion and development of persons with disability]. 30 May 2017. [Online]. [Accessed on 20 April 2022]. Available from: https://www.gob.mx/conadis/articulos/conadis-seis-anos-trabajando-por-un-mexico-incluyente?idiom=es.

Constitución Política de los Estados Unidos Mexicanos [Mexico], as amended DOF 18-11-2022, Diario Oficial de la Federación [D.O.], 5 de febrero de 1917 (Mex.).

Corby, D., Taggart, L. and Cousins, W. 2020. The lived experience of people with intellectual disabilities in post-secondary or higher education. *Journal of Intellectual Disabilities: JOID*, 24(3), pp. 339–357.

Corby, D., King, E., Petrie, M., Reddy, S., Callan, A. and Andersen, T. 2022. Making a case for the inclusion of people with intellectual disabilities in higher education. *Disabilities*, 2(3), pp. 415–427.

Cortés, F. 2015. *Universidad y discapacidad: hacia una realidad incluyente en el marco internacional latinoamericano*. México: UNAM.

Cruz López, Y. and Cruz López, A.K. 2008. La educación superior en México tendencias y desafíos [Higher education in Mexico trends and challenges]. Avaliação: *Revista da Avaliação da Educação Superior (Campinas)*, 13(2), pp. 293–311.

Cruz Vadillo, R. 2016. Discapacidad y educación superior: ¿Una cuestión de derechos o buenas voluntades? [Disability and higher education: a question of rights or goodwill?]. *CPU-e Revista de Investigación Educativa*. 23. [Online]. [Accessed on 5 May 2022]. Available from: http://www.scielo.org.mx/scielo.php?script=sci_arttext&pid=S1870-53082016000200002&lng=es&nrm=iso>. ISSN 1870–5308

Cruz Vadillo, R. and Casillas Alvarado, M.Á. 2017. Las instituciones de educación superior y los estudiantes con discapacidad en México. *Revista de la Educación Superior*, 46(181), pp. 37–53.

De Los Santos, P.J. and Tinoco, D.B. 2013. El proceso de transición a la vida adulta de los jóvenes con trastorno del espectro autista. Análisis de la planificación centrado en la persona [The transition process to adult life of young persons with autism]. *Educar*, 49(2), pp.323–339.

Dickinson, H., Smith, C., Yates, S. & Tani, M. 2021. The importance of social supports in education: survey findings from students with disability and their families during COVID-19. *Disability & Society*. DOI: 10.1080/09687599.2021.1994371

Echarri Cánovas, C.J. and Pérez Amador, J. 2007. En tránsito hacia la adultez: eventos en el curso de vida de los jóvenes en México [In transition to adulthood: life course events of young persons in Mexico]. *Estudios demograficos y urbanos*, 22(1), p. 43.

Economic Commission for Latin America and the Caribbean (ECLAC). 2016. The social inequality matrix in Latin America [Online]. Santiago: ECLAC. [Accessed on 28 June 2022]. Available from: https://repositorio.cepal.org/handle/11362/40668.

Ferrer Cerdà, E. 2001. Los padres ante la transición a la vida adulta de su hijo con discapacidad psíquica [Parents in the transition to adulhood of their children with mental disability]. In: *Atención educativa a la diversidad en el nuevo milenio (XVIII Jornadas de Universidades y Educación Especial), 2–5 April 2001, A Coruña*. [Online]. Spain: Universidade da Coruña, pp. 887–893. [Accessed on 22 May 2022]. Available from: https://ruc.udc.es/dspace/handle/2183/11114?show=full.

Fundación Organización Universitaria Interamericana. 2019. Modelos Educativos Innovadores en Educación Superior/ Fundación Organización Universitaria Interamericana. [Online]. [Accessed on 12 April 2022]. Available from: https://oui-iohe.org/es/premio-mein-2020/.

Grigal, M., Hart, D. and Weir, C. 2012. A survey of postsecondary education programs for students with intellectual disabilities in the United States. *Journal of Policy and Practice in Intellectual Disabilities*, 9(4), pp. 223–233.

Grigal, M., Dukes, L.L. and Walker, Z. 2021. Advancing access to higher education for students with intellectual disability in the United States. *Disabilities*, 1(4), pp. 438–449.

Gobierno de México. 2014. *Programa Nacional para el Desarrollo y la Inclusión de las Personas con Discapacidad 2014-2018* [National Program for Inclusion and Development of Persons with Disability 2014-2018]. 30 April 2014. [Online]. [Accessed 20 April 2022]. Available from: https://www.gob.mx/conadis/acciones-y-programas/programa-nacional-para-el-desarrollo-y-la-inclusion-de-las-personas-con-discapacidad-2014-2018-5882.

Guajardo, E. and Góngora, J. 2018. Estudiantes con discapacidad en la enseñanza superior de México ¿Logran acceder jóvenes con discapacidad a este nivel educativo? [Students with disability in higher education in Mexico. Are students with disability accessing this educational level?]. In: Martínez, M. ed. *Educación Inclusiva en México: Avances, estudios, retos y dilemas* [Inclusive education in Mexico: Advance, research, challenges and dilemmas]. San Cristóbal de las Casas, Chiapas: Universidad Intercultural de Chiapas, pp. 16–52.

Guzmán, P. and Platero, R. 2012. Passing, enmascaramiento y estrategias identitarias: diversidades funcionales y sexualidades no-normativas [Passing, masking and strategies around identity: functional diversities and non-normative sexualities]. In: Platero, R. ed. *Intersecciones: cuerpos y sexualidades en la encrucijada* [Interesections: bodies and sexualities at the crossroads]. Barcelona: Bellaterra, pp. 125–158.

Hart, D., Mele-McCarthy, J., Pasternack, R.H., Zimbrich, K. and Parker, D.R. 2004. Community college: a pathway to success for youth with learning, cognitive, and intellectual disabilities in secondary settings. *Education and Training in Developmental Disabilities*, 39(1), pp. 54–66.

Leite, P. 2020. Encuesta nacional sobre discriminación (ENADIS). 2017 Resultados sobre personas con discapacidad. [National survey on discrimination. 2017. Findings on persons with disability]. [Online]. Ciudad de México: Ediciones Conapred. [Accessed 3 April 2022]. Available from: https://www.conapred.org.mx/index.php?contenido=documento&id=391&id_opcion=147.

Ley General de Educación Superior [Higher education general law], 20 de abril de 2021. (Mexico).

Male, C. and Wodon, Q. 2017. *Disability gaps in educational attainment and literacy*. Washington, DC: The World Bank.

Meresman, S. and Ullmann, H. 2020. COVID-19 y las personas con discapacidad en América Latina: mitigar el impacto y proteger derechos para asegurar la inclusión hoy y mañana [COVID-19 and persons with disability in Latin America: to mitigate the impact and to protect rights to inclusion today and tomorrow]. Santiago: CEPAL. [Online]. [Accessed on 22 April 2022]. Available from: https://hdl.handle.net/11362/46278

Midjo, T. and Aune, K.E. 2018. Identity constructions and transition to adulthood for young people with mild intellectual disabilities. *Journal of Intellectual Disabilities: JOID*, 22(1), pp. 33–48.

Miller, D. and Arvizu, V. 2016. Ser madre y estudiante. Una exploración de las características de las universitarias con hijos y breves notas para su estudio [An exploration on the characteristics of university women with children and brief notes for their study]. *Revista de la Educación Superior*, 45(177), pp. 17–42.

Moreno, M.T. 2006. Integración/inclusión de las personas con discapacidad en la Educación Superior. In: IESALC, ed. *Informe sobre la educación superior en América Latina y el Caribe, 2000–2005: la metamorfosis de la educación superior*. Instituto Internacional de la UNESCO para la Educación Superior en América y el Caribe (IESALC), pp. 144–155.

Morris, J. 2002. *Young disabled people moving into adulthood*. [Online]. York: Joseph Rowntree Foundation. [Accessed on 17 May 2022]. Available from: https://www. jrf.org.uk/report/moving-adulthood-young-disabled-people-moving-adulthood

OECD. 2019. *Higher education in Mexico: labour market relevance and outcomes, higher education*. Paris: OECD Publishing. [Accessed on 21 March 2023]. Available from: https://doi.org/10.1787/9789264309432-en

Padilla Muñoz, A. 2011. Inclusión educativa de personas con discapacidad [Education inclusion of persons with disability]. *Revista Colombiana de Psiquiatría*, 40(4), pp. 670–699.

Pallisera, M., Fullana, J., Vilà, M., Jiménez, P., Castro, M., Puyalto, C., Montero, M. and Martin, R. 2014. Análisis de los apoyos que reciben los jóvenes con discapacidad intelectual en su transición a la vida adulta en España: una investigación a partir de experiencias de profesionales y personas con discapacidad [Analysis on the support provided to young persons with intellectual disability in their trasnition to adult life in Spain: a research from experiences professionals and persons with disability]. *Revista Española de Discapacidad*, 2(2), pp. 27–43.

Patiño Domínguez, H.A.M. 2018. ¿Cuál es el legado de la Universidad Jesuita? Percepciones de los egresados sobre la formación humanista [What is the legacy of the Jesuit university? Perception on graduated students on the humanist formation]. *Revista Latinoamericana de Estudios Educativos*, 48(2), pp. 291–330.

Paz-Maldonado, E. 2020. Systematic review: educational inclusion of university students in situation on disabilities in Latin America. *Estudios Pedagógicos*, 46(1), pp. 413–429.

Pérez-Castro. 2019. La inclusión de los estudiantes con discapacidad en dos universidades públicas mexicanas [Inclusion of students with disability in two public mexican universities]. *Innovación Educativa (México, DF)*, 19(79), pp. 145–170.

Pinilla-Roncancio, M. 2018. The reality of disability: multidimensional poverty of people with disability and their families in Latin America. *Disability and Health Journal*, 11(3), pp. 398–404.

Priestley, M. 2003. *Disability: a life course approach*. Oxford: Polity.

Reyes Lastiri, M.E. 2021. Percepción de indicadores de inclusión en la educación superior: El caso de la Universidad Iberoamericana de la Ciudad de México [Perception of inclusion indicators in higher education. The case of the Iberoamerican university of Mexico city]. [Online] Doctor, Facultad de Educación y Trabajo Social, Universidad de Valladolid. [Accessed on 31 May 2022]. Available from: https://investigacion.ubu.es/documentos/619ca0c4a08dbd1b8f9f1126

Saad Dayán, E., Díaz Barriga Arceo, F. and Pacheco Pinzón, D. 2019. Transición a vida adulta de jóvenes con discapacidad intelectual: análisis de trayectorias de alumnos del programa Construyendo Puentes Capys-Unam [Transition to adult life of young persons with intellectual disability: analysis of trajectories from students of the program Building Bridges Capys-Unam] (Área temática 05 currículo). In: *XV Congreso nacional de investigación educativa, 18 al 22 de noviembre de*

2022, *Ciudad y puerto de Acapulco, Guerrero, México*. Acapulco, México: Consejo Mexicano de Investigación Educativa. [Accessed on 15 May 2022]. Available from: https://www.comie.org.mx/congreso/memoriaelectronica/v15/doc/0777.pdf

Saad Dayán, E., Zacarías Ponce, J. and Buenfil López, C. 2017. 'Construyendo Puentes': Modelo de inclusión educativa universitaria para jóvenes con discapacidad intelectual: alcances y desafíos ['Building bridges': Model of university education inclusion for young persons with intellectual disability]. In: Congreso Nacional de Investigación Educativa - COMIE [Online]. Available from: https://comie.org.mx/congreso/memoriaelectronica/v14/doc/1290.pdf

Secretaría de la Educación Pública 2020. Programa sectorial de educación 2020–2024. Recuperado https://www. dof. gob. mx/nota_detalle.

Skivington, M. 2011. Disability and adulthood in Mexico: an ethnographic case study. *International Journal of Special Education*, 26(3), pp. 45–57.

Smith, C. 2021. Challenges and Opportunities for Teaching Students with Disabilities During the COVID-19 Pandemic. *International Journal of Multidisciplinary Perspectives in Higher Education*, 5(1), pp. 167–173.

Tucker, E.C., Jones, J.L., Gallus, K.L., Emerson, S.R. and Manning-Ouellette, A.L. 2020. Let's take a walk: exploring intellectual disability as diversity in higher education. *Journal of College and Character*, 21(3), pp. 157–170.

Uditsky, B. and Hughson, E. 2012. Inclusive postsecondary education-an evidence-based moral imperative. *Journal of Policy and Practice in Intellectual Disabilities*, 9(4), pp. 298–302.

UNESCO. 2020. *Global education monitoring report, 2020: inclusion and education: all means all*. [Online]. 3rd edition. Paris: UNESCO. [Accessed on 13 May 2022]. Available from: https://unesdoc.unesco.org/ark:/48223/pf0000373718.

UNESCO Institute for Statistics (UIS). 2018. Education and disability: analysis of data from 49 countries [Online]. UNESCO. [Accessed on 18 May 2022]. Available from: http://uis.unesco.org/en/news/education-and-disability-analysis-data-49-countries

Universidad Iberoamericana Ciudad de México. 2016. *Política Institucional de Igualdad y Equidad de Género* [Institutional policy on gender equality and equity]. [Online]. Ciudad de México/Tijuana: IBERO. [Accessed on 14 May 2022]. Available from: https://ibero.mx/sites/all/themes/ibero/descargables/programa-genero/politicas-institucionales-de-igualdad-y-equidad.pdf

Valls Fernández, F. and Martínez Vicente, J.M. 2005. Discapacidad y transición a la vida activa [Disability and transition to active life]. *International Journal of Developmental and Educational Psychology*, 2(1), pp. 761–770.

Wilkinson, V.J., Theodore, K. and Raczka, R. 2015. 'As normal as possible': sexual identity development in people with intellectual disabilities transitioning to adulthood. *Sexuality and Disability*, 33(1), pp. 93–105.

Wolbring, G. 2008. The politics of ableism. *Development*, 51(2), pp. 252–258.

INDEX